TOMMY KOH

Serving Singapore
and the World

TOMMY KOH

Serving Singapore and the World

Editors

Yeo Lay Hwee
Peggy Kek
Gillian Koh
Chang Li Lin

 **WS Professional**

NEW JERSEY · LONDON · SINGAPORE · BEIJING · SHANGHAI · HONG KONG · TAIPEI · CHENNAI · TOKYO

Published by

WS Professional, an imprint of
World Scientific Publishing Co. Pte. Ltd.
5 Toh Tuck Link, Singapore 596224
USA office: 27 Warren Street, Suite 401-402, Hackensack, NJ 07601
UK office: 57 Shelton Street, Covent Garden, London WC2H 9HE

British Library Cataloguing-in-Publication Data
A catalogue record for this book is available from the British Library.

TOMMY KOH
Serving Singapore and the World

ISBN 978-981-3222-37-3
ISBN 978-981-3222-38-0 (pbk)

Desk Editor: Jiang Yulin

Copyeditor: Leong Wenshan

Typeset by Stallion Press
Email: enquiries@stallionpress.com

Printed in Singapore

Preface

Those who know Tommy Koh can imagine how difficult it was to persuade him to allow this collection of essays to be written. Modest to a fault, Prof. Koh resisted our attempts for over a year before our persistence wore him down. He finally gave his blessings to this festschrift on condition that it would focus less on him, and more on the issues that he was involved in so that readers may be informed of their implications for Singapore. He made us promise that all this would be done without lionising him.

Ambassador and Professor Tommy Koh (or Prof. as he is often referred to) turns 80 on November 12, 2017. His lifelong service to Singapore and achievements are far beyond what one book can capture. The essays in this volume represent only a sampling of the institutions, committees, projects, causes and issues Prof. Koh has committed himself to over the years. We have also included a Tributes section to accommodate essays from his classmates, friends and colleagues.

Everyone who contributed an essay to this book had worked closely with him and had a ringside view of how he went about performing his multiple roles every day, or has been friends with him for many years. Just as it was impossible to include everything that he had a hand in, the length constraint did not allow us to include everyone with whom he had worked and whose lives he had touched.

Prof. Koh has remained active and "At-Large" long past his "official" retirement. At Singapore's Ministry of Foreign Affairs, he puts his wisdom, diplomatic agility and resourcefulness at the service of the Little Red Dot, co-chairing the China-Singapore Forum, the Japan-Singapore Symposium, and the India-Singapore Forum, just to name a few important programmes under his charge. He is fully engaged with the academic community as the Rector of Tembusu College, Special Advisor to the Institute of Policy Studies and Chairman of the Governing Board of the Centre for International Law, again, just to name a few of his associations. He actively contributes to the development of knowledge in the various fields that he has worked in and shares his learned opinion on many university-based as well as public and media platforms.

This book is an affectionate, and in no way exhaustive, tribute to Tommy Koh. For purely practical reasons, it is organised under four manageable sections in which Prof. Koh has made a mark over five decades of public service to Singapore and the world, with the four of us editing one section each — diplomacy and international relations, arts and heritage, progressive society, and international law. We hope that this volume will serve not only to honour the record of Prof. Koh, but also inspire a new generation of Singaporeans to cultivate a well-lived life, to serve with moral courage and civic consciousness, and be counted in making the world a better place.

We would like to express our deepest appreciation to all the authors here who took precious time off their busy schedules to share with us their recollection of the work they have done with Prof. Koh. We hope he will forgive them and us, the co-editors, for allowing our admiration and deep affection for him to seep through the pages of this book.

We also wish to thank Prof. Koh's family — Mrs Koh, his children and grandchildren, for allowing us to embark on this book project. A special thanks to Aun Koh for his input for the design of the book cover.

Special mention goes to World Scientific Publishing for being so keen to publish this book and the dedication of members of their team, which includes Chua Hong Koon, Khoo Yee Hong, Jiang Yulin and Jimmy Low.

We owe a great debt to our copy editor, Leong Wenshan, who readily took on the task to help us put our best foot forward on this project.

Our gratitude also to the National Archives, National Heritage Board, National Library Board and National University of Singapore for some of the photos that are included in the book. There are many more to thank for their help along the way. We could not have done this without all of you.

It has been so wonderful to discover how we are a part of a large community that celebrates the deep imprint Prof. Koh has put in our minds and hearts; a living national treasure who is wished many more good years ahead.

For us, working on this book has been truly a privilege and a joy. Thank you all and thank you, Prof. Koh.

Yeo Lay Hwee
Peggy Kek
Gillian Koh
Chang Li Lin

Contents

Foreword

꩜

It is with the greatest of pleasure that I welcome Tommy Koh to the Eighties Club. Fortunately for us, it is no longer as exclusive as it once was.

The tributes in this volume tell the story of Tommy comprehensively. He is admired in Singapore and abroad as a diplomat par excellence, as a distinguished international lawyer and, perhaps most of all, as a cultural patriot and champion of a progressive society. I cannot but concur with the judgments and appreciations so warmly expressed. I cannot think of anyone who deserves the words of praise better than Tommy. That leaves me with little to add, so I shall limit myself to a few personal comments about why I respect him so much.

I first met him when he was a lively student leader on the Bukit Timah campus, active in the University Socialist Club that some of us had founded a few years earlier. Later, I moved to Kuala Lumpur and Canberra and could only follow with admiration his remarkable career from afar.

We met again in San Francisco and Hong Kong some 30 years later and, when Margaret and I came to Singapore, I came to understand even better why so many people feel such affection for him. It struck me that, above all, it is for his love of his country and its people.

This brings me to Tommy's Singapore story as it unfolded for me during the 20 years I have lived here.

When we arrived early in 1996, he invited me to join the National Arts Council that he was chairing. Later, when he moved to chair the National Heritage Board, he asked me to join him there as well. I also worked closely with him on the Board of the Chinese Heritage Centre, one that he did so much to bring to fruition. And then he brought me into the Institute of Policy Studies Board and we were together on the Governing Board of the Lee Kuan Yew School of Public Policy. That was how I saw him at work at close quarters.

Throughout those years, he never failed to demonstrate how deeply committed he was to the city-state's future. His idealism and optimism were infectious. That makes me feel that, with people like him working for Singapore, it is no wonder that it has become the modern state admired by so many.

The significance of its surprising success came to me when I heard Tommy speak of how he had always believed that Singapore could be independent and did not think that it had to be part of the Federation of Malaya. It made me realise that, behind his youthful anti-colonialism, he also had hopes for a republican future free from feudal hangovers, and was ready to draw inspiration from socialist ideals.

Many in my generation had lived with the idea that Singapore, as part of British Malaya, should seek its independence as a constituent state in the Federation. There were strong arguments why Singapore should not join Malaysia unless the conditions were right and I greatly admired those who negotiated uncompromisingly for the best possible terms before joining the larger federation of Malaysia.

I had moved to the Kuala Lumpur Division of the University of Malaya in 1959 and was among those who saw the formula for bringing Singapore into the federation as a step in the right direction. When Singapore was separated, it was a time of sadness for me because I had high hopes for Greater Malaysia. But then I was looking at it from the perspective of someone who had grown up in the Malay state of Perak and understood why Malaysia chose to stay by its constitutional monarchy. And I believed that Malaysia needed Singapore if it were to fulfil its historic mission as a potentially great multicultural modern country in the heart of Southeast Asia.

Tommy, however, was confident that Singapore could go it alone and his arguments for that made good sense. As an independent state, it would be a strategic port that had global reach. Its frontline location in a world that was ideologically divided by the Cold War gave it an importance no other port in the region could match. Tommy was fearful of the ethnic nationalism that had become the centrepiece of politics on the peninsula. He was also opposed to the violence that had become the norm during the long war against communism.

In addition, he believed in the new international world order that was based on respect for the rule of law. His implicit faith was that a plural society led by men and women who were pragmatic and visionary was a good place to start if a new model of a modern state is to be built. On that basis, Tommy dedicated his life to help his people make that model a reality.

Looking back at what he has done unflinchingly for half a century, I have to conclude that this is a man who has become the international voice of his multicultural city-state. In the eyes of all those who have dealt with Singapore, he is the gentle face of a state that punches — and sometimes punches hard — above its weight. And, within the country, his is the voice of sharing, optimism and mutual trust — everything that the small dot of a nation-in-the-making needs to meet the challenges of an uncertain age.

If more Singaporeans were like him, the city's ability to survive and thrive in these tough times would be better assured.

Professor Wang Gungwu
University Professor, National University of Singapore
Chairman, East Asian Institute

Section I

Diplomacy and International Relations

Chapter 1

Diplomacy, International Relations and Singapore's Foreign Policy

Yeo Lay Hwee

Introduction

Looking at our troubled world now, as international politics enters into uncharted waters, I cannot help but wish that the world had more Tommy Kohs.

The world of international relations has changed radically in the last few years because of developments in information and communications technologies, and the disruptions that these technologies have brought to the economy and the socio-political order. The Internet and social media, the diffusion of power and many other forces have combined to undermine some of the traditional assumptions of diplomacy.

Yet, the enduring qualities that led to Tommy Koh's extraordinary diplomatic success — or what Kishore Mahbubani termed as "seven pillars of Tommy Koh's wisdom"[1] — are still very much needed for Singapore, the little red dot, to navigate an increasingly contested and complex world.

Being a small country, Singapore is keenly aware of its limitations in material hard power. Hence it has invested a lot in diplomacy, and in turn "diplomacy has played a significant part in Singapore's success story abroad over the past 50 years".[2]

---

1 See Kishore Mahbubani's essay in this collection.
2 Evelyn Goh and Daniel Chua, *Singapore Chronicles: Diplomacy* (Institute of Policy Studies and Straits Times Press, 2015), p 1.

Singapore has established diplomatic relations with 187 sovereign states and participates in all major multilateral forums and international institutions. Singapore is a founding member of ASEAN and an initiator of various informal multilateral groupings such as the Forum of Small States (FOSS), the Asia-Europe Meeting (ASEM) and the Global Governance Group (3G) to encourage dialogue and cooperation. It is also active in the United Nations (UN), having been non-permanent Security Council member from 2001 to 2002, and its diplomats being called to chair UN conferences such as the UN Conference on the Law of the Sea (UNCLOS) and the UN Conference on Environment and Development, also known as the Rio Conference. And Ambassador Tommy Koh has been one of the stalwarts in Singapore's diplomatic scene, playing an important role in protecting Singapore's interests, promoting regional and global cooperation, and contributing to the building of international norms and institutions vital to the functioning of a rule-based global order.

As reflected in the essays in this section, he has used his immense diplomatic skills to serve Singapore in building bilateral relations with the US, China, Japan and India. When he was Singapore's ambassador to the US, he raised Singapore's stature by securing a congressional address for then Prime Minister Lee Kuan Yew during the latter's visit to the US in 1985. As noted by Ambassador Chan Heng Chee in her essay, "this was a very big deal at that time as Singapore was and still is a tiny country, a micro state in reality." Another of Tommy Koh's important contributions to Singapore-US relations is his role as the chief negotiator of the US-Singapore Free Trade Agreement. In his essay, Daren Tang who was in Tommy's negotiating team captured the "master distiller" at work, sharing some close observations of this chief negotiator and the lessons that he learnt from working with Tommy Koh. Ambassador Tommy Koh's negotiating skills earned him the 2014 Great Negotiator Award given by Harvard.

Tommy Koh also played an important role in facilitating the upgrade of Singapore-China relations, as described in Lye Liang Fook's essay. Koh "toiled behind the scenes to create the right conditions for the leaders of Singapore and China to meet" in the 1970s and 1980s when diplomatic ties were not yet established between the two countries, and played an instrumental role in negotiating an agreement for the establishment of diplomatic relations in 1990. With Japan, Chang Li Lin noted in her essay that Professor Koh was "conferred the prestigious Order of the Rising Sun, Gold and Silver Star by the Japanese government in recognition of his contributions in promoting intellectual exchange and mutual understanding between Japan and Singapore."

His negotiating skill was in full display in regional and multilateral forums, from ASEAN to APEC, and in the drafting of the Dublin Principles, paving the way for the establishment of the Asia-Europe Foundation (ASEF). According to Peggy Kek, "ASEF might not have taken off 20 years ago, if not for Ambassador's legendary diplomatic skills."

He served with distinction in the UN, having been given the privilege of chairing two important global conferences involving all UN member states: the UN Conference on the Law of the Sea (1980–1982) and the UN Conference on Environment and Development (the Rio Conference) from 1990 to 1992, and taking on the role of Special Envoy to the Baltic states to help mediate issues over the withdrawal of Russian troops from the Baltic states. His affable personality, expertise and intellectual prowess and independence of mind have also made him a "model" in Track 2 diplomacy.[3] As noted in Simon Tay's essay, "as a diplomat and negotiator, Ambassador Koh has valued the need to establish and maintain strong networks." He is also a master communicator who often contributes articles to media that are easy to read and to defend ideas dear to him.

Tommy Koh further bolsters official ties by creating greater awareness, understanding and empathy through sharing his perspectives at public outreach events. He is also a prolific scholar contributing regularly to journals and books, to share his thoughts and views on issues pertaining to international law, regional integration, diplomacy and Singapore's foreign policy. Professor Koh's written work, as Ambassador Ong Keng Yong noted in his essay, "is easy to read, often very practical-oriented and most importantly addresses complicated issues in layman's language that can be understood by the general public."[4]

---

3 See Simon Tay's essay in this collection for a description of Track 2 diplomacy.
4 See Ong Keng Yong's essay in this collection.

As we reflect on Tommy Koh's contributions to Singapore and his service to the regional and global community through his role at the United Nations and participation in various regional and inter-regional forums, we can also see how Singapore's foreign policy has evolved.

Singapore's Foreign Policy

Singapore's policies, foreign or otherwise, are dictated by its geographical constraints as a small state without a hinterland or natural resources, and by a deep sense of vulnerability and a strong desire to survive against all odds.

Singapore's overall foreign policy approach would be what I call conservative pragmatism. This is one that is informed primarily by the realist perspective of the international system's anarchical structure, the centrality of state as the key actor, and the belief in self-help. At the same time, it is one that utilises a whole range of tools and instruments, from building a strong military, to a pragmatic approach towards cooperation, active participation in multilateral institutions to emphasising the international norms and principles as embodied in the UN Charter.

Conservative pragmatism has guided Singapore's policymaking since its independence. Though there are several scholars such as Michael Leifer, who have classified Singapore as a realist in its approach towards international relations, realism in itself cannot adequately explain Singapore's foreign policy in the Asia-Pacific. It is rather an eclectic mix of approaches and improvisations, which I see as pragmatism, to ensure the best outcome for Singapore. It understands the constraints of structural power on what a small state can do, and often self-effacingly refers to itself as a price-taker; yet it actively participates in multilateral institutions and creates new institutions to ensure its voice is heard. It is conservative in the sense that it places the highest value on order (which often is seen as the pursuit of balance of power) and less so on the liberal pursuit of justice and liberty.

Singapore's approach to foreign policy served it well during the Cold War era, and also in the immediate post-Cold War period with the US as the sole superpower and its western-centric global order. Singapore subscribes to the view that the US presence in the Asia-Pacific region has fostered peace and stability, and is hence generally beneficial to the countries in the region. With the rapid rise of China, it is all the more important for the US to remain anchored in the Asia-Pacific, and play an active role in upholding peace and stability in the region.

The Association of Southeast Asian Nations (ASEAN) is an important cornerstone of Singapore's foreign policy. ASEAN was founded in 1967 to enable the smaller states of Southeast Asia to have a semblance of autonomy and not become proxies of great power games. It also provided a platform for confidence building amongst the member states — much needed in view of the different colonial histories and different trajectories in gaining independence. Tommy Koh's contributions to ASEAN, according to Ambassador Ong Keng Yong, are legendary. Ong described how Koh has given much of his public life to ASEAN, and not only during this time at the UN, "campaigning for Democratic Kampuchea as part of a consistent and persistent initiative by ASEAN to prevent a *fait accompli* after the Vietnamese invasion"; he was also very much involved in helping move ASEAN into the next stage of its development with the drafting of the ASEAN Charter.

Besides investing in ASEAN, Singapore also rode on the new wave of regionalism in the 1980s that led to the founding of the Asia-Pacific Economic Cooperation (APEC). In his essay, Manu Bhaskaran praised Tommy Koh as a "visionary of his time" for actively involving the business community to bring about a spirit of enterprise and practical mindedness to the APEC process.

APEC was built on the basis of "open regionalism", a concept taken to mean a non-exclusionary approach towards regional economic blocs that are compatible with the global trading system. The 1990s also saw the optimistic belief in growing international cooperation governed by institutions and rule of law, and a proliferation of new cooperative forums. Highly cognizant of these developments and broader trends, Singapore began a policy of actively supporting economic regionalisation and making a concerted effort to strike a balance between globalism and regionalism. It was also active in creating new multilateral forums from the Forum of Small States to the Asia-Europe Meeting (ASEM) and the Global Governance Group. As power became more diffused, Singapore also reached out to establish and strengthen partnerships beyond its immediate neighbourhood to Latin America and the Middle East, and this strategy of diversification could well continue as Singapore faces a more challenging external environment.

The external environment in which Singapore operates has become far more challenging in the second decade of the 21st century. Political and economic risks have increased in almost every region, including the developed West, and not just confined to less developed countries or emerging markets. There is a rising tide of nationalism, which is translating to anti-globalisation and protectionist sentiments. These underlying populist forces which had led to Brexit and Trump's election require Singapore to rethink its foreign policy strategy. Security tensions are rising in many parts of the world, from the intractable conflicts in the Middle East to the provocations from North Korea and heightened tensions in the Eastern part of Europe, the South China Sea and the India-Pakistan border. American ability or willingness to maintain the international order is declining in the aftermath of the long-drawn wars in Afghanistan and Iraq and the financial and debt crisis of 2008–2009. The Trump administration, in giving expression to his "America First" sentiments, portends a transactional, unilateral approach to international relations that would undermine any remnants of the western liberal order that had been in place for the last few decades. Any erratic unilateral policies by the US could also lead to serious miscalculations with potential for widespread chaos and conflicts.

With the unpredictability of the Trump presidency and the increasing assertiveness of China, the decades of sensible "symbiotic" relations between the US and China may be upended. We are therefore heading into uncharted territory, and our policy of not choosing sides between these two powers will come under immense pressure. How will international relations and Singapore's foreign policy evolve in the next decade, and will our diplomacy and diplomats continue to help us successfully navigate this increasingly complex and unpredictable external environment to ensure Singapore's survival for another 50 years?

International Relations and Diplomacy in the 21st Century

Twenty years ago, Amitav Acharya wrote in a book dedicated to Tommy Koh on his 60th birthday, noting that "Koh's career attests to the possibility of conceptualising international relations as an arena for a pragmatic but principled diplomacy, rather than as blind realpolitik and raw geopolitics."[5] He went on to expound on the importance of building international regimes and securing respect for international norms as ways to ensure survival and progress.

Unfortunately, this respect for international norms and rule of law looks set to be sorely tested in the years ahead. We are now going through the gradual decay of the international order that emerged after World War II and transitioning into a future system where the contours and parameters are not yet clear.

Global integration and globalism fostered by the advances in information and communications technologies in the last few decades have created more wealth and lifted millions out of poverty. It has empowered individuals and groups to impact geopolitics through their networks and connections. The same globalising forces and the technological disruptions have, however, also hollowed out the middle classes in the developed countries, and led to rising inequality and greater migration flows that threatened social cohesion in many societies. These have in turn resulted in rising populist and nativist impulses and a pushback against globalisation. Nationalism, identity politics and economic protectionism contribute to tensions within and between countries. Old geopolitical risks such as border disputes and military adventurism can now converge with new socioeconomic risks — from populism, fringe politics and declining trust in elites — to create new tensions, and more instability in regional and global environments.

Uncertainties about the commitment of the US to a liberal global order and an inward-looking Europe will encourage a more assertive China and Russia to stake their claim and carve out their own spheres of influence. Terrorism and other asymmetrical attacks or disruptions caused by dissident groups are likely to increase as empowered individ-

---

5 Amitav Acharya, "Introduction" in Tommy Koh. *The Quest for World Order: Perspectives of a Pragmatic Idealist* (IPS: Singapore, 1997), p.xxx.

uals and groups can leverage new technologies, new ideas and networks to destabilise the current political and economic systems. All these point to a far more volatile future. The US National Intelligence Council's 2017 report has in fact warned that the risks of conflicts between and within nations will increase over the next five years as global growth slows, the post-World War II order crumbles, and nationalism and anti-globalisation sentiments rise.[6]

The world of international relations in which diplomats operate will become more challenging and demanding. The number of actors who can shape geopolitics has grown, and the role of governments in setting and implementing policies is increasingly constrained by different actors with different agendas, making it harder to govern. The traditional functions of diplomacy in the sense of representation, communication and negotiations to manage inter-state relations will be severely challenged. There are now more actors, more channels and more issues to deal with. To a far greater extent than in the past, diplomacy now has to interact and compete with wider dynamics of agency, and to contend with domestic politics societal demands about governance. Diplomacy, for instance, is ineffective against rising sentiments of injustice and inequality among increasingly diverse social groups. But diplomacy, whether traditional diplomacy or public diplomacy, remains important in shaping and crafting new patterns of competition and cooperation between states and other important actors in the international arena.

To cope with a more complex and unpredictable environment, diplomacy can no longer take place only in a closed, hierarchical structure with formal rules and low transparency. The 21st century diplomat must learn to operate in two different spheres — a closed club-like atmosphere, but also an open network with far more diverse players. There will be greater demands for transparency and greater media scrutiny (particularly the social media). The ability to straddle both spheres and to turn the tensions between the two different spheres into creative energies for change and action is important.[7]

---

6 US National Intelligence Council, "Global Trends: Paradox of Progress," January 2017.

7 Andrew F Cooper, Jorge Heine and Ramesh Thakur, "Introduction: The Challenges of 21st Century Diplomacy" in *The Oxford Handbook of Modern Diplomacy*, edited by Andrew F Cooper, Jorge Heine and Ramesh Thakur (Oxford Handbooks Online, 2013).

Here I come back to what Ambassador Tommy Koh has done serving Singapore and the world.

Tommy Koh's Diplomatic Wisdom

Diplomacy will remain an important tool for small nations like Singapore, to create the regional and international space that is needed to survive and thrive. It helps to foster cooperation and is an important element in cementing partnerships and creating change. Singapore is fortunate to have dedicated diplomats like Tommy Koh who help the country navigate the complex foreign policy landscape, promoting Singapore's interests and building Singapore's reputation in the global arena. Although only a little red dot, Singapore has always been known to punch above its weight.

In Ambassador Tommy Koh's 1997 collection of essays *The Quest for World Order: Perspectives of a Pragmatic Idealist*, it was revealed that Koh, an ardent admirer of U Thant,[8] sees himself as a pragmatic idealist who tries to reconcile his optimism, his belief in justice and faith in qualities such as honesty and reciprocity with the realpolitik approach and cynicism that is so commonplace in the world of diplomacy. In Acharya's words: "Koh firmly believes that idealism accompanied by common-sense pragmatism is desirable not just from a moral point of view but also as a practical and efficient way of conducting international relations."[9]

Would Tommy Koh's seven pillars of wisdom, his endearing qualities and enduring optimism continue to be relevant in a fast-changing unpredictable world? My answer is a resounding yes.

We need our diplomats to be tough and charming, principled and pragmatic, ethical and shrewd all at the same time if they are to be able to deal with an ambiguous world. Most importantly, we need them not only to be smart, but to possess the cultural and emotional intelligence, the empathy to feel the prevailing mood, appreciate the differences and understand the context of a situation, and communicate and work with

8 Myanmar diplomat who served as the 3rd Secretary-General of the United Nations.
9 Amitav Acharya, "Introduction" in Tommy Koh. *The Quest for World Order: Perspectives of a Pragmatic Idealist* (IPS: Singapore, 1997), p.xviii.

others for answers and solutions to our problems. But the most important quality of all is dedication and the belief in human agency and the ability to learn and adapt. It is not only the diplomats but all of us who can take inspiration from Tommy Koh's life of service to Singapore and the world.

CHAPTER 2

A Professor and His International Stage

ᴏɴɢ ᴋᴇɴɢ ʏᴏɴɢ

For several years, I have worked with Ambassador-at-Large Professor Tommy Koh at close quarters in a number of forums to project and protect Singapore's national interests, and he never fails to amaze me each time I see him in action. His skills and diplomatic prowess are well known. He speaks clearly and concisely, with an appropriate dose of humour and objectivity. His devotion to making "three points", on the direction of his beloved wife, is a KPI (key performance indicator) that I try to achieve, much to the delight of my own wife who thinks I am too long-winded at times.

Tommy Koh's written work is easy to read, often very practical-oriented, and most importantly, addresses complicated issues in layman's language that can be understood by the general public. It is a joy to read his essays even when they can be lengthy and focused on technical issues such as Law of the Sea. Someone asked me on one occasion how Tommy Koh could possess such deep and wide knowledge. The enquirer said Professor Koh seemed to know every important topic in Singapore's foreign policy and the huge area of international relations. I told the enquirer to take a look at the books and papers in Koh's library. I added that Tommy Koh was also astute in asking the right questions, and always eager to acquire new knowledge. When he taught people, wrote about issues of interest or made speeches in forums worldwide, he would acquire new ideas and skills. He was always learning and digesting what others would tell him, and he repackaged complex issues into simpler formulations for others to appreciate the key points.

Drafting the ASEAN Charter

Indeed, Tommy Koh is the academic par excellence and diplomat *et non erat*. In drafting the ASEAN Charter from 2006 to 2007, he adroitly applied his vast legal knowledge and varied experiences from being a top rules-based champion and negotiator, to persuade, cajole and inspire 10 delegations from the ASEAN family to accept the language and outcome for what he called "the first formal document to institutionalise ASEAN." The Singapore delegation was also a party that had to be convinced of certain phrases and sentences in the drafting of the Charter. I could see the Singaporeans struck with awe whenever Tommy Koh raised diplomatic and legal arguments.

I asked my former Special Assistant in the ASEAN Secretariat, Termsak Chalermpalanupap, who had served four different Secretaries-General of ASEAN, for his recollection of Koh's brilliant manoeuvres in preparing the ASEAN Charter. Termsak replied as follows:

> *Essentially, Tommy was the peace-maker, the mediator and the cheer-leader combined into one. I recall we ran into some difficulty with Cambodia, Laos, Myanmar and Vietnam (CLMV), especially concerning a new ASEAN organ to handle human rights cooperation. At one time, the Charter drafters from the CLMV countries and other ASEAN member states could not even sit together. Tommy had to shuttle back and forth between the two groups to try to wrap up the drafting in time for the leader of the Thai delegation to bring the draft back to Bangkok in time for the Thai Cabinet's approval.*[1]

Nurturing Younger Colleagues

One innovation Professor Koh introduced in the Charter drafting process was the Assistants Group. Each delegation from ASEAN member states was to nominate an assistant to the Head of Delegation and this person would meet the other nine assistants (ASEAN has 10 member states) and brainstorm ideas or consider how to reconcile the competing drafts or wording. The challenge was to have the assistants from the

---

1 Termsak Chalermpalanupap, e-mail message to author, September 29, 2016.

less developed ASEAN countries be given the necessary authority to speak and negotiate. The respective assistants must have the mandate to deliberate the choices with their peers. A number of young assistants intimated to me that they were still "junior" in their own respective bureaucratic systems and never had the kind of authority to negotiate anything previously. In the end, the conclusions of the assistants' deliberations helped to expedite the discussions at the main drafting committee and break deadlocks among "senior" members in settling key texts for the ASEAN Charter.

The nurturing and teaching ways of Tommy Koh probably originated from his years as an excellent professor and Dean of the Faculty of Law at the National University of Singapore. His clarity of thought and constant search for young talented individuals to do more admirable jobs inspired many ASEAN senior officials. These officials would always welcome his suggestions and would give any proposal Tommy Koh made the due consideration. As a Thai negotiator put it, they saw the logic of his "legalese" and the fair-minded approach he espoused.

Sharing Knowledge

Another example of Koh's professorial style is the public forums he initiated at the end of the Japan-Singapore Symposium and the India-Singapore Strategic Dialogue. I am involved in these Track 1.5 forums that regularly bring together Track 1 and Track 2 experts[2] to exchange views on the latest regional and international developments and how they have created an impact on bilateral relations. Tommy Koh would highlight the relevant issues for the public forums and any interested party could sign up to attend, listen and ask questions or make comments. The policy objectives of public messaging and public education are often realised through his open and classy discourse. The interesting aspect of such interactions is the way he could draw out the foreign participants in these Track 1.5 dialogue process and put them through a meaningful engagement with the public at large. The effusive Indian

---

2 Track 1 refers to diplomacy between governments and their representatives; Track 2 experts refer to non-government actors like civil society, academia, businesses and other informal contacts or individual citizens.

and reticent Japanese participants of the government-supported forums would become willing collaborators under the masterful direction of Tommy Koh on the public stage. That is the real treat for me attending these public forums.

Championing ASEAN

Ambassador Koh is more than the public communicator. He is famously recognised in Singapore, ASEAN and the world. He is a brilliant thinker and strategist. Through his years on the international stage, he has honed his skills and reinforced his instinct with an uncanny combination of his disarming *élan* and remarkable presence of mind. When former Australian Prime Minister Kevin Rudd tried to promote the Asia-Pacific community (APc), which is inimical to Singapore's interests and could well undermine ASEAN's strategic relevance, Tommy Koh executed a *coup de grace*. Rudd aimed his APc as a regional institution that would cover the entire Asia-Pacific but with only selective principal members, namely, the United States, China, India, Japan, Australia and Indonesia. There was nothing for ASEAN in Rudd's vision. Such a proposal was criticised by ASEAN leaders and intellectuals who were favourably disposed towards the prevailing mechanisms in regional diplomatic and security architecture.

Despite the criticisms, Rudd raised his idea at the APEC CEO Summit, which was held in Singapore in 2009. Tommy Koh chaired the session that featured Rudd, and popped three questions to poll the large number of CEOs present. The first question was on whether the existing architecture for political and security dialogue in the region had been successful. The vote was 80% "yes". The second question was whether the region needed a new institution, as proposed by Rudd. The CEOs voted 55% in favour. Then the "killer question" came: "Should ASEAN's role as the region's facilitator and catalyst be preserved?" The response was 75% "yes". After the APEC CEO Summit, Rudd convened a specially arranged meeting of regional experts from Track 1 and Track 2 to discuss the APc in Sydney in December 2009. Tommy Koh attended this Sydney gathering. He was very alert and followed the proceedings closely. He expressed his concern at one point with the procedure adopted by the senior Australian in charge of advancing the proposed APc. Koh argued that there was no serious exchange of views on the move to establish a group of eminent persons from the region to discuss a "concert of powers" as a means to manage relations in the region (which would presumably replace ASEAN). Koh also disagreed openly with the suggestion from certain quarters that the ASEAN Regional Forum (ARF) was not useful anymore because of its unwieldy membership. Overall, his succinct articulation of the potential undercutting of ASEAN by any new and hasty assembling of regional big countries, as envisaged by Rudd and his supporters, debunked the rationale for the APc. Tommy Koh stated it this way: "We in ASEAN feel the grouping's long-term goal of peace and stability and the dividends obtained to date should not be minimised or marginalised."[3]

Tommy Koh has given much of his public life to ASEAN. His exploits at the UN and other international forums to campaign for Democratic Kampuchea as part of a consistent and persistent initiative by ASEAN to prevent a *fait accompli* after the Vietnamese invasion of Cambodia in the guise of removing the genocidal Khmer Rouge, are legendary. In fact, today's Cambodia owes its birth to a group of internationalists and principled diplomats fighting the Vietnamese-installed Heng Samrin regime in Phnom Penh. Among them is Tommy Koh who stood tall and prominent. Without them, the history of Southeast Asia, ASEAN and Cambodia will be very different. I should leave it to those directly involved in this fascinating episode of ASEAN diplomatic history to write the story authoritatively.

In closing, Singaporeans must also thank Tommy Koh for his exemplary contribution to nation-building. He is among the pioneer generation of the country's builders. He managed the external dimension after policy decisions had been made by the leadership in Singapore. He had presented a credible and effective foreign policy for the island republic on the international stage. He added much punch to Singapore's diplomacy abroad. The Singapore brand created by Lee Kuan Yew and the political leaders has been enriched by Koh's extraordinary diplomatic agility and resourcefulness. "Prof." or "Professor", as we like to call him,

---

3 Tommy Koh, "Rudd's Reckless Regional Rush," *The Australian*, December 18, 2009.

is always obliging when asked by the government and private sector to undertake all kinds of "national service", for example, serving in statutory boards and chairing committees concerned with policy matters. Simply put, his achievements are far beyond what an outstanding academic from the university appointed into diplomatic service would dare dream to strive for. Singaporeans must appreciate and treasure the results of this man's endeavours for the little red dot.

CHAPTER 3

The Master Multilateral Diplomat: The Seven Pillars of Tommy Koh's Wisdom

✌

KISHORE MAHBUBANI

Over 20 years ago, when I was the Permanent Secretary of the Ministry of Foreign Affairs, I accompanied the then Prime Minister of Singapore, Goh Chok Tong, on an official visit to Germany. During this visit, we took a short boat cruise on a river. On the cruise, Prime Minister Goh asked me, "Kishore, why do we have so few globally recognised diplomats like Tommy Koh and Chan Heng Chee?"

Twenty years later, the same question can still be asked. Tommy Koh's success in multilateral diplomacy, especially in the UN family, is truly outstanding. If Joseph Schooling has won one gold medal for Singapore in the Olympics, Tommy Koh has won many gold medals for Singapore in the field of multilateral diplomacy. Two stand out in particular: his chairmanship of the UN Conference on the Law of the Sea (1980–1982) and his chairmanship of the Preparatory Committee (PrepCom) for the Main Committee of the UN Conference on Environment and Development (the Rio Conference, 1990–1992).

Few diplomats are given the privilege of chairing one global conference involving all UN member states. I have never chaired any. Even fewer are given the privilege of chairing two. What makes Tommy Koh's role in multilateral diplomacy even more striking is that he succeeded in securing a consensus at both these global conferences. Securing consensus among almost 190 countries with vastly different interests is actually harder than winning a gold medal in the Olympics. It takes extraordinary diplomatic skills to succeed.

Prime Minister Goh is right in suggesting that Singapore needs to produce more globally successful diplomats like Tommy Koh. The goal of this essay, therefore, is a simple one: to spell out the qualities that led to Tommy Koh's extraordinary diplomatic success. I would like to suggest that Tommy Koh has seven pillars of diplomatic wisdom. Future Singaporean diplomats could try to replicate these seven pillars to achieve similar success.

Pillar One: Being Ethical

The first pillar is that Tommy Koh is always ethical. This may come as a surprise to many readers. Many people believe in the well-known adage: "An ambassador is an honest gentleman sent to lie abroad for the good of his country." Yet, Tommy Koh never told any lies. Indeed, he confirmed the wisdom of the famous British diplomat Sir Harold Nicolson, who said that the most important quality of any diplomat is truthfulness.

Tommy Koh has confirmed this in one of his essays. He said:

> Machiavelli also advised the prince that "it is necessary to be a great pretender and dissembler." In my experience, this is bad advice. In the community of nations, some governments and diplomats acquire a reputation for duplicity and dishonesty. Is a government or a diplomat with a reputation for veracity and integrity more likely to succeed in promoting the country's interests than one with a reputation for duplicity? I think the answer is yes to the former.[1]

In the multilateral context, Tommy Koh's integrity was also a huge asset. His shining integrity led diplomats from all over the world to trust him. It is traditional for diplomatic gridlocks to emerge at major global conferences. When this happened, many chairmen would set up small negotiating groups to solve the gridlock. Tommy Koh resisted

---

1 Tommy Koh, "Can Any Country Afford a Moral Foreign Policy?" in *The Quest for World Order: Perspectives from a Pragmatic Idealist* (Singapore: Marshall Cavendish Academic, 1997), 2.

this practice as he believed in openness and transparency. In one of his essays, he explained his methods:

> *The UN has 192 member states. Most international conferences are attended by all the member states of the UN and sometimes, even more. It is difficult to conduct negotiations with so many interlocutors. It is, therefore, always tempting for the chairman to set up a smaller nego-tiating group. One should always resist this temptation unless one has the blessings of the plenary to do so. During the fourth and final session of the UNCED Preparatory Committee, the Committee requested me to take over the negotiations of the text of the Rio Declaration of Prin-ciples from the chairman of the Third Committee. I agreed to do so on the condition that the negotiations be conducted in a group of 16, eight each from the Group of 77 and OECD. The plenary agreed and the 16 members of the negotiating group were chosen, not by me, but by the two interest groups. We completed our negotiations in two days and the result of the small group was subsequently ratified by the plenary. In Rio, all the negotiations were conducted in the presence of all delegations. It was hard, but we succeeded in negotiating and adopting by consensus, the 500 pages of Agenda 21. My advice to conference chairmen is to avoid setting up small negotiating groups in secret. Why? Because the secrecy will be exposed, the product of the small negotiating group will be repudiated and your credibility will be destroyed.*[2]

This episode also demonstrates that both the developed and devel-oping countries allowed Tommy Koh to work with small groups repre-senting them because they trusted him to be fair and ethical.

Of course, being ethical can also create disadvantages in multilat-eral diplomacy. In 1981, Tommy Koh was persuaded to run for the Presidency of the United Nations General Assembly. He ran against two candidates: Ambassador Ismat Kittani from Iraq and Ambassador Khwaja Mohammed Kaiser from Bangladesh. His two competitors campaigned ferociously. Tommy Koh took the ethical route. He said he would not campaign and would leave it to the UN member states

---

2 Tommy Koh, "The Art of Chairing Conferences: Lessons Learnt," in *The Tommy Koh Reader: Favour-ite Essays and Lectures* (Singapore: World Scientific, 2013), 240–241.

to decide. As a result, even though Tommy Koh was better known and more highly respected, he was eliminated in the first round of voting.

Pillar Two: Shrewd Understanding

The second pillar of Tommy Koh's wisdom is that he is shrewd. Traditionally, many ethical people tend to be politically naive. However, Tommy is not. He understands the complex political dynamics that go into a global negotiating process. Timing is always critical in trying to broker an agreement. Tommy Koh has given an example of how wrong timing can lead to failure. During the Rio PrepCom process, Working Group III (on law and institutions) elected Bedřich Moldan of Czechoslovakia as its chairman. Tommy Koh explained what happened:

> One of the items on its agenda was the drafting of the Rio Declaration on the Environment and Development, popularly referred to as the Earth Charter. At the beginning of the fourth substantive session, Moldan offered a compromise draft consisting of 10 principles and three prerequisites. He moved too soon. Also, his draft was viewed, rightly or wrongly, by the developing countries as favouring the viewpoint of the developed countries. Because of this, the developing countries refused to continue to negotiate under his chairmanship.[3]

In contrast to the failure by Moldan, Tommy Koh was able to produce success after success whenever he chaired the meetings. His success was a result of a shrewd understanding of when the conditions were right to push for an agreement, as well as his ability to foster the right conditions. For example, according to James Sebenius and Laurence Green of the Harvard Business School:

> In 1978, Koh was appointed to chair a key negotiating committee of the overall LOS (Law of the Sea) conference that dealt with the financial terms of contracts to mine the resources of the deep seabed and ocean

---

3 Tommy Koh, "The Earth Summit's Negotiating Process," in *The Tommy Koh Reader: Favourite Essays and Lectures* (Singapore: World Scientific, 2013), 491.

floor. Deep disagreements over the implementation and financing of so-called deep seabed mining stood in the way of the 150+ participant nations reaching agreement on the overall convention .... Carefully introducing outside experts while balancing formal meetings with non-binding gatherings, Koh incrementally built both momentum and consensus for a remarkably creative agreement on seabed mining. In 1980, Koh's group reached agreement on a text used directly by the convention. His unexpected success led the grateful LOS delegates to elect him to be president of the overall LOS conference, which finally produced a treaty — a "constitution for the oceans" — ultimately ratified by 165 nations and signed by an additional 15 countries.[4]

Pillar Three: Personal Charm

The third pillar of Tommy Koh's wisdom is that he is always charming. Personal charm is one of the most underrated features of diplomacy. When I arrived at the UN in August 1984 to take on the impossible mission of succeeding Tommy Koh as the Singapore Ambassador to the UN, I quickly learned that personal charm went a long way in multilateral diplomacy. Soon after I arrived, I discovered that one of the most popular and effective diplomats to the UN was the Ugandan Ambassador to the UN, Olara Otunnu. He managed to singlehandedly broker an agreement to select Javier Pérez de Cuéllar as the Secretary-General of the UN in 1982. Olara was remarkably effective even though he came from a broken country, Uganda, which had just emerged from Idi Amin's disastrous rule in 1979.

Olara was also a great admirer of Tommy Koh. Indeed, everyone I met on arrival in the UN in 1984 on arrival was an admirer of Tommy Koh. His charm would win over everybody. Since a strong sense of humour is a quality not normally associated with being a Singaporean, it is essential to emphasise here that Tommy Koh had a superb sense of humour. He would tell self-deprecating jokes. And after he had rammed through a difficult agreement, he would proudly announce to his audience, "My mother will be very proud of what I have done."

---

4 James K. Sebenius and Laurence A. Green, "Tommy Koh: Background and Major Accomplishments of the 'Great Negotiator, 2014'", *Harvard Business School Working Paper 14–049* (2014): 3.

Pillar Four: Toughness

The fourth pillar of Tommy Koh's wisdom is that he is very tough. Most charming people tend to be soft and pliable. Tommy Koh is the opposite. Whenever it is necessary, he is prepared to be tough. When the chairmen of the sub-committee of the Rio PrepCom failed to achieve their tasks, Tommy Koh replaced them. As he has said in his essay on the Rio negotiating process:

> As one who attaches great value to loyalty and friendship, I have always found it very hard to abandon a colleague. However, I felt duty-bound to put the best interests of the Conference before friendship and loyalty. The fact that both Ricupero and Alders[5] succeeded in their work showed that I was right to make the personnel changes.[6]

Equally important, Tommy Koh could be very tough whenever he wielded the gavel at international conferences. Tommy Koh was not afraid of confronting strong and important delegations at the UN if he felt they were being unreasonable. As he has explained in one of his essays:

> However, if you judge that the delegation is acting unreasonably, you must have the courage to confront that delegation. At the fourth session of the UNCED Preparatory Committee, Israel was the only delegation which opposed the adoption of the Rio Declaration of Principles. At the Earth Summit, Saudi Arabia insisted on deleting the whole chapter, on Climate, from Agenda 21. I overruled Israel and Saudi Arabia and requested them to challenge my ruling which I was prepared to put to the vote. They were angry, but declined to challenge my ruling because they knew that they did not have the support to overturn my ruling.[7]

---

5 Rubens Ricupero, the Brazilian Ambassador, and J. M. G. Alders, the Dutch Minister for the Environment.
6 Tommy Koh, "UNCED Leadership: A Personal Perspective," in *Negotiating International Regimes: Lessons Learned from the United Nations Conference on Environment and Development (UNCED)*, ed. Bertram I. Spector, Gunnar Sjostedt and I. William Zartmann, (London: Graham-Trotman/Martinus Nijhoff), 167.
7 Tommy Koh, "The Art of Chairing Conferences: Lessons Learnt," in *The Tommy Koh Reader: Favourite Essays and Lectures* (Singapore: World Scientific, 2013), 242–243.

Pillar Five: Being Principled

The fifth pillar of Tommy Koh's wisdom is that he is principled. He stands by his principles, even when it is not popular to do so. In the UN, Tommy Koh, as an avid defender of international law, would consistently take a strong stand against the invasion and occupation of a small state by a larger one.

It was easy for Tommy Koh to take a principled stand against the Vietnamese invasion of Cambodia in 1978 and the Soviet invasion of Afghanistan in 1979, because Singapore was clearly closer to the United States during the Cold War. There were few political costs to criticising the Soviet Union then. However, Tommy Koh had to pay some political costs when he also strongly criticised the invasion of Grenada by the United States in 1983.

I know that Tommy Koh's principled stand at the UN against the American invasion caused some discomfort in Singapore. The feeling among some in the Ministry of Foreign Affairs then was that since the United States was a good friend, Singapore should not have been so tough in its criticisms. Tommy Koh, however, insisted on being principled. In his statement to the UN Security Council on October 28, 1983, he said:

> Mr President, it is easy enough for us to demonstrate our adherence to principle when to do so is convenient and advantageous and costs us nothing. The test of a country's adherence to principle is when it is inconvenient to do so. I find myself in such a situation today. Barbados, Jamaica, the United States and the Member States of the Organisation of East Caribbean States are friends of my country. It is extremely convenient for me to acquiesce in what they have done or to remain silent. To do so will, in the long run, undermine the moral and legal significance of the principles which my country regards as a shield. This is why we must put our adherence to principle above friendship. This is why we cannot condone the action of our friends in Grenada.[8]

---

8 Tommy Koh, "The Situation in Grenada," statement delivered to the UN Security Council on October 28, 1983, in *The Tommy Koh Reader: Favourite Essays and Lectures* (Singapore: World Scientific, 2013), 197–198.

Some years later, when the then Prime Minister Lee Kuan Yew met George Shultz, then Secretary of State in the US, he told Mr Shultz that he would have crafted the speech on Grenada differently. Clearly, Lee Kuan Yew was not happy with the approach Tommy Koh had taken. Yet, I know that Tommy was unfazed by this. When he believed that he had taken a principled stand, he would stay the course.

Pillar Six: Pragmatism

The sixth pillar of Tommy Koh's wisdom is that he can also be very pragmatic. Probably the biggest diplomatic disappointment that Tommy Koh suffered in his entire career was when the US government, under the leadership of President Ronald Reagan, decided not to sign the UN Convention of the Law of the Sea (UNCLOS) in 1982. In a *Wall Street Journal* commentary by William Clark and Edwin Meese from the Reagan administration, they wrote that the real reason Reagan rejected UNCLOS was that "no nat[ional] interest of ours could justify handing sovereign control of two-thirds of the earth's surface over to the Third World." President Reagan had also privately written in his diary on June 29, 1982, "Decided in [National Security Council] meeting — will not sign 'Law of the Sea' treaty even without seabed mining provisions."[9]

I remember discussing with Tommy this American decision to walk away from UNCLOS. He saw it clearly as an act of bad faith. The US had negotiated hard and secured many key concessions on issues that were vital to American interests, such as freedom of navigation in international waterways and Exclusive Economic Zones (EEZs). Even though the US did not sign UNCLOS, it knew that it would enjoy the benefits of these concessions as others would respect these provisions. At the same time, the US did not want to sign UNCLOS as it would tie American hands on deep seabed mining. In short, the US wanted others to be bound by the rules that benefited it, but it did not want to be bound by the rules that benefited others.

Tommy Koh felt deeply betrayed by this American decision as he had negotiated in good faith with them. In a remarkable irony of history,

---

9 Ronald Reagan, *The Reagan Diaries*, ed. Douglas Brinkley (New York: Harper Colllins, 2007), 140.

Tommy Koh was posted as Singapore's Ambassador to the US in 1984, two years after the American decision to walk away from UNCLOS. Despite his sense of personal betrayal, Tommy continued working pragmatically with the Reagan administration. Indeed, he did a brilliant job as the Singapore Ambassador. He secured the highest honour that any Singapore leader has ever received in Washington D.C., where Prime Minister Lee Kuan Yew was invited to address a joint session of the US Congress on October 9, 1985. I was personally present on the occasion. I learnt at first hand what a diplomatic coup Tommy had secured.

Similarly, in multilateral negotiations within the UN, Tommy would be equally pragmatic. He knew when to make significant concessions to secure an agreement. In an essay, Tommy Koh has noted that negotiations can only succeed with a spirit of give and take on both sides, including:

> ... willingness to make a small concession, in a matter of secondary importance to my country, in order to achieve an agreement on a package deal which is of fundamental interest to my country. In other words, I must be flexible and accommodating. However, when my fundamental interest is at stake, I must be firm and let my negotiating partner know that it is a point on which I have no flexibility.[10]

Pillar Seven: Dedication

The seventh pillar of Tommy Koh's wisdom is that he is dedicated. It is truly amazing how long Tommy has worked in the field of multilateral diplomacy. He began his career with the Ministry of Foreign Affairs as the Singapore Ambassador to the UN in 1968. Forty-nine years later, in 2017, he remains an Ambassador-at-Large with Ministry and continues to be involved in all kinds of diplomatic negotiations, formally and informally, on behalf of Singapore. There is virtually no one in Singapore who can match his long record of dedicated service to Singapore.

His dedication to serving Singapore's diplomatic interests explains his willingness to take on a whole variety of diplomatic assignments.

---

10 Tommy Koh, "Eight Lessons on Negotiations," in *The Tommy Koh Reader: Favourite Essays and Lectures* (Singapore: World Scientific, 2013), 237.

He has handled sensitive global negotiations, like UNCLOS and the Rio Conference. He has also handled sensitive bilateral negotiations like the agreement reached between Singapore and China on issues involving Taiwan. Tommy Koh has written in an essay stating:

In 1990, I was asked to lead a delegation to negotiate an agreement with China for the establishment of formal diplomatic relations between our two countries. At our first meeting in Beijing, the Singapore side explained to our Chinese friends that although we wanted the negotiation to succeed, we were not prepared to humiliate Taiwan, to abrogate our existing agreements with her or for our leaders to give up their right to visit Taiwan, in their individual and private capacities. The negotiations were successfully concluded and formal diplomatic relations were established in October 1990.[11]

In addition, he delivered a political miracle by managing to secure an agreement on the complex document called the ASEAN Charter within a year. It's hard to imagine anyone else succeeding in such a delicate exercise.

Another equally delicate exercise was the negotiation Tommy undertook to secure an agreement between Russia and the tiny Baltic states of Estonia, Latvia and Lithuania, "to facilitate the complete withdrawal of foreign military forces from the territories of Estonia, Latvia and Lithuania."[12]

With this remarkable track record of dedicated and effective diplomacy, Tommy Koh will clearly go down in Singapore's history as the number one Singapore diplomat. Quite amazingly, he could also go down in world history as one of the most effective multilateral diplomats ever. Tommy deserves every tribute he has received. And we should continue to learn lessons from his wisdom.

---

11 Tommy Koh, "Confessions of a Lucky Negotiator," *The Straits Times*, May 7, 2014, http://news.asiaone.com/news/singapore/confessions-lucky-negotiator.
12 United Nations General Assembly, "Resolution Adopted by the General Assembly, United Nations General Assembly 47th Session, Agenda item 139, March 24, 1993, http://www.un.org/en/ga/search/view_doc.asp?symbol=A/RES/47/21.

Chapter 4

Tommy Koh: The Master Distiller and His Legacy as a Negotiator

———— ❧ ————

Daren Tang

On the morning of November 17, 2000, I opened *The Straits Times* to a huge headline "US, S'pore Eye Free Trade Pact", announcing that the US-Singapore Free Trade Agreement had been launched. Barely two minutes later, my then boss, the late S Tiwari, called and asked if I had seen it. Before waiting for my answer, he told me to hurry to the office. I gulped my breakfast down and rushed in.

Thus began a frantic and intense two-and-a-half-year journey as a member of the US-Singapore FTA team, whose Chief Negotiator was Ambassador Tommy Koh and whose leadership of that negotiation would shape and influence my professional life in many ways.

For those who have not been involved in international negotiations, it seems to be a world of mystery, drama and glamour, populated with characters from a Le Carre novel whose protaganists look like Nicole Kidman or Tom Hanks. The reality is of course far more prosaic. What often happens is that teams of subject matter experts meet at conference venues, sit across one another in rooms and attempt to make sense of what can be very different perspectives and approaches on issues that have to be addressed in the negotiations. Sometimes the subject matter is straightforward and the context almost amorous — for example, a Twin City agreement. And at other times, the topics are devilishly complex and the environment fraught with tension, for example, climate change negotiations. Whatever the context, the most common mistake a negotiator makes is to approach negotiations as a purely intellectual exercise, and to assume that the most rational and intelligent solution to a negotiating problem will carry the day. The truth is that rationality is often just the starting point for gaining credibility, and that negotiations are far more often about relationships and the dynamics of the process.

A few days after the announcement of the launch of negotiations, the entire negotiating team finally met in a sprawling room in the Ministry of Trade and Industry. It was the first time I had seen so many people representing virtually every government ministry in Singapore assembled at one location. The more senior officers knew each other fairly well and went around saying hello, whilst those who were more junior hung at the back, eyeing the scene and absorbing the atmosphere. There was a nervous energy and people either spoke too quickly or too quietly.

Finally, Tommy Koh walked in. He immediately struck me as quite different from the other civil servants I had worked with. It started with the hair, which, for a civil servant, was long. Yet it was groomed and swept back in a way that paired perfectly with the pace and cadence of his speech, which tended to the professorial. His hands would assume a gentle chopping motion as he made his points, more tai chi in its feel than karate. There was a genteel confidence to his manner, and a calm that radiated through the unspoken anxieties in the room. In time to come we would take it for granted, but at that first meeting it stood out sharply. Towards the end of negotiations that same preternatural calm would help pave the way for conclusion, when there were often tense moments, both internally and externally.

Another quality was soon to be evident at that first meeting — a striking and uncanny ability to take the most mundane observations and even incoherent responses from the members of the team, and paraphrase them elegantly into something that made perfect and natural sense. This was a master distiller at work. It was an ability that I would see in action time and again as we worked together over the next few years.

In negotiations, whether corporate, governmental or international, the messenger is often as important as the message. Knowing how to phrase something appropriately, and with the right amount of sweetness — or tartness, as the case may be — and at the right time to the right person, can make the difference between a breakthrough or a breakdown in discussions. This is something that comes with experience and perhaps sensitivity; the former is something that can be picked up, the latter perhaps not. In Singapore's case, there has always been a willingness to take young and smart people and throw them into the fray of negotiations. The upside of this is that these young people soon pick up the ropes, and those that don't sink, will swim. But the downside is that the lack of experience may sometimes lead to unskilful interventions or engagements that raise temperatures unnecessarily, or cool the negotiations too quickly, both equally undesirable.

In such a team, it is crucial to balance youth with experience. Watching Tommy Koh gave us an insight into how to engage with the opponent on the other side. His ability to disarm was unparalleled. He would combine some soothing turn of phrase with the appropriate body language to signify openness and receptivity. He never took umbrage easily, or gave in to apoplectic fits, no matter how unreasonable the demands. We learnt from him how to explain the uniqueness of Singapore in a way that was self-deprecating and illuminating, often as a prelude to an effective explanation of why we took a certain negotiating position.

One of his favourite tactics was to turn the table around and point out the absurdity of the request being sought by asking the other side if they would have agreed to it if we had sought the same. And he prodded us internally when he felt that there were certain policies or practices which could do with a rethink, or had become obsolete and had to be dropped. When all else failed, he always made a point wrapped around a homily which he claimed had been given to him by his wife. And as we all know, no one quite dares to dispute what one hears from one's spouse. So that invariably settled the matter!

His interest in the younger members of the team was also unusual, often singling us out in fulsome terms to others that embarrassed us. Yet what was even rarer was that he took an interest in not just tutoring us in negotiations, but the larger and broader things in life. In complex negotiations like the US-Singapore FTA, what happens is that there are close to 20 negotiating groups undergoing concurrent negotiations. Each group sits in their separate room, and the Deputy and Chief

Negotiators float from room to room, sometimes sitting in on the especially difficult ones, hoping that their presence would lend some progress to the recalcitrant team. What happens though is that at the end of the day, all teams will meet to brief the Chief Negotiator on the salient events of that day. After these serious work meetings, he would hold off dismissing us until he shared a list of interesting artistic or cultural events happening that evening. In fact, at one session I joined him to watch Lee Huei Min's debut at Wigmore Hall in London, and learnt that the violin which she played on was a 1704 Guarnerius filius Andreae. He was in a celebratory mood, and shared with me that he had played a role in getting sponsorship for her to play this violin when he was Chair of the National Arts Council. Many other colleagues were the beneficiaries of his forays into these events, and he was a civilising influence in a world that was often steeped in the rough and tumble of negotiations. He was the first negotiator I saw who was able to adroitly and skilfully combine negotiations with diplomacy, and taught me that in negotiations, we are seen and judged as representatives of the country whose flag we fly.

One of the earliest lessons we learnt from Tommy Koh was the ability of food to bring people of all nationalities together. He called it "*makan* diplomacy" and under his tutelage we practised it to a high degree of polish by the time we finished the USSFTA. He always made sure that our counterparts were well fed, but it was not merely a gustatory gesture. Food was the jumping point for understanding the cultural context of the cuisine and other excursions into history and society. Nevertheless, we saw the earthy effects at the negotiating table, when after a satisfying lunch, our counterparts would be far more amenable to what seemed uncompromisingly difficult in the morning, or would be too drowsy to really object to a position we were advocating.

We did not tell Ambassador Koh this, but some of us also played "*makan* diplomacy" in a perverse fashion, by using it to put the other side into a position of some discomfort when we felt they deserved to be roughed up a bit. I recall feeding one particular intransigent negotiator durian puffs, and one other group brought their entire team of disagreeable counterparts to the spiciest fish head curry restaurant in Little India. By and large though, "*makan* diplomacy" drew on the truism that people bond over food, and that this in turn made it easier to break the ice and build familiarity so that candid conversations could be had on what needed to be done to move the negotiations forward.

One of the toughest things in negotiations is to build respect and yet bring barriers down. Respect at the negotiating table is earned through command and mastery of subject matter, or display of a trait, e.g., prodigious stamina in negotiating stubbornly until the wee hours of the morning, that serves one's country well. (My ex-boss, S Tiwari, was a particularly practised exponent of this). But this does not mean that the other side feels warmth or a certain closeness. And this is what sets apart the good negotiators from the great ones.

Intellectual capacity and technical knowledge are crucial elements in taking the negotiation process from the start to a state where the issues and differences have been defined, but it is often not enough to take it to closure, where the issues have to be ironed out, and the differences transcended. This requires creativity, and often, "constructive ambiguity" — an entirely apposite phrase that I first heard from Tommy Koh. The rub is this: constructive ambiguity requires trust, which is relational in nature. What we all learnt from Tommy Koh was not just that this was important, but how to go about building it. He taught us that one needed to get to know one's fellow negotiators not just across the negotiating table, but also in a social setting. He humanised the whole process, and made us understand that we were not just dealing with the representative of a sovereign state, but a human being whose perspective of the world had an impact on negotiations and was worth knowing. It was an invaluable lesson for a young officer whose experience of government was still very much within the rational and technical domains. He opened our eyes to the intangible and relational aspects of negotiations, which like dark matter, exerts a heavy influence on the negotiations even if initially unseen.

I worked with Tommy Koh at a fairly late stage in his career as a diplomat and negotiator, and never had the chance to see him in action in the contexts which made him renowned throughout the diplomatic world — his chairing of the negotiations that led to the 1982 UN Convention of the Law of the Sea, or the 1992 Rio Summit. Of course, I had older colleagues who had worked with him in those projects, and their anecdotes confirmed to me that some of his characteristics I witnessed as a negotiator; his ability to distil a point, his even-temperedness and bonhomie, his adroitness in managing negotiation dynamics were present even early on. However, I had a small flavour of what he had to navigate when I was chairing the IP negotiations in the Trans-Pacific Partnership Agreement (TPP).

The USSFTA was a complex FTA given the breadth of its impact on our economy, and the ambition of the disciplines. Moreover, as everyone knows, the US has a complex set of domestic checks and balances that engenders difficult internal negotiations. However, it is still ultimately a set of negotiations between just two countries. In a multilateral setting like the TPP, the Law of the Sea or the Rio Summit, the number of participants can be the entire international community, and negotiation dynamics multiply in complexity.

In the TPP, there were just 12 countries, but at the table a wide variety of groupings around the Pacific Rim — the NAFTA Parties, Latin America, the Commonwealth, South East Asia, North East Asia, were represented. On every issue — and in modern FTA negotiations, the issues run well into the high hundreds — views on each issue could be split three or four ways. In such a context, managing the dynamics became absolutely crucial to a successful outcome, and I found myself drawing time and again on the lessons that I had learnt during my years working under Tommy Koh.

First, to be on top of all issues technically in order to build basic credibility. Second, to quickly distil the essence of any point being made, and communicate this in the right way to the right person at the right time. Third, to understand, nurture and manage the relationships between the different negotiators through a combination of formal and informal means, including settings where people can let their guard down and start to build trust. Fourth, to bring some humanity to the negotiations by understanding each negotiator as a human being bringing his or her prejudices and perceptions to the table, and in so doing, allow for a more skilful way of managing the negotiation dynamics. Lastly, taking an interest in helping those more junior or less experienced in the team to feel confident in bringing their own value to the negotiating table, and mentoring them in not just negotiations but in being a good ambassador for the country.

Of course, practising these was not easy, and it was just 12 countries. I can only imagine the challenges that Tommy Koh had to handle in navigating the incredible complexity of a multilateral negotiation at the global level, and pulling it off in a way that earned the respect, goodwill and admiration which I saw time and again in his meetings with foreign dignitaries. But I am fortunate to have seen him in action in a smaller, more intimate setting, and those of us who have worked with him and have learned much will impart these lessons in turn to those that we work with. This will be part of his legacy for Singapore.

CHAPTER 5

Singapore's Envoy to the United States (1984–1990)

CHAN HENG CHEE

By the time Tommy Koh arrived in Washington D.C., his reputation had already preceded him. He had spent 13 years as Singapore's Permanent Representative at the United Nations (UN) in two stints spanning three and 10 years, respectively. He had chaired and concluded the United Nations Law of the Sea negotiations, UNCLOS, a marathon that lasted 10 years but nonetheless left behind a document which to this day is quoted frequently and by which small and medium countries protect their interests, waters and territories. He was also at the UN when Vietnam invaded Cambodia on December 25, 1978 and completed its takeover in January 1979. ASEAN took the Cambodian issue to the UN and Tommy Koh and the Singapore team played an active role working with the other ASEAN members to put pressure on Vietnam through the UN, to withdraw its troops and presence from Cambodia, and agree to a comprehensive political settlement, which included UN-supervised elections.

Securing Lee Kuan Yew's 1985 Congressional Address

There were three key developments in Singapore-US relations that marked the tenure of Tommy Koh's ambassadorship in Washington from 1984 to 1990. The most memorable was Prime Minister Lee Kuan Yew's official visit in 1985 to Washington and his address to the joint session of Congress. Singapore was offered the full trappings of a state visit with a state dinner, even though Singapore's protocol designates that only a president can do state visits while our prime ministers do official visits. This was a very big deal at that time as Singapore was and still is a tiny country, a micro state in reality. But Prime Minister Lee was held in high regard by successive presidents of the United States, from Lyndon B. Johnson to Richard Nixon, Gerald Ford and Ronald Reagan. He was particularly good friends with President Nixon and President Reagan.

Securing a visit and good meetings in Washington for Prime Minister Lee Kuan Yew was not a difficult exercise. It was one which every Singapore Ambassador to Washington found to be a relative breeze and continued even after Lee Kuan Yew was no longer the prime minister. But Ambassador Tommy Koh was not satisfied to leave it at that level. He wanted to do something special during this visit that had not been done before: to address the joint session of Congress. Prime Minister Lee had never done this before. In fact his initial reaction to the idea was: Why would Congress even want to listen to a small country like Singapore?

For that matter no leader from Southeast Asia had addressed Congress before. Ambassador Koh set out to work the Washington political process to secure this honour for Singapore. It was not an easy process though he knew Secretary of State George Schultz well and was personal friends with many senators and congressmen on the Hill. As always, domestic politics, or rather Congressional politics, between the White House and Senate made it tougher for the agreement to be obtained than realised. According to Bilahari Kausikan, Singapore's then First Secretary in the Washington mission, Speaker Tip O'Neill held off signing on to the joint session (his agreement was essential) because he was trying to squeeze concessions from the White House on issues of his concern. It was not till the very day that Prime Minister Lee Kuan Yew landed in Washington that the Singapore embassy learned that the joint session was on. Ambassador Tommy Koh had asked Secretary Schultz to make a crucial call to Tip O'Neill, which finally achieved the result.

Prime Minister Lee made a brilliant and influential speech in Congress and to this day that speech is remembered in trade circles. Lee Kuan Yew tried to address the protectionist sentiments that were gathering in America at that time. He cleverly made the link between democracy and free trade. He told Congress that if the United States was interested to promote democracy abroad, it could not do so by closing its markets to the outside world — especially to developing countries that were seeking to improve their economic prospects and develop a middle class. Prime Minister Lee reminded Americans of the crucial link between a liberal political order and the liberal economic order. The speech had an enormous impact in Washington. A visit such as this certainly raised the profile of Singapore. It took an ambassador to facilitate this extraordinary opportunity and a prime minister with a grasp of geo-strategy, gravitas, eloquence and charisma to use this platform to "to hit a home run" as they say in America.

Rallying US and ASEAN Support for Cambodia

A major preoccupation of the Singapore embassy during this time was the Vietnamese occupation in Cambodia. Ambassador Koh had been working this issue at the United Nations with the other ASEAN countries. At the UN his work was to rally international public opinion and votes against Vietnam to demonstrate that the international community was against the invasion and occupation, and the Vietnamese puppet regime of Hun Sen. In Washington the work of the Singapore embassy was to seek the support of the United States to include the murderous Khmer Rouge as a member of the Coalition Government of Democratic Kampuchea (CGDK), the Cambodian resistance coalition at the time. The Khmer Rouge was anathema to most governments, particularly the governments of the West because the Pol Pot regime was responsible for the wanton killings of hundreds of thousands, if not millions, of its population. Singapore's task was to explain to the Reagan officials that while they had strong human rights objections to the Khmer Rouge, there were sound strategic reasons why the latter should be included.[1] Bilahari Kausikan, now an Ambassador-at-Large, recalled that it was not a difficult sell. The Reagan officials in the context of the Cold War grasped the argument. The more difficult part was to

---

1 Bilahari Kausikan, "The Myth of Universality: The Geopolitics pf Human Rights," IPS-Nathan Lectures No. IV, Singapore, April 29, 2016.

persuade the officials to provide non-lethal assistance to the coalition. Their reservations came from the post-Vietnam syndrome that this could lead to the US being drawn into another war.

Ambassador Koh used all his persuasive powers and his friendship with the Chairman of the House Sub-Committee of the Asia-Pacific, Congressman Steve Solarz to get Congress to provide US$5 million in overt aid to the coalition fighting forces. He and the Embassy would have lobbied many of the members of Congress as well to get the assistance passed. Kausikan had wondered why a liberal Congressman like Solarz would support this when it was explained to him that a substantial number of Solarz's constituents were former refugees from the Soviet bloc. "They hated the Soviet Union. Since the Soviet Union was supporting Vietnam, they were for anything against Vietnam," Kausikan recounted.

After I arrived in Washington in 1996 as Singapore's Ambassador to the United States, I came to know Steve Solarz well. By then he had lost his seat in Congress but we became good friends. Solarz recalled having dinner in Ambassador Koh's residence one evening. Boneless chicken was served. Half way through the meal, Solarz choked on the boneless chicken! An ambulance was called, and as he was escorted out the door by the nurses, Solarz, with his irrepressible humour, turned around and called out, "Tommy, you got the wrong one. I voted for you."

The "Hendrikson Affair"

One difficult episode in Singapore-US relations during Ambassador Koh's tenure was what came to be known as the "Hendrikson Affair". It involved a junior diplomat from the United States embassy in Singapore who was found to have crossed the line in diplomacy by "interfering" in the internal politics of Singapore. Hank Hendrickson was alleged to be contacting opposition party leaders to encourage them to stand in the elections against the government of the day and offering resources. In American diplomacy there was no wrongdoing at all. After all American foreign policy is about values and the promotion of values. American diplomats believe they are doing the right thing to promote democracy and human rights wherever they are posted. Singapore took a tough position against the diplomat and asked him to leave the country; in other words, Singapore "expelled" him.

This took place in 1988. Secretary of State George Schultz summoned Ambassador Koh, who had never seen him angrier. He could not believe his good friend Lee Kuan Yew would take such an action against a friendly country, one that enjoyed warm bilateral relations otherwise. Singapore was not a communist country or a Soviet ally; this was a very serious move. But Singapore decided to take a tough line against foreign officials interfering in their domestic politics, and still does, even though it could be a powerful country and a friend. They wanted to make an example of Hendrickson. As a response, the US immediately asked a junior diplomat from the Singapore embassy, Robert Chua,[2] to leave the US. This tit-for-tat in diplomacy happens. The episode ended when Prime Minister Lee proposed to the US to go for international arbitration to look into the case. He may have known that the US would not bring such a case to arbitration, but the offer allowed Singapore to appear to end on a high note.

This diplomatic strain took place at a time when Singapore saw its political scene bubbling with activism beneath the surface and above. Former Solicitor-General Francis Seow had just been arrested a week before Hendrickson's expulsion. A year earlier, in 1987, the "Marxist Conspiracy" was unveiled by the government as a security threat. A few Catholic priests had begun to flirt with liberation theology, and with church workers, social workers, students and professionals, set out to mobilise workers to oppose the government. They were following the school of neo-Marxist Latin American writers such as Paulo Freire who wrote the influential *Pedagogy of the Oppressed*.

During the "Hendrickson affair", the friendships that had been established by Ambassador Koh, and his history of nurturing good relations with Americans at all levels, took the sting out of the day-to-day relations that would have been quite prickly as he went about his official business. This is what good diplomats do for their countries in times of strain in relations. Fortunately, this period did not last too long.

---

2 Robert Chua would later be appointed Singapore's ambassador to Myanmar.

Negotiating the US-Singapore FTA

One final development which must be included in a look at Ambassador Tommy Koh's contributions to the Singapore-US relationship is his role as Chief Negotiator of the US-Singapore Free Trade Agreement (USSFTA). The decision to do the FTA was delivered at a night golf game between Prime Minister Goh Chok Tong and President Bill Clinton in Brunei, on the sidelines of an APEC meeting. This has been documented in a book edited by Ambassador Koh himself on the FTA and in many media articles. He was the Chief Negotiator who dealt with the difficult issues that his Deputy Chief Negotiator Ong Ye Kung and the team could not resolve with their counterparts. The American Chief Negotiator was Ralph Ives. What the chief negotiators from both sides could not resolve went forward to the Minister of Trade and Industry George Yeo and United States Trade Representative Robert Zoellick for their negotiation.

Ambassador Koh who spent his time in Washington cultivating the American chambers of commerce found residue goodwill towards him, adding to the immense reservoir of support the Singapore embassy had cultivated from Ambassador to succeeding Ambassador. Ambassador Koh had also cultivated the leadership of the AFL-CIO[3] and could call on labour leader John Sweeney and his team to talk about the FTA. So while the unions, especially Teamsters' Union, came out against the FTA — as they would every FTA that came before Congress for passage — the negotiations were prevented from worsening, thanks to the positive groundwork built over the years. Overall, Tommy Koh's leadership of the remarkable team of negotiators helped achieve our objective. It was good teamwork.

Upon his return from the United States and in the years that followed the end of the Cold War, the rise of new powers, the collapse of Lehman Brothers, and the humbling of the US economy, Tommy Koh, now an Ambassador-at-Large with the Ministry of Foreign Affairs, spoke up against voices that were quick to point to the end of the US as

---

3 American Federation of Labor and Congress of Industrial Organizations

a predominant power.[4] He truly admires the United States and holds the country in deep affection, and maintains many of the ties built over the years he had spent in the US.

It is evident today that the Singapore-US relationship is broad-based and strong, and Tommy Koh is one of the key diplomats from Singapore that helped to achieve this.

---

4 Tommy Koh, "Why the US will Still be No. 1 in 2039" and "Reports of America's Sorry Demise May Just Be a Little Bit Exaggerated" in *The Tommy Koh Reader: Favourite Essays and Lectures* (Singapore: World Scientific, 2013).

CHAPTER 6

Engaging China and the China-Singapore Forum

⚬⚬⚬

LYE LIANG FOOK

Facilitating the Upgrade of Singapore-China Relations

Professor Tommy Koh is most noted for upholding Singapore's foreign policy interests and expanding its international space, especially in his earlier capacity as Singapore's ambassador to the United States (US), and as Singapore's permanent representative to the United Nations (UN), where he also served as President of the third UN Conference on the Law of the Sea and chaired the Rio Conference. What is less known but no less important is his contribution to the upgrade of Singapore-China relations in the 1970s and in 1990, and for sustaining the positive momentum of this relationship in the 21st century through a bilateral platform known as the China-Singapore Forum, where he was the co-chair, together with Ambassador Yang Wenchang of the Chinese People's Institute of Foreign Affairs.[1]

Professor Koh toiled behind the scenes to create the right conditions for the leaders of Singapore and China to meet officially for the first time. In the early 1970s, China signalled its readiness to improve relations with its neighbours, and Malaysia proceeded to become the first ASEAN country to establish diplomatic ties with China in May 1974. Although Singapore was not ready for formal ties with China due

---

1 Ambassador Yang Wenchang stepped down as President of the Chinese People's Institute of Foreign Affairs in 2016. His successor is Ambassador Wu Hailong.

to sensitivities involving its much bigger neighbour, Indonesia, it saw the importance of improving relations with Beijing.

One of the earliest formal contacts between Singapore and China occurred when Professor Koh was appointed Singapore's permanent representative to the UN for the second time from 1974 to 1984. In October 1974, he organised a dinner hosted by Singapore's Foreign Minister S. Rajaratnam for the leader of the Chinese delegation to the UN General Assembly, Qiao Guanhua, who was then Vice-Minister for Foreign Affairs. The dinner went well and Qiao invited Rajaratnam to lead a goodwill delegation to China, that went not long after in March 1975. In the absence of diplomatic ties, the details of Rajaratnam's visit were thrashed out by Professor Koh working closely with his Chinese counterpart to the UN, Ambassador Huang Hua. The two of them went on to organise the visit by Lee Kuan Yew to China in May 1976, the first by a Singapore prime minister. During that visit, Lee Kuan Yew called on the ailing Chairman Mao Zedong.

Professor Koh played a similar instrumental role in another milestone in the Singapore-China relationship in 1990. In August of that year, Indonesia established formal ties with Beijing, clearing the way for Singapore to follow suit based on its earlier commitment to be the last ASEAN country to normalise relations with China. In the same month of August 1990, Professor Koh was appointed the leader of the Singapore delegation to negotiate an agreement with the Chinese assistant foreign minister Xu Dunxin for the establishment of diplomatic relations.[2] After three rounds of negotiations, the two sides agreed on the text of a memorandum of understanding (MOU) to establish formal ties on September 18, 1990 at the premises of the renowned state guesthouse known as Diaoyutai in Beijing. The MOU was signed by Singapore Foreign Minister Wong Kan Seng and Chinese Foreign Minister Qian Qichen at the UN on October 3, 1990.

Apart from his contributions in negotiating the MOU to establish diplomatic ties and facilitate visits by Singapore leaders to China, Professor Koh has continued to play a role in promoting Singapore-China

---

2 Professor Koh met Xu Dunxin again at a welcome dinner the night before the 10th China-Singapore Forum in Beijing in October 2015. The meeting was of added significance as it took place on the 25th anniversary of the establishment of diplomatic relations.

relations through the China-Singapore Forum. This is a "Track 1.5" forum that seeks to promote dialogue and understanding on issues of common interest, not only among officials and diplomats but also among businessmen, academics, think-tanks and media representatives from both sides. Since its inaugural meeting in 1998, the forum has met a total of 12 times. Over the years, the forum has progressed from an ad hoc meeting to a regular platform where participants meet annually (alternating between Singapore and Beijing) to exchange views in a frank and open manner in a closed-door setting. In addition to the closed-door discussions, each China-Singapore Forum has a public outreach component where selected delegates from both sides share their views on issues of topical interest to a general audience.

Over the past several years, I have been a member of the Singapore delegation led by Professor Koh to the China-Singapore Forum. I highlight here what I think are salient points he made during the forum in three main areas: Singapore-China relations; China-ASEAN relations; and Singapore's relations with the major powers. In these three main areas, Professor Koh had stated, elaborated or reaffirmed Singapore's position on issues raised by our Chinese counterparts. A seasoned diplomat with a warm and friendly demeanour, Professor Koh has been able to put across Singapore's views in a manner that the Chinese side can readily understand and even accept although they may not always agree with us. On occasions where there are differences of opinions, Professor Koh was extremely effective in conveying the Singapore perspective in a firm but polite manner.

Keeping Bilateral Differences in Perspective

One of the key takeaways for me during the discussions on the Singapore-China relationship is how far ties have progressed over the years and hence the importance of keeping any differences between the two countries in perspective. I recall Professor Koh reiterating on a number of occasions that Singapore-China relations are broad, deep and multifaceted. Apart from robust economic cooperation, there are frequent exchanges of high-level visits and extensive people-to-people ties. The two countries collaborate not just on government-to-government projects (with the third such project in Chongqing officially launched in November 2015), but also on other key private sector-driven projects. Furthermore, there are several institutional mechanisms overseeing bilateral ties such as the Joint Council for Bilateral Cooperation, the China-Singapore Leadership Forum, the Singapore-China Social Governance Forum, and seven other Chinese provincial-level economic and business councils. These mechanisms have helped to generate a positive momentum through reviewing existing areas of cooperation and identifying new areas for the two countries to work on, such as community building, urbanisation and financial services.

In my view, the points made by Professor Koh above have become much more salient in view of the current differences between Singapore and China, especially over China's perception of Singapore's biased position on the South China Sea issue. In other words, the South China Sea issue should be put in perspective and not come to define the Singapore-China relationship. Overall, this relationship is still fundamentally sound and substantive.

Bringing China-ASEAN Relations Back to a Positive Footing

At one recent China-Singapore Forum, I recall Professor Koh making the observation that China-ASEAN relations had undergone three distinct phases. In the first 30 years, from 1949 to 1979, China-Southeast Asia relations were marked by acrimony because China was exporting revolution abroad. In the next 30 years, from 1979 to 2009, China embarked on a charm offensive in Southeast Asia and was regarded as a good neighbour, generous friend and benefactor of ASEAN. However, since 2009, there was a change in China-ASEAN relations caused by a shift in the nature of China's foreign policy and diplomacy towards more assertiveness, and the increasing competition between China and the US in the Asia-Pacific. In view of this development, Professor Koh made three suggestions to improve China-ASEAN relations and to reduce tensions in the South China Sea.

First, he urged China to accelerate the pace of negotiations with ASEAN for a Code of Conduct in the South China Sea. Second, Professor

Koh called on China to work with other ASEAN claimant states to seriously consider the possibility of implementing a joint development project, which could completely change the atmosphere and tone of China-ASEAN relations. He recalled that "this was an idea put forward many years ago by Deng Xiaoping who once said that sovereignty issues were very hard to settle" and had suggested that claimant states set aside their differences and concentrate on "joint development and sharing of benefits from such development." Third, Professor Koh noted that the South China Sea was one of the few semi-enclosed areas in the world where there were no existing cooperative mechanisms for relevant countries to cooperate to conserve the marine environment and biodiversity. In his view, it would be a "good thing if China and ASEAN could jointly take the initiative to convene a meeting of the littoral states in the South China Sea to consider how they can cooperate with one another to conserve the marine environment and biodiversity in the area."

Reaffirming the Principle of Singapore's Ties with the Major Powers

I remember Professor Koh elaborating on Singapore's foreign policy orientation vis-à-vis the major powers on occasions when some Chinese delegates expressed unhappiness with what they saw as warm and close relations that Singapore had with Washington. To a large extent, they mistakenly regard Singapore for being a US ally and for siding with the US against China. This was especially so when Singapore reiterates the importance of freedom of navigation and overflight in the South China Sea, even though this iteration is based on Singapore's own perspective as a small, vulnerable and extremely trade-dependent country.

To counter such a view, Professor Koh would state that Singapore seeks to be friends with all, including all the major powers. In particular, he would clarify that Singapore is a close friend of the US but not an ally. If Singapore were a US ally, it would not have broken ranks with the US by becoming a founding member of the Asian Infrastructure Investment Bank, initiated by China. Nor would Singapore be proactive in supporting China's One Belt, One Road initiative as evidenced by its participation in the third government-to-government project that centres on Chongqing, building on the basis of its two other government-to-government ventures in Suzhou and Tianjin. Singapore has therefore consistently and actively supported China's efforts to grow its economy and to modernise ever since Deng Xiaoping's reform to open the Chinese economy to the world. In other words, what Singapore did and is doing are not the actions of a US ally but a good friend and partner of China.

Conclusion

To me, Professor Koh has played a key and invaluable role by working indefatigably behind the scenes to lay the groundwork for the establishment of diplomatic ties between Singapore and China, and continuing to work to broaden and strengthen relations even after formal ties were established. In an earlier period, he helped to upgrade Singapore-China relations by organising the visits by Foreign Minister Rajaratnam and Prime Minister Lee Kuan Yew to China in 1975 and 1976, respectively. The visits by these two Singapore leaders helped pave the way for Deng Xiaoping's visit to Singapore in 1978 where Deng was struck by the extent of Singapore's socio-economic progress since his last visit in 1920.[3] Thereafter, Deng saw in Singapore a reference model for China's next phase of development.

After formal ties were established, one of the instrumental ways in which Professor Koh has continued to promote bilateral ties is in his capacity as the co-chair of the China-Singapore Forum. Through the forum, the members of the Singapore delegation with Professor Koh as its leader have shared Singapore's perspectives on issues of common concern with our Chinese counterparts. In turn, the Singapore delegates have been able to gain better insights to China's position on various issues. Although there may not always be a consensus on the topics discussed, the China-Singapore Forum, which now convenes on an annual basis, has become a regular platform for representatives from different ministries and agencies and also from the other sectors to interact. In addition, each side would usually submit a report on the outcomes of

---

3 In 1920, Deng Xiaoping transited Singapore for two days enroute to France on a work-study programme. At that time, Deng's impression of Singapore was that of a poor, fishing village.

every China-Singapore Forum to their respective foreign ministries for information and for follow-up action where needed.

With China's growing clout, and with the shift in the balance of power between China and the US being played out in the region, the room for manoeuvre for small states like Singapore has become much more challenging. Bearing this trend in mind, the importance of the China-Singapore Forum as a regular forum to promote understanding and bridge differences as well as to clear up any misconception and misunderstanding is likely to become more important. In this regard, having an astute, calm and steady hand as embodied by Professor Koh, and his role as leader of the Singapore delegation, is an indispensable asset.

CHAPTER 7

Keeping the *Kizuna*[1] Strong

—∿—

CHANG LI LIN

Professor Tommy Koh has a deep appreciation of Japan. He has an optimistic view of Japan because he sees Japan's many strengths, which are often under-estimated.[2] He believes that the people of Japan and the values that they embody such as resilience in the face of adversity; the quality of the Japanese workforce; their work ethic and culture of excellence; their pursuit of excellence in science, technology and innovation; and their soft power, will stand them in good stead in the international arena.

It is with this openness and optimism in mind, that Professor Tommy Koh has guided the Japan-Singapore Symposium (JSS), since its formation, as a "Track 1.5" forum[3] where representatives from Singapore and Japan can conduct frank exchanges over regional and international issues, and offer constructive suggestions in building a deeper trust and mutually respectful relations.

The Japan-Singapore Symposium (JSS) was launched in 1994 by then Prime Minister of Japan, Murayama Tomiichi and former Prime Minister of Singapore, Goh Chok Tong. The Institute of Policy Studies (IPS) was appointed the secretariat from Singapore. The JSS was organised with

---

1 "Bonds of friendship" in Japanese.
2 Tommy Koh, "Japan's Prospects and Challenges — A View from Southeast Asia", speech delivered at the International House of Japan on the occasion of its 60th anniversary celebrations, October 3, 2012, Tokyo, published in *The Tommy Koh Reader: Favourite Essays and Lectures* (Singapore: World Scientific Publishing Ltd, 2013), 265–280.
3 Track 1.5 type forums involve a broader section of the society beyond government representations, such as non-government organisations, businesses and civil society groups.

the support of the Ministries of Foreign Affairs of Singapore and Japan. Professor Tommy Koh, who was Director and then Chairman of IPS, has played an important role in keeping the JSS relevant for more than a decade. He took over the chairmanship and built on the foundations set by the past Singapore chairmen, the late President S R Nathan and Ambassador Lim Chin Beng, and strengthened the regular meeting as an important platform for engagement between Singapore and Japan. JSS is usually attended by representatives from different sectors; academia, government, media and the private sector from the two countries are brought together to exchange views on issues of mutual interest and help foster closer ties between the two countries. The symposium comple-ments the regular exchanges at the official level, and is held alternating between Singapore and Japan. The symposium is usually held biennially but there were some occasions where it was held outside of its normal schedule.[4]

During the 8th JSS, Yutaka Banno, then State Secretary for Foreign Affairs of Japan, reiterated the importance of JSS as an "invaluable asset for Japan, which places importance not only on the strengthening of our bilateral relations but also on the development of the East Asian region as a whole."[5]

After World War II and the Japanese occupation of Singapore, Singapore and Japan have gradually rebuilt their relations between the governments and the people over the years. In 2016, Singapore and Japan celebrated the 50th anniversary of the establishment of dip-lomatic relations. Over the last five decades, the bilateral relationship has deepened and broadened, with cooperation at many levels, and in a wide range of areas including economic, social, cultural, research and development, among others. A mark of the comfort and trust between the two countries can be seen in the signing of the Japan-Singapore Economic Partnership Agreement (JSEPA) in 2002. JSEPA was Japan's first bilateral economic partnership agreement and Singapore's first with a major trading partner. In 2015, Japan was Singapore's eighth largest

---

4 JSS has taken place in 1994, 1996, 1998, 2001, 2003, 2006, 2009, 2011, 2013, 2014 and 2016.
5 "Post-Disaster Japan and its Regional Diplomacy", Keynote Address by Yutaka Banno, State Secre-tary for Foreign Affairs of Japan at the 8th Japan-Singapore Symposium, April 25, 2011, http://www.mofa.go.jp/announce/svm/address110425.html

trading partner and second largest investor, while Singapore was Japan's top Asian and fifth largest foreign direct investor.

More recently, as parties to the Trans-Pacific Partnership (TPP), Japan and Singapore, among others, had worked hard to facilitate the conclusion of this free trade agreement among Australia, Brunei Darussalam, Canada, Chile, Japan, Malaysia, Mexico, New Zealand, Peru, Singapore, the United States and Vietnam. It was unfortunate that the Trump administration withdrew the US from the TPP. Japan and Singapore remain committed to the ratification of TPP. Even before the election of Donald Trump, Professor Koh had warned of the trends seen in the US and Europe — of populist politicians purveying anti-globalisation and anti-free trade rhetoric. He saw the need for Singapore and Japan, two trading nations, to work together to ensure an open and liberal international trading system.

Singapore and Japan also share many common interests on regional and international issues and collaborate closely under Singapore's largest and most successful joint training programme with another country — the Japan-Singapore Partnership Programme for the 21st Century, to provide technical assistance to third countries.

As a member of the IPS secretariat that co-organised the JSS, I have observed at close quarters how Professor Koh worked hard to ensure that each JSS would be timely and topical, making sure that the meeting would discuss issues that could help Singapore and Japan participants better appreciate each other's perspectives. Over the last decade, like Singapore, the Japanese government also appointed different chairmen successively to represent Japan and to co-organise the JSS. Professor Koh was able to work with each of them, and deliver the necessary outcomes.

Because Professor Koh has established himself as an honest broker, he is able to explain the alternative points of views on contentious issues, and put across different views for Japan's consideration, with the hope that these will enable the decision-makers to make choices that would benefit regional stability. Professor Koh occupies a unique position, as he is also the co-chair of the Track 1.5 meeting with China and also the India-Singapore Forum. He is also involved in regular meetings with his American and European counterparts. As such, he understands the views of the stakeholders of the region and works to bring them together and build consensus. In 2009, Professor Koh was conferred the prestigious Order of the Rising Sun, Gold and Silver Star by the Japanese government, in recognition of his contributions in promoting intellectual exchange and mutual understanding between Japan and Singapore. Professor Koh is the 10th Singaporean to receive this award. Other recipients include Mr Lee Kuan Yew.

One particularly memorable meeting took place in 2011, when the 8th JSS was held in Singapore. Just prior to the meeting, the Tohoku region was struck by a strong earthquake, and Japan had to deal with the aftermath of the triple tragedy of the earthquake, tsunami and nuclear plant disaster. In spite of the national tragedy, the Japanese decided to proceed with the meeting in Singapore a month later in April, and also took the opportunity to publicly acknowledge the help and support they had received. There had been a spontaneous outpouring of support by Singaporeans following the earthquake and tsunami, culminating in one of Singapore's largest-ever relief contributions being raised.[6] Close to S$35.7 million was raised by the people in Singapore. Four rebuilding projects undertaken by the Singapore Red Cross were completed and Singapore has also committed to support six additional rehabilitation projects in the Tohoku region. As a show of support, Singapore President Tony Tan visited one of the projects in Tohoku as part of his state visit to Japan in December 2016.

In Professor Koh's opening remarks at the 11th JSS in 2016, he noted that in the last 50 years, Japan and Singapore have enjoyed robust political, business, cultural, defence and people-to-people ties. There is a high level of comfort and mutual trust between the leaders of both countries. And to take the relations even further, the State Minister for Foreign Affairs of Japan, Seiji Kihara announced during his keynote speech that the Japan-Singapore Symposium would be held annually rather than biennially.

This was a crowning acknowledgement of the important contribution that the JSS makes to the thriving relations between Singapore and Japan, and we have Professor Koh to thank for it.

---

6 Transcript of Keynote Address by Minister for Foreign Affairs Dr Vivian Balakrishnan at the 11th Japan-Singapore Symposium, International House of Japan, April 26, 2016, https://www.mfa.gov.sg/content/mfa/media_centre/press_room/pr/2016/201604/press_20160426.html

CHAPTER 8

Professor Tommy Koh's Contributions to APEC

—⚬—

MANU BHASKARAN

Through an illustrious diplomatic career littered with many achievements, Professor Tommy Koh has been involved in several initiatives that have helped transform the Asian region for the better. One area where his contribution was profound, but perhaps understated, was in supporting initiatives such as the Asia-Pacific Economic Cooperation (APEC), now the leading Asian-Pacific regional forum that has helped expand regional cooperation, trade and investment. Koh also played key roles in the establishment and development of associated institutions such the Pacific Business Forum (PBF), which eventually became the APEC Business Advisory Council (ABAC). In so doing, Koh not only helped Singapore expand its connectivity and "soft power" but he also contributed greatly to creating a more vibrant and peaceful region.

A Deep Belief in the Asia-Pacific's Economic Integration

Much of Koh's involvement with APEC reflected his deep conviction in the capacity of enhanced regional integration to create a more peaceful and stable world, one that would work for the benefit of the region's peoples. This came out clearly, for example, in his speech at the 68th Session of Economic and Social Commission for Asia and the Pacific in May 2012. Here he outlined three reasons why regional economic integration deserved the support of everyone.

First and foremost, he saw such integration as a means of promoting peace and preventing war in a region that had seen too much turbulence.

Second, and more pragmatically, he saw economic integration bringing the benefit of economies of scale to the countries of the region, which in turn would attract more investment and lead to even higher economic growth.

Third, reflecting his humanist inclinations, he wanted economic integration because it would help to create more jobs and enhance human welfare.

Promoting Regional Integration via APEC

These passionate convictions explain why Koh was prepared to devote his time and energies to the APEC ideal. APEC has been a game-changer for the economic integration in the Asia-Pacific region that Koh believed in. APEC's Bogor vision of free trade and open investment by 2010 for developed economies and 2020 for developing economies helped to mould the thinking of political leaders, spurring them to recognise the value of deepening economic relations among its members. Partly as a result, trade barriers have fallen and regulations have undergone major tweaks to boost trade amongst member economies.

The numbers speak for themselves in a region that has enjoyed a dramatic increase in prosperity: Average tariffs fell to 5.2% in 2012, down from 17% in 1989 while total trade in the APEC region expanded sevenfold over the same period, a pace of growth well ahead of other regions of the world. This flourishing regional trade has helped to lift millions of people out of poverty, and led to societal changes such as a fast-growing middle class forming in just over two decades — changes that achieved the promotion of human welfare that he saw as one of the key benefits of regional economic integration. Residents of the member economies have seen their per capita incomes rise by 36% between 1989 and 2012. In short, the region has been brought far closer together as a result of APEC and its economic integration agenda.

Driven by his belief in promoting mutual understanding and cooperation between peoples of different races, religions and countries, Koh has long championed the importance of APEC not only to Singapore but also to its allies. For example, Koh had authored the article "Chile in the World: A View From Singapore" in 2004, which was in equal parts a celebration of warm ties as it was an espousal of the importance of openness and APEC to both countries. The piece was also dotted with many surprising examples — politically, societally and culturally — in which Singapore and Chile were similar despite seemingly significant geographical, historical and cultural differences.

In his inimitable diplomatic style, Koh always had a way of bringing countries together. Coupled with his belief in the value of expanding economic integration among countries, Koh naturally became one of APEC's most earnest supporters; and one who earned the trust of every member country.

Bringing Enterprises to APEC

As a visionary of his time for the liberalisation of trade and investment in the region, Koh knew that they were goals that could not be fully accomplished without the involvement of the business sector. The business sector could bring a spirit of enterprise and practical-mindedness to the APEC initiative. This is encapsulated in his astute observation that "APEC is emerging as an economic community because of the strong economic linkages... that are forged not by government or the bureaucracy, but by a multitude of business enterprises."[1] Not surprisingly perhaps, this combination of pragmatism and idealism made him a natural choice to help bring into fruition a new initiative aimed at unlocking the powers of enterprise to bring Asian-Pacific economic cooperation to new heights.

Though APEC was inaugurated in 1989, the inaugural Leaders Meeting was held near Seattle, US, only in 1993 under the chairmanship of then-President Bill Clinton. The event brought together top leaders representing the APEC member countries. At the meeting, the leaders decided to reach out to the business circles of APEC to identify

---

1 Tommy Koh, "Towards a Productive Asia-Europe Business Relations," speech delivered at the Asia-Europe Business Conference, Jakarta, July 9, 1997, in *Asia and Europe: Speeches and Essays by Tommy Koh*, eds. Yeo Lay Hwee and Asad Latif (Singapore: Asia-Europe Foundation and World Scientific, 2009), 29.

issues and obstacles to regional trade and investment that they could begin to address. This would also encourage the further development of business networks throughout the region. The representatives decided that establishing a forum was the best way to accomplish this. Thus was born the Pacific Business Forum (PBF), which was later rechristened as the APEC Business Advisory Council (ABAC).

The Pacific Business Forum was arguably the first time that an official, independent business forum was integrated with a yearly summit of a major grouping of economies. Before the PBF, there was a dearth of engagement between government officials and the business community and its attendant captains of industry — in spite of the fact that economic development was often at the top of the agenda in regional and international meetings between political leaders. With this practice, APEC leaders made a significant departure from the deliberative process of old and were able to speak to and hear directly from the business community via appointed PBF members.

The decision to establish the forum was conveyed by then-Assistant US Trade Representative Sandra Kristoff to Koh, who had assumed duties as Ambassador-at-Large with the Government of Singapore in addition to his responsibilities as head of Singapore's Institute of Policy Studies. Credentialled, possessing a wealth of experience in international law and a natural diplomat to boot, Koh was Kristoff's first choice for Convenor of the inaugural meeting of the PBF and to act as its Secretary. A staunch believer in the merits of free enterprise and trade and in Singapore's ability and need to contribute to this goal, Koh duly accepted the request and went on to serve as the Executive Secretary of the APEC Pacific Business Forum from 1994 to 1995.

The PBF which became the ABAC was thus a story of the world's most powerful political leaders deciding to engage the people who are often most directly involved in economic development — the business community. Over the years, the council has put gentle pressure on the governments to press on with its goals of liberalisation and economic integration. When the APEC CEO Summit was convened in Peru in November 2016, the council completed its 24th year in operation. Koh's early contribution to its now successful and long-running legacy speaks volumes to his diplomatic capabilities and the values central to his work.

How APEC/ABAC Helped Promote Singapore's Regional Presence

APEC and ABAC served as crucial conduits through which stronger relations between Southeast Asia and other regions were forged. They were also important channels to build Singapore's reputation as a regional player. Singapore's ever-present role in APEC and ABAC served to broaden the island's connectivity beyond its immediate neighbours, whilst also contributing to strengthening ASEAN's relevance on a global platform. Singapore worked hard to sustain the trans-regional forums, making it a credible and relevant "friend to all". Koh's contributions to these efforts ranged from the small to the momentous, and were part of his legacy for Singapore in promoting trade, investment, peace and understanding across the region. In doing so, Koh showed that Singapore had something of substantial value to offer to the world.

Vital Contributions in View of Current Challenges

Koh has remained the go-to person in Singapore's foreign policy circles, negotiating sensitive matters such as the Pedra Branca dispute with Malaysia and representing the country on the international stage. He remains resolute in his belief in deepening relationships within the Asia-Pacific region, which led him to offer his voice to numerous publications and speeches that were well-received by APEC and other inter-regional forums. Today, he continues to serve many organisations, including his roles as the Ambassador-at-Large for the Ministry of Foreign Affairs, Special Advisor for the Institute of Policy Studies and Chairman of the Centre of International Law at the National University of Singapore.

Worryingly, we are also beginning to see a rising wave of anti-globalisation sentiment that threatens to unravel the constellation of networks — political, economic, cultural or otherwise — and the trust that had been painstakingly built across the region through decades of trade, friendly relations and goodwill between one another. In his first executive order, the US President Donald Trump who ran on a protectionist agenda, withdrew the US from the Trans-Pacific Partnership agreement.

In the light of such troubling challenges, institutions like APEC and ABAC become all the more important in maintaining the region as an open and integrated one. It will be diplomats and political leaders who have Koh's combination of passionate convictions and hard-headed pragmatism who can help ensure that economies remain open and free to trade, business and investment. In that way, values and themes that define Koh's life's work and helped him promote APEC and ABAC — trust between nations; diplomacy; economic cooperation — may have become even more crucial now than ever.

CHAPTER 9

Regional Integration for Peace, Prosperity and People: Tommy Koh and Europe

—❦—

YEO LAY HWEE

Ambassador Tommy Koh spent almost 20 years in the United States and is well known as Singapore's former ambassador to the United Nations in New York (1968–1971; 1974–1984) and then as our ambassador to the United States from 1984–1990.

He served with distinction and helped put Singapore on the world map during his time at the UN. His skills as a diplomat and negotiator had seen him being thrust in the forefront of several UN Conferences, and he performed his tasks as chair of these meetings with flying colours. He was President of the Third United Nations Conference on the Law of the Sea from 1980 to 1982, which resulted in the United Nations Convention on the Law of the Sea (UNCLOS), an international agreement that was successfully concluded in 1982 after almost 10 years of negotiation. UNCLOS came into force in 1994 and since then 167 countries and the European Union (EU) have acceded to this agreement. Ambassador Tommy Koh also chaired the United Nations Conference on Environment and Development in 1992, also known as the Rio Summit, a 10-day meeting that resulted in several important political declarations and legally binding agreements.

The Baltic States

Lesser known perhaps, but no less important are his contributions to Europe, and his strong belief in the European integration process despite the current problems faced by the European Union.

In 1993, after his successful chairing of the Rio Summit, he was called upon by the UN again, this time for a mission to the Baltics to help mediate the demand of Estonia, Latvia and Lithuania for the full withdrawal of the Russian troops from their territories.

The three Baltic countries, Estonia, Latvia and Lithuania, were independent countries after World War I, but were relegated to the Soviet sphere of influence by the then infamous secret Molotov-Ribbentrop Pact of 1939 (also known as the Nazi-Soviet, or the German-Soviet Pact). This secret pact was terminated by Germany in 1941 when the Germans launched war against the Soviet Union, and the Baltic states were occupied by the Germans from 1941 to 1944. The Soviet Union regained control of the Baltic states towards the end of World War II, and then annexed them as part of the Soviet Union after the war.

The Baltic states began to agitate for independence in the late 1980s with the onset of glasnost in the Soviet Union. Their independence was formally recognised by the Soviet Union only on September 6, 1991 and they were admitted to the UN on September 17, 1991. However, an estimated 200,000 Russian troops remained in these three countries. Russia had refused to agree on a definite date for complete troop withdrawal citing the need to be assured of the protection of the rights of Russians living in Estonia and Latvia. Talks on the withdrawal stalemated in 1993, and Ambassador Tommy Koh was sent as Special Envoy to help with the mediation between Russia and the Baltic states.

As he took on the role, he prepared himself amply, spending months reading on the histories and cultures of the three Baltic states and their relations with their immediate neighbours. He was also astute enough to enlist the help and support of the European Community (now the European Union), and other relevant organisations and players to work towards a successful mission. The agreement with Lithuania was easiest to achieve because of the small Russian population and there were no bases of strategic importance. Negotiations with Estonia were the hardest because of the presence of the Paldiski Nuclear Submarine Base, and the high number of Russians living in Estonia. The stalemate was broken, and Ambassador Koh's mission — with help from countries like Sweden and Denmark and pressure from the US, resulted in a deal that allowed Russian army veterans and demobilised personnel to obtain permanent residence in Estonia.

Engagement between Asia and Europe

Ambassador Koh's involvement with Europe did not end there. He went on to play an important role in strengthening the engagement between Asia and Europe.

Building on the idea that was first floated during the Europe-East Asia Economic Summit held in Singapore and organised by the World Economic Forum, Singapore under then Prime Minister Goh Chok Tong proposed to his French counterpart during the official visit to France to create a link between Asian and European leaders. This led to the launch of the Asia-Europe Meeting (ASEM) in 1996, involving 10 Asian countries, comprising then the seven ASEAN countries plus China, Japan and Korea, and the 15 European Union member states and the European Commission.

The inaugural ASEM Summit was held in Bangkok and was a huge success with substantive discussions and several new initiatives. One of these initiatives proposed by Singapore was to set up an Asia-Europe Foundation (ASEF) to foster stronger ties amongst the peoples of Asia and Europe through intellectual, cultural and people-to-people exchanges. Ambassador Koh with his diplomatic savvy and negotiating skills was given the task to negotiate with the other 25 ASEM partners on the establishment of ASEF. Having successfully led the negotiations, navigating the different interests and cultural differences, ASEF was inaugurated in February 1997, and he was appointed as the Executive Director (1997–2000).[1]

Ambassador Koh's understanding and appreciation of the history of Europe, and his admiration for the post World War II European

---

1 His role as ASEF's founding Executive Director is discussed by Peggy Kek's essay in this collection.

integration project that brought about decades of peace and stability in the European continent, have won him many friends amongst the Europeans. He has also received numerous awards from European governments for his relentless efforts not only to foster deeper understanding and broader exchanges between Singapore, Asia and Europe, but also to promote environmental and legal issues important to the global community. These included Commander, Order of the Golden Ark from the Netherlands; Commander, First Class of the Order of the Lion of Finland; Grand Officer, Order of Merit of the Grand Duchy of Luxembourg; Officer in the Legion d'honneur from the French Republic; and the Encomienda of Isabel la Catolica from His Majesty King Juan Carlos of Spain.

Rallying for Europe Today

In recent years, the European Union has been confronted with several challenges. From the sovereign debt crisis to the migrant crisis, and the British vote to leave the EU (Brexit) at the June 23, 2016 referendum, Ambassador Koh has unequivocally spoken out to remind us of the reasons behind the European integration project. Swimming against the tide of anti-Europe sentiments, It Is a timely reminder to us of this huge political experiment undertaken by the Europeans in search of peace and a more civilised way of managing differences and reconciling different national interests. He wrote several articles in "defence of Europe", encouraging Europeans to keep faith with their vision of an economic and monetary union and to overcome the Brexit challenges to emerge stronger and more united.[2]

In his defence of Europe, he stood in contrast to many policymakers in Singapore who tend to be eurosceptics because they look at international relations through a very classic realist lens. Instead, Ambassador Koh, who considers himself a pragmatic idealist, can see the idealism and aspirations in the European project, and has the faith that peaceful cooperation, rule of law and strong institutions can be potent weapons

---

2 See Tommy Koh and Yeo Lay Hwee, "Keep Faith with Europe's Vision of Economic Monetary Union," *The Straits Times*, January 9, 2014; and Tommy Koh and Yeo Lay Hwee, "In Defence of Europe," *The Straits Times*, December 15, 2011.

against self-seeking behaviour of states, and that national and regional interests can be reconciled. In that sense, Ambassador Koh embodies the true spirit of Singapore — a country that is pragmatic but not afraid to be a contrarian of prevailing views, and willing to go against the convention.

While accepting that the European integration project cannot be a model for Asia, he has not failed to recognise the tremendous attraction and achievement of the European Union in bringing peace to Europe. On many occasions when he was invited to speak on EU-ASEAN and Asia-Europe relations, he would remind the audience of the underlying principles and goals of regional integration — to bring peace and prosperity for the people. As ASEAN forges its own regional path and seeks to maintain its relevance in the regional order in the Asia Pacific, it is worthwhile to draw lessons from the European integration project. Similarly, China and Japan, in seeking a path forward in their relations, could also look at the historical reconciliation of France and Germany and reflect on the lessons that can be learnt from the history of Europe.

Ambassador Tommy Koh's support for Europe is however also not without criticisms. In his desire to see more genuine engagement and dialogue between Asia and Europe, he had on several occasions implored Europe to be less arrogant in order to engage Asia more deeply. While Asia has been learning from Europe for centuries, it is also time that Europe learns from Asia on how to manage diversities and make multiculturalism work, and to be more outward-looking.

Brexit, as Ambassador Tommy Koh said in one of his latest essays, is a wake-up call for Europe. While the EU should be proud of what it has achieved so far, "putting an end to half a century of conflict" and keeping the peace in Europe for more than 60 years, moving forward, it has to undertake bold reforms to "bring it closer to the people of the Union."[3] Europe is not yet a failed project and European leaders must have the belief and confidence that they can remake Europe to become even more open, more competitive to sustain their quality of life. It has to prepare its young people for competition and not protect them from competition.

---

3 Tommy Koh, "Why I Think the EU Will Survive," *The Straits Times*, 29 June 2016.

Hence, it is crucial that the EU resists the desire to look inward and withdraw into Fortress Europe as we witness the rise of far right and fringe parties extolling anti-immigrant, anti-trade and anti-globalisation sentiments. Instead, Europe should work with Asia to find an inclusive growth model, defend the multilateral global trading system to "reinvigorate its economy", and continue to be a beacon of peace and prosperity. Do not allow the populists to have their way. As the EU marks the 60th anniversary of the signing of the Treaties of Rome (March 1957), it should reaffirm what it has achieved so far and pledge to fulfil another 60 years of peace and prosperity through open and inclusive policies.

CHAPTER 10

A Founding Vision to Connect the Peoples of Asia and Europe

⌒⊷⌒

PEGGY KEK

Tommy Koh once called the Asia-Europe Meeting (ASEM) process a "journey of rediscovery".[1] In his typical succinct manner he described ASEM as a house with four pillars of engagement between the political leaders, government officials, business communities and the civil societies of the two regions. The task of connecting the fourth pillar — civil societies — was the mission given to the Asia-Europe Foundation, or ASEF.

ASEF might well not have taken off 20 years ago, if not for Ambassador Koh's legendary diplomatic skills. Through a blitz of multilateral and bilateral consultations and negotiations among ASEM partners, he succeeded in drafting the so-called *Dublin Principles* in Ireland, to pave the way for the establishment of ASEF.[2] Named after the city where it was adopted, the document spells out the new organisation's mandate and the key principles upon which it would operate.

A Founding Vision

The mission statement of ASEF reads "to bring about better understanding between Asia and Europe through intellectual, cultural and

---

1 Yeo Lay Hwee and Asad Latif, *Asia and Europe: Essays and Speeches by Tommy Koh* (Singapore: World Scientific, 2000), 100.
2 Ibid., 168–171.

people-to-people exchange." Tommy Koh, the founding Executive Director from 1997 to 2000, had a clear vision of how ASEF would fulfil its mission, by playing the multiple roles of interpreter, intellectual entrepreneur, cultural impresario, network creator and clearing house of information.[3]

ASEF sought to help "interpret important developments taking place in one region to the people of the other region" such as the 1997–1998 Asian Financial Crisis, the launch of the single currency in Europe and the first democratic Indonesian elections in 1999. Through projects such as the Asia-Europe Classroom and the Asia-Europe Young Leaders Symposium, ASEF created new networks between the two regions of entrepreneurs, curators, teachers, youths and students. Playing the role of clearing house, ASEF set up inventories of ASEM activities as well as exchanges between think-tanks in Asia and Europe.

Strategic flagship projects helped to build the ASEF brand quickly. Project names like the Asia-Europe Lecture, Europe-Asia Forum and the ASEF Summer School helped to reinforce the linking of the words "Asia" and "Europe" and familiarity with the new acronym "ASEF".

Tommy Koh's leadership focused on relevance and ownership. Under him, ASEF projects and activities aimed to be useful not just to the two regions' civil societies but also to the politicians and senior government officials. Between 1998 and 2000 he led a roadshow to introduce the new European single currency (the Euro) to audiences in Beijing, Hong Kong and Singapore. With the help of his French deputy, Pierre Barroux, heads of French financial institutions leading the launch of the Euro were invited and participated enthusiastically in the roadshow.

To be genuinely relevant, ASEF could not, and did not, shy away from controversial topics. A case in point: the Asia-Europe Young Parliamentarians Meeting in the Philippines in 1998 provided the two regions a new platform for parliamentarians and future political leaders to meet and give a fresh take on the then highly contentious issue of Myanmar/Burma.

---

3 Ibid., 132–135.

To extend the sense of ownership to partner countries and the European Commission, Tommy Koh instructed ASEF programme directors to organise activities in as many different countries as possible, rotating regularly between Asia and Europe. For instance, the Asia-Europe Young Leaders Symposium debuted in Japan and moved to Austria, Korea and Ireland; the Informal Human Rights Seminar Series was launched in Sweden in 1998 with subsequent editions hosted by China and France.

Lest ASEF was perceived as a solely Singaporean initiative, Tommy Koh shrewdly insisted that the Programme Directors personally presented their portfolios at the ASEF Board of Governors Meetings. The directors serving during his term came from China, Germany, Singapore and the United Kingdom and the simple procedural decision helped to emphasise the multilateral ownership of ASEF.

Riding on Tommy Koh's Coat-Tails

As the first Executive Director, Tommy Koh did three important things to give ASEF a running start. He created important connections for the organisation. He raised its profile very quickly. He initiated a body of projects that led the way in scale, tone and level of ambition for future ASEF projects.

ASEF greatly benefited from his international stature and reputation. He had been Dean of the Law School at the National University of Singapore and was one of the most senior diplomats at the Ministry of Foreign Affairs. Many potential partner organisations that did not know him in person already knew him by reputation and were therefore open to working with the fledging organisation.

Some people, including Tommy himself, had initially referred to him as an Americanist taking on the job of a Europeanist. While it is true that Tommy had spent 20 years in the United States in the 1970s and 1980s, he had in fact been back in Singapore, in Asia, for almost seven years by the time he began his tenure at ASEF. During this time, he had been the Director of the Institute of Policy Studies (IPS) and the founding Chairman of the National Arts Council in Singapore. These were ideal roles that allowed him to renew ties and develop networks in Singapore and the region. The IPS job enabled him to expand the networks in the academic and think-tank world that he had already built during his time in Washington and New York. As cultural impresario, ASEF facilitated artistic collaborations between artists from the two regions and convened many forums for discussion and exchange between professionals and organisations such as publishers, television executives, film festivals and museums. These would not have happened without the contacts he brought from his tenure at the National Arts Council.

Riding on the good Ambassador's coat-tails, ASEF, the new kid on the block, was able to partner established names like Chulalongkorn University, *Die Zeit*, INSEAD, Japan Foundation, Raoul Wallenberg Institute and Visiting Arts UK within a very short period of time. In three and a half years, Tommy Koh had helped ASEF to arrive on many prominent stages in Asia and Europe in a way that few others could have done. And he had become very much a Europeanist.

Personal Attributes

The *Dublin Principles* were adopted in December 1996 and in record time ASEF was launched on February 15, 1997, witnessed by the ASEM Foreign Ministers who were meeting in Singapore. ASEF had been set up in double-quick time and was under tremendous pressure to produce results. This was only possible with Tommy Koh's passion and energy.

Michael Reiterer, a senior European Commission official who was involved with the development of ASEF from the beginning, wrote:

> *[Tommy Koh] came with a devoted team to Brussels and gave us the impression that ASEF was already up and running at full speed because he spoke to the point, conveyed a strong sense of purpose and presented his arguments in a statesman-like manner. When I then came to Singapore to see ASEF at Nassim Hill, any last doubts were gone.*[4]

---

4 Michael Reiterer, e-mail message to author, October 24, 2016.

His ability to focus strategically on the big picture and not be sidetracked by obstacles on the way was complemented by his naturally optimistic nature. Sir Tim Lankester, the ASEF Governor for the United Kingdom from 1997 to 2011 made this observation:

> *Tommy could so easily have been put off by the less than enthusiastic attitude of one or two members. But that is not Tommy's style: if he believes strongly enough in something, he won't be put off by the pessimists.*[5]

Although usually mild mannered, Tommy became quite fierce when he was confronted by what he considered unreasonable behaviour from a member state. He refused to budge when the Governor of a member country threatened to withdraw its contribution unless ASEF agreed to co-fund two of its projects.

ASEM members helped to reduce ASEF's running costs by seconding their nationals to join the Singapore-based management team. Another advantage of this international team was the diverse networks that each member brought to the organisation. However, this diversity also brought its challenges. The different working cultures did not always meld naturally and easily. The team had to establish a level of comfort and trust. The differences sometimes produced disagreements and misunderstandings.

In this regard, Tommy Koh's patient, non-confrontational and unflappable nature was crucial to keeping ASEF on an even keel. One day, after a fraught discussion over a complex project, one hot-headed staff slammed down some files on a table and stormed out of the meeting that Tommy was chairing. We were stunned, expecting him to call the staff back. But he waited a few moments, and then quietly adjourned the meeting.

As the youngest and only woman member of Tommy Koh's management team then, I've always felt fortunate that my age and gender were never obstacles to him. When an organisation in Korea refused

---

5 Tim Lankester, e-mail message to author, October 15, 2016.

to collaborate with ASEF because they felt insulted that he had sent a young woman to negotiate with them, he refused to give in. Instead, he simply sent me back to Seoul, this time to negotiate with a different organisation.

Working with Tommy Koh was filled every day with unlimited opportunities to learn. He always took younger colleagues with him to meetings to watch and learn as well as to enable us to build our networks. But he was also a tough boss. I remember the first time I worked on a press release for him, I had to work and rework the press statement until past midnight before he was satisfied with every single word. Another time we were in Hong Kong on a Friday, after a long week. We were up at 4 a.m. to get to the TV studio for his interview on the morning show. Then we went to our conference venue. After the conference ended at 5 p.m., we rushed to the airport barely in time to catch our flight. Upon check-in, he said to me that he wanted the trip report by the time we landed in Singapore! And in this push to achieve excellence, he set the example.

A talented communicator, Tommy Koh's ability to distil big chunks of information into his trademark "three points" is legendary. His gift for communicating in plain language was a huge asset throughout his tenure at ASEF, but especially so in the beginning when he had to write and speak extensively to convey the aspirations and ambitions of the nascent organisation to very different audiences.

He spoke to audiences in think-tanks and diplomatic academies, at business forums and arts conferences, from Thailand to Finland. He was a tireless writer, churning out pieces for newspapers ranging from Singapore's *The Straits Times* to Spain's *El Pais*, journals such as *Politique Etrangere*, magazines such as *Newsweek* and even an editorial for a UNESCO website. As these were done in the early days of blogs and well before the era of social media and explosion of online platforms such as *Huffington Post*, they were noteworthy achievements.

Tommy Koh also brought his sophisticated and compelling persuasiveness to ASEF, honed from his experiences at the highest levels of diplomacy. These were particularly useful in managing the international board of governors, who each came with his and her own expectations of ASEF. The governors also represented different levels of commitment from partner countries.

ASEF governor for Denmark and former Danish Ambassador to Singapore, Jørgen Ørstrøm Møller, in describing Tommy's "irresistible drive to bring about a better world", said:

He is constantly advocating reconciliation, negotiations, and respect for others warning against belligerent attitudes. These characteristics served him well when appointed the first Executive Director of ASEF.[6]

In sum, Tommy Koh led with passion and conviction but he wasn't just an idealist. He was a strategic thinker with a lofty vision, but also a pragmatic doer with many creative ideas. He called himself a "pragmatic idealist". Having worked on the concept of the foundation, he immediately set about bringing it to life in concrete steps.

Leaving a Lasting Legacy

One of the earliest projects ASEF implemented was an Asia-Europe Editors' Roundtable, where participants were presented with the findings of a study that looked at how the Asian and European media covered the Hong Kong handover from Britain to China. The study sparked an animated conversation. The media started to take notice of ASEF. In a creative move, Tommy Koh had given the Public Affairs unit, which was responsible for media relations, an additional programmatic mandate. The Public Affairs unit convened events such as colloquia for journalists on the 1997–1998 Asian Financial Crisis and the Indonesian elections in 1999. This ensured that Public Affairs did not just enlist the media's help to publicise ASEF activities, but also organised programmes that were for their benefit. Tommy Koh reasoned that if editors and journalists found ASEF useful, they would be more engaged and supportive of ASEF. On this, he was to be proven right on numerous occasions throughout his tenure.

It was also his idea for ASEF to organise events around ASEM Summits and other significant ministerial meetings to augment the visibility of the foundation. This made it possible for government officials (who

---

6 Jørgen Ørstrøm Møller, e-mail message to author, September 29, 2016.

ultimately held the purse-strings) to not only observe the work of ASEF up close, but also to participate in some of these events as well. Examples of these were the arts events held in London in Spring 1998 during the time of ASEM 2, the second summit meeting of ASEM leaders.

Today while ASEF has added the themes of sustainable development and public health to its work, the legacy of Tommy Koh's visionary and creative leadership continues. In July 2016, ASEF organised the 8th edition of the Editors' Roundtable on the sidelines of the ASEM 11 Summit in Ulaanbaatar, Mongolia. In November, the 16th Informal ASEM Seminar of Human Rights took place in Beijing, China.

Sir Tim was clear:

> *Tommy Koh is one of the great international public servants of his generation. True dedication to the public good of one's own country is rare enough; even rarer is true commitment to the public good of the wider international community. ASEF was Tommy's brainchild. As its first executive director, he got it off to a very good start. Without Tommy's leadership, ASEF could easily have been just another pious ASEM hope.[7]*

---

7 Tim Lankester, e-mail message to author, October 15, 2016.

CHAPTER 11

Expertise, Personality, Persistence: Different Diplomatic Tracks and Tommy Koh

SIMON SC TAY

Introduction

There is no doubt that Ambassador Tommy Koh is one of the most successful and respected diplomats from Singapore. His distinguished service for Singapore is detailed in other contributions in this book, especially during his appointments at the United Nations and in Washington DC. So too are his contributions to Singapore as Ambassador-at-Large after his return to the country and the work he has undertaken on behalf of the international community — most notably, in chairing the UN Conference on the Law of the Sea, and the Rio Conference.

This essay seeks to examine a lesser known aspect of Ambassador Koh's work in what has been termed "Track 2" diplomacy.

Track 2 diplomacy describes the dialogues and interactions among analysts, activists, experts and policymakers in more informal and non-official settings. The process interacts with government policies and actors, and the actors seek to influence policy outcomes. Attention in recent years has grown for "Track 2" processes. In a globalised and far more complex world, there is increasing recognition that non-state actors are often important or even essential in addressing larger-scale and transborder issues.

This essay begins by outlining what Track 2 diplomacy is, the differences between "Track 2" and intergovernmental diplomacy and their relationship to each other. The essay will then consider Ambassador Koh's role in notable Track 2 undertakings. In conclusion, the essay will offer some thoughts about the future links between Track 2 and intergovernmental diplomacy and the possible roles for future diplomats and policy advocates.

It is not common that a full-time diplomat of standing can and should play a substantial role in "Track 2" diplomacy, which is, by definition, informal and non-official. Many ambassadors, high officials and even ministers have served loyally and well without so much as writing a commentary for the media (even if speeches are inescapably part of their duties), and they have not sought to influence public opinion or government policy by any means other than through the official channels.

Ambassador Tommy Koh, however, has. He has served effectively in the world of states and official diplomacy but has also managed to be active in Track 2 dialogue processes. By so doing, he has helped build bridges between the world of governments and the non-governmental world. In our complex world, multi-level and multi sectoral governance is needed to address key issues and his example is one that is worthy of study and emulation.

Different Tracks, Different Characters

International law and diplomacy are traditionally seen as the exclusive domain of states.[1] These traditional views have been questioned in today's globalised world. Governments alone cannot solve complex, global issues such as climate change and sustainable development. While governments do remain necessary, they are often in themselves insufficient. There is increasing recognition that non-state actors — private sector corporations, experts, non-governmental organisations, and the media — are important and indeed essential to help shape policies.

---

1 This remains the conventional view, even if the laws created by states may recognise and grant certain limited rights to international organisations or even, in the field of human rights, to individuals.

Relationships between the governmental and these non-governmental sectors are shifting. Top-down hierarchies are being supplemented or indeed in some cases supplanted by processes that allow for a two-way flow as well as for more bottom-up initiatives by non-state actors. Among the diverse non-state actors too, there is a growth in peer-to-peer codes of conduct and market norms in their relationships. These create a "horizontal" form of governance, quite different from the top down rules and laws issued by state authority.[2]

In this context, "Track 2" diplomacy is of increasing significance. It is a term that has come into use to contrast to the official inter-governmental diplomacy, also known as "Track 1", conducted by professional diplomats representing states (or in some cases international organisations). Track 2 is practised by non-governmental organisations and think-tanks, experts and eminent persons, including officials in their private capacities.

The term emerged earlier in the United States[3] and is often used in conflict resolution efforts, as part of the effort to lowering the tension that might already trouble official, inter-governmental relations. However, Track 2 has come to be applied and practised in ASEAN and Asia with special characteristics and on a much wider range of issues. A number of studies on the phenomenon in Asia are centred on the ASEAN network of think-tanks focused on strategic and international studies, known as the ASEAN-ISIS network.[4]

Whereas inter-governmental meetings are often more formal and scripted, Track 2 in Asia and ASEAN is often used as a mode of dialogue that allows more informal and interactive discussions and exchange of views.[5] In such settings, Track 2 assists to improve communication and forge a better understanding of one another's point of view as well as seeks to introduce new ideas and fresh thinking.

---

2 For a survey of the changes, see Moises Naim, *The End of Power: From Boardrooms to Battlefields and Churches to States, Why Being in Charge Isn't What It Used to Be* (New York: Basic Books, 2013).

3 Wikipedia attributes the coinage of the term to Joseph V. Montville. See William D. Davidson and Joseph V. Montville, "Foreign Policy According to Freud," *Foreign Policy* 45(1981): 145–157.

4 See Hadi Soesastro, Clara Joewono and Carolina Hernandez, *Twenty Two Years of ASEAN ISIS: Origin, Evolution and Challenges of Track 2 Diplomacy* (Jakarta: CSIS, 2006).

5 See entry for "Track 2" in *The Asia Pacific Security Lexicon*, eds. David Capie and Paul Evans, (Singapore: ISEAS, 2002), 213–216.

While separate and distinct in character, Track 2 seeks to inform official debates and influence policy outcomes, and this ambition distinguishes Track 2 dialogues from academic debates and discussions. Even if Track 2 experts come from academic and professorial backgrounds, they engage on questions of policy, rather than theory and observations.

The Track 2 effort to inform and influence policy leads to two work streams. The first is to seek the participation of officials, in their private capacity in the Track 2 dialogue itself or engage and brief officials on Track 2 findings and recommendations.[6] The second is that Track 2 participants share their views with the wider public, whether through their own publications or via the media, with the aim to shift public opinion and indirectly influence the policymaking context.

Tommy Koh in Track 2: Expertise and Personality

There are a number of characteristics that distinguish Track 2 from official Track 1 diplomacy and, to a considerable extent, these then influence the degree and extent to which a particular participant is more or less well suited to Track 2 processes, and can be effective even without the grant of official appointments and titles.

One of these characteristics is expertise. Many professional diplomats shift their area of focus from assignment to assignment over the course of a career, as required by their governmental duties. In contrast, Track 2 participants more often build up expertise in specific areas over many decades and generally stay within these defined areas. Expertise lends legitimacy to their inputs, especially when they are not officially appointed to take up these issues.

A second characteristic is the importance of personality. Track 2 discussions tend to favour participants who are comfortable in informal give-and-take, rather than adhering strictly to a pre-determined policy position. This is important as Track 2 dialogues seek to inject fresh and different perspectives into policy prescriptions as well as find creative compromises.

---

6 The term "Track 1.5 diplomacy" is sometimes used by some analysts to define a situation that is initiated by government, where official and non-official actors both engage.

A third and connected characteristic is that of independence of mind. Voicing individual opinion in dialogues and, even more, in commentaries in the media are a key part of Track 2. While knowing prevailing government policies, Track 2 participants must be open to the need to go beyond the existing conventions. Not all officials are comfortable to do so.

Ambassador Tommy Koh has demonstrated strengths in each of these areas. Even as Ambassador-at-Large, he has continued to hone his independent point of view and make this known at various dialogues and through speeches and public commentaries. While remaining loyal to his office, there have been occasions where he has taken license to express personal opinion that may run ahead of where governments stand.

In so doing, he has drawn on the experience and expertise he has developed in identified areas including the environment, institution-building and international law, as well as the skills he has garnered in negotiations. He has also demonstrated his ability to communicate and interact effectively not only with other government officials but with the broadest range of non-state actors, including academics and experts, non-governmental organisations and leaders from the private sector.

In this respect, one might even draw a distinction between *Ambassador* Tommy Koh — and the roles he has played in official diplomacy, and *Professor* Tommy Koh, who has been active, comfortable and effective in Track 2 diplomacy. A few specific contributions are noted below.

The Environment

Chairing the preparatory process for the then path-breaking initiative for the 1992 UN Conference on Environment and Development (UNCED or Earth Summit), Professor Koh developed a high international standing and expertise on the environment. In Track 2, he has applied these strengths to two key concerns facing the region.

One of these is the haze pollution caused by land and forest fires in Indonesia and other parts of Southeast Asia, a complex and global-scale problem that has reoccurred since the 1990s. After the severe haze episode of 1997–1998, Professor Koh was a prime mover in bringing the issue to the attention of the United Nations Environment Programme. In the media, he has written and given speeches quoted by the media to call for laws to be enacted to punish corporations that illegally used fire to clear the land, which caused the haze. Professor Koh did so in advance of the Transboundary Haze Pollution Act that was passed by the Singapore Parliament in 2015.[7]

Today, he serves as co-chair of an International Expert Body on Transboundary Air Pollution, initiated by the Singapore government but comprising international experts sitting in their individual capacity. Together with co-chair, Professor S Jayakumar, Singapore's former foreign minister and deputy prime minister, they have penned commentaries that acknowledge the complexity of the issue but consistently call for cooperation and action to stem the problem within the context of international law.[8]

A second environmental issue on which Professor Koh has played a role in Track 2 diplomacy concerns water — a vital issue for the region and global community. He served as the inaugural chairman of the governing council for the Asia-Pacific Water Forum (APWF), an initiative set up by Japan's former premier, Ryutaro Hashimoto. Established in 2006, the APWF convened the first-ever Asia Pacific Water Summit in Beppu, Japan, to bring to the attention of regional leaders issues on access to clean water and other related water issues. Six years later, a second summit was convened in Chiang Mai, Thailand.

In these years, the APWF process chaired by Professor Koh has developed into the region's key network on water issues, with an open and inclusive membership that includes governments, both at the national and local levels, international organisations, water providers, the private sector, academia, the media and the civil society. With Professor Koh as chair, the work of the APWF is respected for its credibility

---

7 See Tommy Koh and Ewing-Chow, "The Haze and the Law," *The Straits Times*, June 27, 2013. It may be noted that Professor Koh had previously made similar calls in the early 2000s, as did the Singapore Institute of International Affairs, a think-tank chaired by the author of this essay.

8 See S Jayakumar and Tommy Koh, "The Haze, International Law and Global Cooperation", *The Straits Times*, October 6, 2015. See also S Jayakumar and Tommy Koh, "Sovereignty, Jurisdiction and International Law", *The Straits Times*, June 25, 2016, which explains the international law basis for Singapore's national law to punish transboundary haze pollution.

and integrity and contributes to official global and also sub-regional efforts to promote water issues.

ASEAN

Ambassador-at-Large Tommy Koh chaired the drafting committee for the ASEAN Charter, which was completed in 2007. The Charter was ratified and came into force in 2008 and serves as the first formal and written "constitution" for the regional group. At that point, given his long service abroad at the UN and in the United States, he was not a recognised ASEAN expert. But Professor Koh drew from his experience in multilateral diplomacy to go on to contribute most notably on institution-building and rule-making in ASEAN.

In early 2013, when Brunei chaired the group, I was asked to gather experts from across ASEAN for a dialogue with officials in their governments and, although still a serving Singaporean official, Professor Koh was a key participant in that dialogue. Professor Koh has also edited a book about the drafting of the ASEAN Charter. In commentaries for the media, he has shared his views on key concerns for ASEAN, especially in the group's relations with China.

Major Powers

A third area in which Professor Koh has notably contributed to relates to Singapore's relations with the major Asian powers. Professor Koh has long served as the chair for key meetings with China, Japan and India.

These meetings have been co-chaired by Professor Koh and owe much to his personal networks and high standing. It is otherwise not apparent why such larger countries would wish to engage a much smaller country like Singapore on a bilateral basis.

Additionally, for many years, Professor Koh served as one of the co-chairs for the esteemed Williamsburg Conference that is convened by the Asia Society of the United States. This was a multilateral dialogue structured to allow conversations on regional and global strategic issues among experts and also sitting officials, from Asia on one side and the United States on the other.

Conclusion

As a diplomat and negotiator, Ambassador Koh has valued the need to establish and maintain strong networks. His work testifies that personal relationships can buttress official ties, and that the sharing of individual opinions and perspectives in the media and other platform can assist understanding and empathy, over and above the official government statement.

In the vast body of his work, the personal outlook, character and skills of Ambassador Tommy Koh have been used in tandem with official mandates and processes. When we look even briefly at what he has done in Track 2 however, we realise that these personal attributes are not merely ancillary but have allowed him to be effective in areas outside of officialdom.

Section II

The Arts, Culture and Heritage

CHAPTER 12

Tommy Koh and the Ideal of a Well-Lived Life

———⟡———

KWOK KIAN-WOON

How does Professor Tommy Koh get to do all that he does — not only in his illustrious service as a Singaporean diplomat, but also in wider public life, especially as a tireless champion of the arts and heritage? A day in the life of Tommy Koh, which appears to last more than 24 hours, may go like this: a swim with Mrs Koh before sunrise, a breakfast meeting, the official opening of a public event (with him speaking as a most congenial guest of honour), back-to-back meetings throughout the day (all involving complicated issues and requiring his legendary negotiation skills), an evening exhibition opening or a community event (again with him as guest of honour), dinner at a state function (where he strengthens the ties between international leaders) and, when he finally gets home, hours of reading, as well as writing his articles and speeches, which share, among other things, his vision of a more humane Asia. In recent years, too, the rare "free" evening may be blessed with spending time with his grandchildren, who do not always receive top priority if Prof. Koh were invited to grace yet another official event; this is because he would not bring himself to turn it down even when he could cite family life or the need for more rest as perfectly acceptable reasons. What Tommy does in a day may well be what very busy persons in professional and public life do in an entire week. In the process, and with his characteristic generous spirit and amiable personality, he touches the lives of many in Singapore and beyond.

How does Prof. Koh do it all? First, I would like to give a short answer to the question by recalling a statement about Tommy that was purportedly made by a first-generation Cabinet leader. I have heard this statement from several sources over the decades and am inclined to repeat it: "Tommy Koh is a Boy Scout."

I always thought that the statement portrays Tommy accurately and positively because it connotes the values of honour and integrity and the spirit of volunteerism and civic-mindedness. Boy Scouts are, ideally anyway, conscientious to a fault; for example, they are expected to leave a campsite cleaner than they found it. Labouring under such expectations, they also become adept at solving all kinds of problems and mobilising teams to work in unison. Tommy exemplifies the ethos of constantly making the world a better place, as complicated as human beings are and as intractable as some human problems can be.

There are countless examples of Tommy's public spiritedness, whether in agreeing to take up appointments — such as chairing the National Arts Council (NAC; 1991–1996) and the National Heritage Board (NHB; 2002–2011) — or supporting public causes, gracing public occasions and sharing his insights in forums and articles. A quick example here would suffice. For the conference "We Asians: Between Past and Future" organised jointly by the Singapore Heritage Society, the National Archives of Singapore, and the Japan Foundation in 2000, I invited Tommy to serve as the guest of honour. Tommy, although eminently qualified, hesitated because he did not think that he had the right credentials. But within a couple of days, he accepted the invitation. He opened his speech by saying that he did so not because he was a "serial masochist", but because of the communitarian value of "helping each other" that he had "internalised".[1] I am tempted to say that the Boy Scout ethos deeply ingrained in Tommy Koh always places priority on the common good at the risk of the individual becoming a serial masochist.

In writing this essay, I couldn't help but ask Tommy about the "Boy Scout" statement, which he confirmed was made by Lim Kim San, the minister who was credited with initiating Singapore's public housing

---

1 Kwok Kian-Woon, Indira Arumugam, Karen Chia and Lee Chee Keng, eds., *We Asians: Between Past and Future* (Singapore: Japan Foundation Asia Center, National Archives of Singapore and Singapore Heritage Society, 2000), 9.

programme.[2] However, Tommy went on to quickly qualify that the statement did not imply what I had naively thought. In this case, "Boy Scout" was not a term of endearment, although it might have been said in an avuncular tone. (In an earlier time, Mr Lim and the Kohs were neighbours, and Tommy would address him as "Uncle"). Instead, the epithet signified a certain soft-headedness and lack of ruthlessness, which disqualifies one for high political office, especially — it was pointed out — the prime ministership, which Tommy assured all that he would not aspire to. Such indeed was the hard-headed and muscular mindset that undergirded Singapore's post-independence transformation, as exemplified by the first-generation Cabinet ministers led by then Prime Minister Lee Kuan Yew.

How does Tommy Koh get to make all his public contributions? I offer a longer answer, which has everything to do with his belief that the arts and heritage constitute an intrinsic part of a well-lived life — and, by extension, they should have an indispensable place in a good society and in national development, fully deserving of individual commitment and public support. Translating this belief into both his personal life and his public role, as the essays in this section amply demonstrate, Tommy Koh has been an indefatigable advocate of the arts and heritage, as well as an exemplary participant in public discourse.

Before I draw out the impetus behind Tommy's many cultural contributions, an overview of the essays in this section may be helpful. Khor Kok Wah takes us back to Tommy's chairmanship of the newly created NAC as a statutory board, unleashing a whole slew of initiatives that supported artists and arts groups, encouraged new artistic creation, and promoted arts appreciation and arts philanthropy. These positive developments notwithstanding, Kok Wah also highlights the NAC's controversial move to stop funding performance art following an incident in 1994, in effect, as some artists have suggested, banning an entire art form. Although this was later rescinded, and as other instances have shown, it is perhaps impossible to conceive of a more autonomous arts council in Singapore, one that is not caught between state decisions and

---

2 Tommy Koh, personal conversation with the author, January 17, 2017, Nanyang Technological University, Singapore. The author would like to thank Professor Koh for permitting him to report this part of their conversation.

artistic considerations, with the former invariably prevailing over the latter. Under these circumstances, we should appreciate Tommy Koh's efforts in speaking up for artists and the arts, often behind the scenes and also publicly, as in his defence of The Necessary Stage when a *Straits Times* article cast aspersions on its two founders.

Ever the pioneer, Tommy served as the chairman of the first Censorship Review Committee (1991–1992). In his essay, Koh Buck Song recalls Tommy's pivotal role in selecting the 18 members, ensuring both diversity and cultural literacy, and building consensus towards moving "public opinion in the general direction of accepting greater liberalisation of regulations on the media" — well before use of the Internet became ubiquitous. This is not the place to discuss the meanings of artistic freedom and the contrasting positions on censorship in the media and the arts. It may suffice to highlight Buck Song's claim that, given the expected opposing views in the Committee, Tommy's skilful and fair chairmanship led to "the advances achieved… in opening up space for expression." He also adds that there are "divides that do not lend themselves to easy resolution, even with the skill of a Tommy Koh." This observation highlights the paucity of the necessary competencies for engagement on censorship issues and the urgency for developing them as such issues continue to be debated. In this regard, we should take a leaf from Tommy's emphasis on listening and clarifying the stakes from various viewpoints.

Most members of the arts community have witnessed and appreciated the publicly visible role of Tommy Koh, but many artists have also experienced having him as a keen supporter of their individual artistic journeys and a good number as a personal friend. In this connection, Jeremy Monteiro's account captures the spirit of friendship extended by Tommy to an artist, in this case, a jazz musician whose art was not formally recognised as such. Jeremy also highlights Tommy's ability "to move about freely through all levels of society and facets of life in Singapore." This is also fondly recounted by Danny Yeo, who was tasked with organising the first Singapore Hawker Masters awards. Danny requested Tommy to chair the inaugural judging panel, although he "figured that a man of his stature might not have the time or patience to go around nibbling on prata and slurping up laksa with us." Tommy, who is a small eater, rose to the occasion — "over countless bowls of wanton noodles and plates of chicken rice" — with humility, grace and "acute tastebuds". He proved himself as at home with Maxwell Food Centre hawkers as he is with Michelin chefs.

In his capacity as chairman of the National Heritage Board for 10 years, Tommy led the most significant growth of state-sponsored museums in Singapore. In his essay, Michael Koh sets out Tommy's seminal contributions as a unifying and visionary cultural leader, "fund-raiser extraordinaire" and the quintessential cultural diplomat. Kenson Kwok, the founding director of the Asian Civilisations Museum and the Peranakan Museum, shares his memories of Tommy's support for the two museums, as well as his chairmanship of the judging panel for the design of the National Gallery. In his account of Tommy's support for the Singapore Art Museum, Kwok Kian Chow highlights the centrality of artists and artistic work in the NHB chairman's vision, with special emphasis on the artistic creativity of the Southeast Asian region. Tommy did not shy away from sharing his personal preferences in art, and he made a plea for greater "accessibility" in museum programming, but he also argued against "dumbing down" and "underestimating our citizens".

Tan Tai Yong was recommended by Tommy to chair the National History Museum Board. The historian's earliest personal encounter with Tommy in 1997 left him convinced that "[Tommy] understood that history is a contested terrain and that both the victors and the vanquished would have their respective versions of the past... [and] understanding history from only one perspective would be limiting." Two decades later, such an open-minded approach to Singapore's "national history" has yet to be fully appreciated by many politicians, civil servants, and even some academics.

Tommy Koh's open-mindedness is undoubtedly cultivated by his love of reading, which as Paul Tan reminds us, was cultivated from young by a father who, in addition of having a home library, "indulged his son's love of the written word with book purchases, which must have been a luxury in pre-independent Singapore." Paul also refers to Tommy's personal efforts in promoting reading, including running a book club, and encouraging young writers like himself — and all this on top of ensuring that NAC provided significant support for the literary arts. Tommy's love of reading is again highlighted by Elaine Ng, who also provides an overview of Tommy's many efforts in supporting the mission of the National Library Board. Elaine's title, "Tommy Koh: A Reader and a Gentleman", is telling; it suggests that the pleasures of reading (which should be made accessible to all) and the cultivation of social virtues are certainly not unrelated.

This leads me to my larger argument. Tommy's family upbringing, as he has recalled on several occasions, was instrumental in developing his love of the arts and heritage, which lies at the heart of his public contributions. This is most clearly articulated in the two opening essays of *The Tommy Koh Reader*, where he paid tribute to his parents. Among other things, they shaped not only his aesthetic sense, but also his moral outlook and his emphasis on tolerance, respect for others, "the courage to stand up to bullies and fear no one", and the joy of living.[3] What I wish to highlight here, however, is how Tommy internalised this inheritance "that no money can buy" in making his public contributions. In lieu of a detailed exposition, I shall illustrate this by referring to Tommy's well-known status as a diplomat, and it may suffice to cite the "Great Negotiator Award" that Harvard University conferred on him in April 2014. And this is one of Tommy's chief lessons on what it takes to be a successful negotiator:

> *Negotiation is also an art because a good neighbour should also have a high emotional and cultural intelligence. There is increasing recognition of the fact that we both think with our heads and our hearts. To succeed in a negotiation, we should aim to connect with our negotiating partner cognitively, emotionally and culturally.*[4]

Indeed, this kind of "multiple intelligence" appears to be in short supply in Singapore, as much as it is personified in Tommy Koh, who has put it to good use in advancing Singapore's national interests. But this also begs the question of how such intelligence is — and can

---

3 Tommy Koh, *The Tommy Koh Reader: Favourite Essays and Lectures* (Singapore: World Scientific, 2013), 7.
4 Tommy Koh, "Confessions of a Lucky Negotiator," *The Straits Times*, May 7, 2014.

be — developed by a nation and its citizens, paying serious attention to the arts and heritage.

I also take this opportunity to make a few more points in appreciation of Professor Tommy Koh. In a newspaper article published in early January 2015, Tommy raised his concerns about inequality and poverty in Singapore, highlighting especially the challenges faced by needy students and the elderly poor. Tommy added:

> *I would like to see Singapore grow in cultural and political maturity. A culturally mature people accept diversity and welcome different points of view. A politically mature society is one in which the vanquished are gracious in their defeat and the victors are magnanimous in their victory.*[5]

Tommy's column elicited a rebuttal from the press secretary to the Minister for Education, disputing some of the facts used by Tommy and arguing that "broader financial support doesn't mean more students are poor."[6] In his reply, Tommy acknowledged that his article may have "over-represented the extent of student poverty", but he insisted that "one cannot deny that student poverty exists" in spite of government action. Tommy gave examples of how private charities, in which he has served as a trustee, have made a positive difference, including in arts education, citing bursaries for needy students at Nanyang Academy of Fine Arts, LaSalle, and the Intercultural Theatre Institute: "The bursaries are a lifeline to some. Without our help, they would most likely have to abandon their studies or work part-time. The needs exceed our ability to help."[7] Just as books and reading materials are now available to all in our public libraries, education (and especially arts education) should be made more accessible to those from poorer families.

In speaking up on such occasions, Prof. Koh has exemplified the combination of cultural and political maturity that he envisions for Singapore, just as he has done as so as a great negotiator, thinking with his head and heart. This also illustrates the virtue of moral courage

---

5 Tommy Koh, "Three Wishes for the New Year," *The Straits Times*, January 3, 2015.
6 Ho Hwei Ling, "Broader Financial Support Doesn't Mean More Students are Poor," *The Straits Times*, January 9, 2015.
7 "Prof Tommy Koh Replies," *The Straits Times*, January 9, 2015.

that Tommy learnt from his father, a virtue that the morally complex contemporary world could do with more of. Such courage requires a mature moral perspective on the part of citizens, especially those who play the role of intellectuals, including those who are working within the "Establishment". For me, one of Prof. Koh's most profound intellectual contributions is his nuanced articulation of such a moral perspective in the case of foreign policy:

> *... there will be situations, hopefully rare, when a government will be confronted by conflicts between its national interest and its fidelity to law and morality. In such situations, a government may feel compelled to subordinate considerations of law and morality to its national interest. In extreme cases, when the survival of a state may be in question, a government may feel justified in acting beyond the law. In such situations, it is important for the politician or diplomat to have a bad conscience, to be aware of the damage that his [or her] action will inflict on the international system, so that the moral values will survive their violation.*[8]

In conclusion, allow me to say that this "practical idealist" position is indeed morally demanding on the part of the politician or diplomat — and by extension, the citizens who vote in the government of the day and endow it the legitimacy to define the "national interest", which in turn justifies official policy. Tommy's moral perspective could also be appropriately extrapolated to other spheres of power beyond foreign policy. This is not the place to offer an evaluation of its implications for the arts and heritage, and indeed for the realisation of Tommy's vision of a culturally and politically more mature Singapore. As an analogy, for example, in situations when state authorities and official cultural bodies may justify acts of censorship in the name of national interest, wouldn't it be important for politicians and arts administrators to have a "bad conscience" and be conscious of the costs and consequences that their actions entail for artistic creativity? More generally, does the lack of such

8 Tommy Koh, "Can Any Country Afford a Moral Foreign Policy?" Speech delivered at the School of Foreign Service, Georgetown University, Washington DC, November 18, 1987. Reproduced in Tommy Koh, *The Tommy Koh Reader: Favourite Essays and Lectures* (Singapore: World Scientific, 2013), 220.

conscience among citizens also mean that a nation's economic prosperity and political stability are predicated on the impoverishment of moral and intellectual questioning? And does this make a nation stronger in the longer run?

However, it is my duty here to suggest that the exercise of moral reasoning also lies at the heart of Tommy Koh's ideal of a well-lived life. And it is one deeper source behind the kind of energy that he invests in his public service and in his wider humanitarian efforts. We all know Prof. Koh not as the "serial masochist", but as the serial consensus-builder, the serial arts and heritage lover, the serial reader, the serial Asianist and ASEAN champion, the serial public thinker, and even the serial foodie. But underpinning these many roles — and buttressing Tommy's public persona — is a human being who has a moral vision, which is constantly tested by the times we live in. Few will ever really know about his nights of Gethsemane — those moments of conscience when he wishes that moral and aesthetic values were not violated, that he could have prevented their violation, and that such values would survive in spite of their violation.

But all of us would appreciate that, given the serial Boy Scout that he is, our good Professor Tommy Koh will always do his best to keep that precious moral flame alive.

CHAPTER 13

Tommy Koh and the Arts

——— ❦ ———

KHOR KOK WAH

Tommy Koh's leadership of the arts in Singapore from 1991 to 1996 was characterised by three elements: a pioneering spirit, a progressive outlook and most importantly perhaps, an ability to rally people together.

An Arts Pioneer

Newly returned from diplomatic service in America, one of Tommy Koh's first appointments was as Chairman-designate of the National Arts Council (NAC).

Among other significant initiatives, NAC was a new entity proposed in the 1989 "Ong Teng Cheong Report" of the Advisory Council on Culture and the Arts, which promised a new cultural era for Singapore.

All legal and administrative preparations for NAC's birth were in place. George Yeo had taken over the Ministry of Community Development — his first Ministerial appointment — renaming it Ministry of Information and the Arts (MITA). He avoided the word culture as it conjured the image of a totalitarian state. He promptly asked Tommy to head NAC, an outfit expected to be forward- and outward-looking, fresh and nimble.

NAC's first Executive Director was Foo Meng Liang, then MITA Deputy Secretary for Culture as well as a stalwart of the Government Administrative Service, a HR specialist and a literature lover who was also a published poet. Meng Liang gave us good direction and guidance under Tommy's leadership. Both gave us latitude to develop our respective plans. Staff members came from MITA's Arts Division mainly, but also the National Theatre Trust, the Singapore Cultural Foundation and the Festival of Arts Secretariat, all predecessor organisations of NAC. They included Liew Chin Choy, Leen Kim Swee, Teo Han Wue, Lee Soon Hock and me, each looking after a specific area. We were ably supported by Chua Ai Liang, Goh Ching Lee, Elaine Ng, Lim Mee Lian, Stacey Tan, Valerie Lim, Catherine Ho, Corrine Tan, Foo Yoke Guan, Ching Keow Yung, Seah Woo Lye, Jumirah Nomopawiro, Soh Guek Keow, Angeline Tan and other colleagues, many of whom remain in the arts today. We were excited to help start up a brand new statutory board with Tommy and Meng Liang, and to be its first batch of employees.

Our first management meeting with Tommy was memorable. After preliminary greetings he promptly and solemnly announced that the higher-ups had given him the option to replace the whole lot of us with completely fresh blood. A tense moment, which was short-lived, as he promptly announced he had decided otherwise!

NAC's pioneering years saw Tommy presiding over a number of significant initiatives that would have a lasting impact. In its first two years alone NAC launched major new arts initiatives for community outreach, events, artist recognition, facilities, sponsorship and grants.

Tommy's vision for the development of young arts audiences was that "every student should, during his or her four years in secondary school, have the opportunity to visit a museum, see a play, listen to a concert and watch a dance performance." Instead of dwelling on large number targets, he made his targets simple, down-to-earth, and easily understood by all stakeholders. In January 1993, with partial Tote Board funding, NAC's Arts Education Programme (AEP) was launched to give students arts experiences and exposure. The programme underlined NAC's first attempts at significantly scaling up community and youth outreach. By 1996, the number of AEP activities had increased three-fold from 384 in 1993 to 1,132, reaching 118,000 students in 215 schools.

The Young Artist Award was inaugurated in 1992, complement-ing the Cultural Medallion Award instituted in 1979 for established artists, and harking the arrival of a new generation of younger artists. Its first recipients were Jamaludin Jalil (for dance), Ong Keng Sen and Lim Jen Erh (theatre), Shane Thio and Jennifer Tham (music), S. Chandrasekaran (visual arts), Liang Wern Fook (literature) and Lee Tiah Kee (photography). Keng Sen, Jennifer and Wern Fook have since gone on to receive the Cultural Medallion.

A new Festival of Asian Performing Arts, organised in alternate years to the then biennial Festival of Arts, underlined our connection with Asian arts whilst being open to arts from around the world. I recall the inaugural Festival in November 1993, organised by Liew Chin Choy, and watching a mind-blowing dance by Cloud Gate from Taiwan in their first performance in Singapore. A depiction of the 1949 flight of Nationalist troops across the straits to Taiwan, it was one of my most moving and memorable arts experiences and received a long standing ovation from the full house at Victoria Theatre.

The first Singapore Writers' Week to become independent of the Singapore Arts Festival was held in 1991 and has developed into an annual Singapore Writers Festival today. In 1992 the SPH/NAC Short Story Competition in four languages was organised for the first time. In 1995 the first Poems on the MRT were launched.

In 1992 the nation's premier arts event, the Singapore Festival of Arts, initiated a homecoming series, inviting pianists Margaret Leng Tan and Koh Joo Ann, and violinist Siow Lee Chin to return home from successful international careers to perform for Singaporeans. The Festival also commissioned playwrights Kuo Pao Kun and Michael Chiang, and choreographers Anthony Then and Goh Soo Khim to produce and stage new works. It also presented Ninagawa from Japan, Shanghai Theatre Academy, Dallas Symphony, London City Ballet and Paco Pena Flamenco Guitar and Dance Company, among others.

NAC continued organising and evolving numerous events inherited from its predecessors such as the Singapore Art Fair and the National Music Competition.

Also in 1992, NAC started a Special Accounts Scheme to receive donations on behalf of arts organisations. This scheme was instrumental in providing tax exemption for donors and significantly helped arts groups in their sponsorship drive.

In the same year NAC launched five new grant schemes to support theatre, travel, publishing, seed funding and scholarships. Among the recipients of these new grants were The Necessary Stage, Yan Choong Lian Dance Troupe, Sriwarna, Singapore Indian Fine Arts Society and Sarkasi Said (for travel); Heng Siok Tian, Lew Poo Chan and Goh Sin Tub (for publishing); and TheatreWorks, Teater Ekamatra and Practice Performing Arts Centre (for theatre).

During the first years of NAC, we refurbished Kallang Theatre, Victoria Theatre and Singapore Conference Hall. These theatres as well as Drama Centre played a big role in developing our performing arts groups, and in presenting them as well as foreign groups to Singaporeans. Kallang was the venue for larger-scale Singaporean works, plus musicals from the West such as *Cats*, *Les Miserables* and *Phantom of the Opera*.

The Arts Housing Scheme started way back in 1985 with Stamford Arts Centre and Telok Ayer Performing Arts Centre. The main initiators were Ng Yew Kang and Juliana Lim, both pioneer arts administrators. As it made a big difference to arts groups who could now secure space for their work and development, we developed the scheme further. In 1993 we provided the Singapore Indian Fine Arts Society with new premises at the former Rangoon Road Primary School. 126 Cairnhill Arts Centre (1993) housed groups like Act 3 and The Necessary Stage. Selegie Arts Centre (1996) still houses the Photographic Society of Singapore. And the Waterloo Arts Belt (1995) comprised conserved bungalows housing the Dance Ensemble, Chinese Calligraphy Society, Action Theatre and Young Musicians Society. Today the former two tenants remain, while the latter two have been replaced by Centre 42 and The Theatre Practice. Telok Kurau Studios housed 26 artists in 1997, the first and only visual arts studio complex.

In 1994 Tommy successfully lobbied the Urban Redevelopment Authority to provide NAC with a 30-year lease at the former premises of Tun Sri Lanang Secondary School at Goodman Road, which we then passed to LaSalle College of the Arts. A major acquisition for NAC, it is now known as the Goodman Arts Centre and houses NAC's own offices as well as other arts organisations and venues. Two years later NAC secured St Anthony's Convent, outbidding other contenders, and handed it over to Nanyang Academy of Fine Arts.

These interventions on behalf of numerous arts organisations and our two arts schools were critical in facilitating their development.

An Internationalist

Within three months of NAC's establishment Tommy led us in signing an MOU with the Scottish Arts Council. The MOU triggered exchanges such as the performance in Singapore of Scottish percussionist Evelyn Glennie and the attachment of NAC officers to the Scottish Arts Council. More importantly the MOU started NAC's path of international work.

In 1994 we sent a travelling exhibition to Hong Kong and China called "Window on Singapore Art". The 31 Singapore artists represented included our pioneer artists Chen Chong Swee, Georgette Chen, Cheong Soo Pieng and Liu Kang, as well as Tang Da Wu, Ong Kim Seng, Jaafar Latiff, Chua Ek Kay, Salleh Japar and Jimmy Ong. Throughout the initial years of NAC and beyond we actively collaborated with ASEAN neighbours. In 1994 alone we organised Singapore's participation in ASEAN's Theatre Festival, Photo Exhibition and Art Workshop and Exhibition.

The Travel Grant started during Tommy's time helped numerous artists travel to present their works overseas. It enabled TheatreWorks' *Madame Mao's Memories* to be staged at the Edinburgh Fringe Festival, and the Modern Art Society to present exhibitions in Japan and New Zealand. In 1992 it helped the Singapore Symphony Orchestra to tour France, Belgium, Romania, Turkey and Egypt.

Progressive Leadership

I recall an incident when NAC management recommended against helping or collaborating with a commercial entity, as its motivations were profit-oriented and not aligned with ours. Our usual partners then were mainly non-commercial players such as fellow government agencies or non-profit arts groups. When Tommy read our recommendation, he wrote a vehement file note scolding us for not being pro-business, and instructed us to read a book on government, business and their collaborative potential! That admonishment started a mindset shift.

At that time commercial aspects of arts promotion were being undertaken by the Economic Development Board. They supported projects such as Tresors, a commercial art fair from overseas which remained here for a few years, as well as the musicals of Andrew Lloyd

Webber and Cameron Mackintosh, for which we had to negotiate rentals at Kallang Theatre. NAC management played hardball with Cameron Mackintosh over these rental negotiations and at one point Tommy chaired a meeting between the two parties to help us reach agreement.

Rallying Stakeholders

Within a few months of NAC's formation, Tommy set up a Panel of Arts Advisors, which included Kuo Pao Kun, Choo Hoey, Edwin Thumboo and Masuri bin Salikun. He appointed many artists to various arts resource panels and held numerous dialogues to get feedback, explain his plans and seek collaboration.

In 1992 Tommy, already a member of the Esplanade Steering Committee, was appointed Chair of the Users Advisory Group for the project, comprising artists from drama, dance, music, visual arts as well as related users. It was an important job. Naturally there was much antic-ipation over this icon of a centre, what was in it for user-practitioners, and how its design must be made useful for one and all. In 1994, in this capacity and as NAC Chairman, Tommy was given the difficult task of explaining why the government had decided mid-stream to reduce the Esplanade project by one third. Furthermore he had to explain why the amputated part had to be a cluster of smaller spaces, comprising a medium-sized theatre (750 seats), an adaptable theatre (400), a develop-mental theatre (200) and an outdoor pavilion. The arts community felt betrayed on both counts. They sensed that the smaller, sacrificed spaces were more relevant to their needs compared to the concert hall (1,600) and the lyric theatre (2,000) that remained in the building plans. The artists felt the latter would only cater to expensive international shows inaccessible to ordinary citizens.

Many felt the stage was set for Esplanade to assume the epicentre of our arts scene, while the rest of the arts venues remained at the periphery. In one big meeting with artists, including Kuo Pao Kun, Tommy took great pains to explain the government's position against much scepti-cism. His audience was not fully convinced but because of Tommy's persuasive powers, they understood where he was coming from — the government's need to be mindful of a potential public outcry against the full cost of the project ($600m), the relevance of the two big halls to our global hub aspirations, and the fact we already had a number of smaller venues elsewhere. Tommy's involvement helped placate protesters, gave an understanding of the government's position and provided a pathway for Esplanade to win over its audiences later.

And in April 2017, the government announced that the Esplanade would add on a much-needed, long-awaited mid-size (550 seat) theatre by 2021.

Another area where Tommy put his personal charm and diplomatic skills to good use was in arts sponsorship. His chairmanship and championship of the arts provided a certain public credibility, desirability and validity to the arts and perhaps a certain glitter as well. It cannot be denied that the arts often thrive on such matters, though many of us believe the substance of the arts exists in its own right, independent of public perception or support. As chief host at our annual Patron of the Arts Awards and similar events, Tommy would make speeches on the value of the arts for its own sake and for the sake of personal fulfilment, community, nation and business. In typical fashion he would, at the start of each speech, greet friends and arts partners personally by name, say that he wanted to make three points, and then proceed to make those three points simply but convincingly. The media would cover these speeches and events and celebrate top corporate donors and sponsors. They typically included the likes of Shell, SPH, UOB, Shaw Foundation, SIA, GK Goh, Tote Board and Singapore Tourism Board. Arts sponsorship increased seven-fold during Tommy's watch, from $8.4m in 1991 to $57.1m in 1996.

Artists, the Media and Their Public

On the flip side, Tommy did not shy away from fronting difficult or controversial official positions to protect what was deemed to be prevailing public values on what is acceptable or not acceptable in art. In 1994 an incident triggered NAC to stop funding performance art, as well as forum theatre, both relatively new, scriptless art forms. In an event organised by 5th Passage, artist Josef Ng snipped his pubic hair during his performance. It was in protest against recent police action targeted at members of the gay community, and the ensuing media coverage of such action. Josef Ng's performance was in turn sensationalised by an article with a graphic photo on the front page of *The New Paper*. The article triggered negative public reaction and concerns over performance art and artists who practised it, and the direction they seemed to be taking. Many observers construed that it was the government, especially the law enforcement agencies, which took exception to Josef Ng's performance, and that the NAC had no choice but to intervene. NAC's credibility took a hit among artists and audiences who embraced contemporary art. They felt the government could have taken more time and given more consideration before deciding to stop funding performance art and forum theatre. The policy was subsequently reviewed and funding restored some years later when contemporary art forms had become more established and embraced by artists and audiences.

A month after the 5th Passage event, *The Straits Times* published an article "Two Pioneers of Forum Theatre Trained at Marxist Workshops" referring to Alvin Tan and Haresh Sharma, the Artistic Director and Resident Playwright, respectively, of The Necessary Stage (TNS). To all who knew TNS and its leaders, the article was sensational and outrageously biased in painting the two artists and their company in a politically sinister light. To set the record straight and shore up support for TNS, Tommy responded in a letter published in the same paper two days later:

> *I would like to point out respectfully that your report has a slant which tends to put TNS in a bad light. TNS has a good track record and is one of the most promising theatre groups in Singapore.... The NAC will continue to support TNS as long as it keeps up its good work. The only exception is that the NAC will not provide assistance to TNS to stage forum theatre.*[1]

Tommy's letter underscored his consistent concern for and defence of artists whom he felt were deserving of support, or were being unfairly treated or targeted by the media or other parties. At the same

---

1 Tommy Koh, Letter to the Forum, *The Straits Times*, February 7, 1994.

time he upheld the government's recent position on forum theatre. Today TNS, under Alvin and Haresh, is among our most established theatre companies, enjoys strong support from NAC, Esplanade and corporations, and continues to make a deep impact on its audience and our arts scene.

Conclusion

Tommy continued to be a keen champion of the arts after his NAC days. He took on new roles as the Chairman of the National Heritage Board, as patron of arts organisations and artists, or supporter in his personal capacity. In 2015 for instance he launched *Singathology*, a two-volume collection of new literary works by celebrated Singapore writers to mark Singapore's 50th Anniversary. The launch was held at the new National Gallery which he had played a significant role to realise.

When Tommy stepped down from chairmanship of NAC in 1996, the arts scene and NAC had progressed along a steep curve. Together with his NAC colleagues and the arts community, he had set a new and lasting momentum. He made his leadership available to all stakeholders who wished to see the arts progress. His untiring declarations on the worthiness of the arts converted many over time. He brought his skills and personality to bear on Singapore's goal of becoming a culturally vibrant society.

CHAPTER 14

Tommy Koh on the Censorship Review Committee 1991–1992

⚜

KOH BUCK SONG

Fundamental Shifts in Media and Arts Censorship

A number of people the world over have had the chance to see Tommy Koh — the quintessential, consummate Singaporean diplomat — in action, chairing a meeting on the international stage. There, he would never fail to impress his interlocutors and audiences, exuding his typical charm, as he brings yet another diverse group closer towards consensus. Fewer would have had a similar vantage point in the more unusual context of a domestic setting charged with more strongly divided individual agendas. Of course, in Singapore, his public service appointments have included being the Chairman of the National Arts Council and National Heritage Board, as well as many other committees. But the members of these less contentious boards were unlikely to have come from as disparate starting positions as the 18 people who served under his chairmanship on the Censorship Review Committee (CRC) of 1991–1992, to help change the media and arts landscape of Singapore forever.

Younger people today might find it hard to imagine that, in the early 1990s, Singapore was a much more innocent place. This was when media and arts censorship had real teeth, before the advent of widespread use of the Internet, when no pornographic materials could be viewed, obtained or displayed openly at all. This was a time when some fundamental shifts were being proposed for the very first time by the government of the day in what media and arts materials could be allowed into the public domain. Hence, on this committee, there were meetings in which metaphorical swords were crossed during debates on issues of personal morality, values and beliefs. Tommy's flair, fairness and flexibility as a committee chairman were called for on many an occasion. He never disappointed, nor was he ever slow to exercise his skill, as a chairman, to deal with, or to defer — and thereby defuse — significant instances of emerging major clashes of opposing positions, whenever these arose. As a result, the advances achieved on this committee in opening up space for expression have remained a vital part of the broad legacy that Tommy has left in the sphere of media and arts censorship.

The CRC is a citizens' committee formed every five to 10 years to review all the country's regulation policies on all types of media and arts content except mainstream media. Everything else, from stage plays to calendars, came under scrutiny. Not only did I have the chance as a member of the 1991–1992 CRC to observe Tommy at work, up close, over the course of more than a year of committee meetings, I also had the opportunity later to compare this CRC with two other CRCs — when I served once more as a member of the 2002–2003 CRC and, for a third time, on the 2009–2010 CRC as Deputy Chairman, to become the only person to have served on all three CRCs.

The 1991–1992 Censorship Review Committee

The 1991–1992 CRC was a panel that started the process of transforming the media and arts landscape of Singapore like never before. It was a game-changer indeed, in many ways. As it turned out, in effect, the work of this committee contributed significantly also as part of Singapore's transition from Third World to First, by updating and modernising the country's censorship standards that were then behind the times in several important aspects. For films, there was no proper classification system to speak of. All films then were treated the same way in terms of censorship standard. Even the PG (Parental Guidance) category did not exist. Everything had to be censored to General standard — essentially cut, if necessary, to make it suitable for viewing even by an unsupervised primary school child.

As this was the very first time that changing the country's film censorship system was being contemplated, the committee's discussions on this topic were conducted on the basic level of first principles. Sometimes, time had to be spent even to settle very simple questions of what kind of scenes in a movie should be censored, such as the specific details of what exactly would be considered nudity. Whenever this happened, Tommy displayed always the patience of a saint, and often the wisdom of a sage. These facets of his character are perhaps honed from his long, broad and deep experience of foreign relations for many years. He seemed well-versed in one chief reality that a diplomat involved in negotiations to do with culture has to become accustomed to — the time and effort needed to seek, and to secure, what little common ground there might be in between the mounds of self-interest that inevitably dot the landscape of any coming-together of groups of human beings. The appeal to the greater good, founded on a common commitment to tolerance, harmony and mutual respect, continues to be a precious value in artistic and socio-political discourse in Singapore.

Tommy's leadership was seminal right from the very start of the year-long censorship review process from May 1991 to September 1992, in the very composition of the CRC itself. He exercised care in playing a key role in selecting members from the whole spectrum from conservative to liberal, on a panel that had representatives ranging from 20-somethings to leading figures of the religious establishment. Indeed, his selection could even be said to have been made to ensure the inclusion of members relatively better versed in culture, with a greater level of such representation than on later committees, including the scores of similar citizens' panels since then. He was not afraid to include among the CRC's 18 members four writers, four journalists and two artists. Tommy could do this because he himself was confident in his own ability to carry the day for what would eventually be a fair consensus in the public interest. In this way, the foundation that was laid in articulating the case from artistic perspectives established important benchmarks for future discussions of these same issues.

In helping to select, and then gather and lead this disparate group, all with active minds and strong individual voices, Tommy's personal influence and vast network were vital attributes. At that time, a key feature of the political backdrop to the formation of this CRC was the then-recent leadership handover in the late 1990 from Singapore's first prime minister, Lee Kuan Yew, to his successor, Goh Chok Tong. Mr Goh would not long after campaign under what he called his "consultative style" in the August 1991 "snap" General Election, held in the midst of the year-long work of this CRC. In the early months of the CRC's work, George Yeo, then Minister for Information and the Arts, was an active speaker in public discourse, arguing for the advantages of opening up Singapore's media and arts landscape. Tommy, then recently returned from having served as Singapore's Ambassador in the United States and the United Nations between 1968 and 1990, was, in many ways, the perfect choice as Chairman of the 1991–1992 CRC, to help move public opinion in the general direction of accepting greater liberalisation of regulations on media and the arts.

Trying to Define Artistic Merit

Part of the maturing process of developing more open mindsets on censorship — and, by extension, on the whole outlook on life — involved coming to grips with what precisely is meant by the term "artistic merit". It was the first time that the question of artistic merit was raised for public discussion, to introduce the idea of considering the context of an artistic work when deciding whether it should be censored. Some broad guidelines were suggested, captured in Annex D of the 1991–1992 CRC Report, titled "Definition of the Term 'Artistic'". The tentative, progressive nature of this Annex is a badge of Tommy's open-mindedness and willingness to allow room for the exploration of questions that have no immediate definitive answer, of ideas that live mostly in the realm of the intuitive and instinctive. On this topic, especially, he showed his affinity with, and affection for, the world of the arts — something so close to his heart that he continues to speak with passion on the subject whenever he can, in all spheres and occasions, from launching a book for a lone aspiring writer to addressing a conference audience of thousands of subject experts on, for instance, the value of culture as part of what makes a city liveable. Giving his backing to what he sometimes liked to call "lost causes", he would even put his personal reputation on the line to champion the arts. What he has said, and continues to say, on this topic remain vital for the support for the place of the arts in society till today.

One of the thorniest issues that the 1991–1992 CRC reviewed was whether "greater leeway" — a much-used term in those days, much less so of late — should be accorded to depictions of homosexuality in film and other media. The consensus of this CRC moved — ever so slightly, and reluctantly on the part of some members — towards giving more room for such depictions, except for those deemed to be seeking to "glorify" homosexuality. It is a measure of how the dominant argument on this topic has evolved over the years; the current benchmark in the mid-2010s is to question materials that appear just to "normalise" homosexuality. Shifting from watching out for materials that "glorify" to those that simply "normalise" is a mark of moving the line backwards rather than forwards, at least from the viewpoint of those who would like to see increasingly more tolerance, if not acceptance, of such depictions. On such issues, Tommy showed empathy for freedom of expression, and deep understanding of its value to society. He would suspend quick judgement as far as possible in earlier rounds of discussion, to afford space to listen to views from both sides of the divide.

Another area that sometimes came under heated debate was whether to allow more expression of religious doubt. This was a topic seen in more "black-and-white" terms in the early 1990s, when much less depiction and discussion were allowed on anything related to religion. This was long before the subject opened up, with developments starting with the global "war on terror" following the 9/11 attacks in the United States in 2001. Here, Tommy exercised caution, perhaps applying self-restraint in curbing his own instincts to expect that most people would be able to show good judgment.

Religious doubt and homosexuality are examples of divides that do not lend themselves to easy resolution, even with the skill of a Tommy Koh. Yet another issue was also debated at length — summed up in the proposal to lift the ban on the women's lifestyle magazine *Cosmopolitan*

oh: Serving Singapore and the World

racy articles", including those giving advice to mainly young women readers on aspects of lifestyle, relationships and sex. But there was not enough support from the CRC to make it to the final list of recommendations. It was to take another 11 years, and some more energetic debate on the 2002–2003 CRC, to finally allow the magazine to be sold on newsstands in 2004. It took another year of civil service administrative work for the recommendation to be implemented — 22 years after *Cosmopolitan* was first banned. This was an issue on which Tommy had a firmer personal position, but even so, he did not impose his own stand on the committee, respecting the beliefs and standpoints of those members who opposed allowing the magazine for sale. Nonetheless, the way that Tommy, with his voice of conscience and compassion, managed the balanced airing of positions on these debates enhanced understanding of the core issues, and left crucial markers of the ground that was gained in arguing for more acceptance of diversity.

A Quest for Consensus, That Carries on Today

One of the last meetings of the 1991–1992 CRC was, for me, particularly memorable. As the date drew closer for the committee to have to conclude its deliberations, the Chairman had to exert himself more than usual to move the discussion along. Watching Tommy get the job done was like a Harvard class in negotiation, a rare instance of seeing him working at a crunch, under time pressure to meet a deadline. His primary method was first to propose a consensus conclusion on each unsettled discussion point. Then, he would say he was going to press ahead to move on to the next point, unless there were strenuous objections. And so, this process continued down the list of items, one by one, until all the recommendations were done, and the masterclass was complete.

The ground-breaking achievements of the 1991–1992 CRC as a service to Singapore were due, in no small part, to the dedication with which Tommy Koh fulfilled his duty. This he never fails to do, with an unshakeable sense of public service and a fair-minded regard and respect for the common man. And this, I am sure, is also the case on all the many other committees he has led, always applying his generosity of heart as much as his breadth of mind. This is how he devotes due attention and loving care to every important detail, ranging from the most global of questions that could affect the future of all humanity, down to the most insular aspect that might just have some chance, however small, of contributing to the betterment of his fellow citizens. The quest for consensus carries on today.

CHAPTER 15

A Heart for the Written Word

~∞~

PAUL TAN

A Prodigious Reader

That the founding chairman of the National Arts Council is a prolific and sensitive reader is of little doubt to anyone who knows Tommy Koh. In fact, most times those of us who know him wonder where he finds the time to read and think about the works he has read, given his multiple responsibilities and interests. We are amazed — especially in this day and age of short attentions and easy Google searches — at how he liberally quotes off-the-cuff from them.

Perhaps it is from the discipline of chairing the numerous public panels featuring public intellectuals and writers, as well as adjudicating in competitions like the Commonwealth Writers' Prize.

It is well chronicled that Professor Koh grew up surrounded by books, thanks to a father who had a library at home and who indulged his son's love of the written word with book purchases, which must have been a luxury in pre-independent Singapore.

What is perhaps less known is Professor Koh's behind-the-scenes encouragement of the growth and support of the literary arts here in Singapore. The successful Singapore Writers Festival, now into its 20th edition, started modestly as Singapore Writers Week during Professor Koh's tenure as the Chairman of National Arts Council (NAC). What was then a component of the Singapore Festival of the Arts has evolved into a dedicated annual fest of the written and spoken word, loved particularly by literary aficionados and aspiring writers, featuring leading poets, novelists and thinkers from Singapore and around the world.

Professor Koh's Book Club

For instance, most people are not aware that Professor Koh ran a book club for a number of years, which met at the (now-defunct) Pines Club along Stevens Road. It focused on non-fiction works and gathered some of the brightest minds in Singapore. Meira Chand, one of our country's foremost writers and author of *A Different Sky*, was a regular guest. She reminisced:

> *There can be few book clubs like Tommy Koh's book club. Rather like Tommy himself, it was unique. As important as the literature discussed was the intellect and graciousness that surrounded it… and I was honoured to be included…. The discussion spawned from the mainly non-fiction books was fierce and stimulating. Yet, as important as all of this was the food we ate and the wine we drank, all chosen personally by Prof. Koh in the midst of his frenetically busy schedule. The books examined and discussed were often deep and dense and highbrow. While others with lesser jobs hurried in with a cursory reading or even no reading at all, Prof. Koh prepared for each meeting with extraordinary commitment and detail, putting everyone else to shame. He saw straight to the literary heart of a book in a way few of us could match, and his notes for discussion points were always copious. This was work that could not be delegated. He read and absorbed each book in the most meticulous way, whether it was the writings of Henry Kissinger or Joseph Conrad. Where Prof. Koh found that time in the midst of such an intensely busy life I will never know, but I believe the pleasure and insight he finds in literature is but a reflection of the depth and compassion of his remarkable personality.*[1]

---

1 Meira Chand, e-mail message to author, September 9, 2016.

A Thoughtful Gesture

While I did not have the opportunity to be part of this convivial book-talk, I do have a personal anecdote that clearly illustrates Professor Koh's passion to help artists and writers.

In the 1990s, I won literary awards for two collections of poetry, *Curious Roads* and *Driving Into Rain*, which, perhaps given the quieter cultural climes then, received a lot of media buzz and critical attention. As a young writer with little understanding of how the publishing world worked and heady with the thrill of winning the prizes, I, along with other writers, had thought the national awards and the ensuing publicity meant that the works would sell widely, and that the publisher would be proud of and find success with these new award-winning titles in their catalogue.

Unfortunately in 2001, the publishing house decided to close down the imprint that had featured the competition winners. They wrote to the affected authors to return their rights to them and gave them a chance to buy remaining unsold copies. The publisher must have had over-optimistic sales projections, which they had missed. Ominously the publisher said they would pulp the rest of unwanted copies. Obviously, this caused distress among the affected authors.

I wrote to Professor Koh, although he had stepped down from NAC, with an inner instinct that he would understand and try and help. And indeed he did, replying promptly and expressing concern at the sad state of affairs. A meeting was then convened with senior NAC staff — I was not working at the Council then — to explore options.

In the end, the Council was able to nudge the publisher to donate some of the unsold books to the Singapore International Foundation (who would then dispatch the books to libraries overseas). There was no way to save the rest of the books but for me at least, it was a salutary lesson on the books business, the limits of our market and the importance of managing one's expectations. More importantly, needless to say, the writers and I were grateful to Professor Koh for his timely intervention, and the efforts undertaken by the NAC team.

Just like in his book clubs, when it came to speaking at the Singapore Writers Festival's events, Professor Koh was scrupulous in his preparations, gently probing his interviewees (which included the late President SR Nathan on his memoirs) and generous in his approach and acknowledgment of everyone involved. In particular, the last always came effortlessly to him, in part thanks to Professor Koh's prodigious memory!

Keep Listening, Keep Reading

The fact that Professor Koh always found the time for individual writers and artists and creative talents, continues to inspire me today as someone working to advocate and champion the arts in the Arts Council. As I tell my fellow colleagues, we must be good listeners and seek to understand, rather than be quick to explain or judge, and be able to communicate clearly and consider the listener and their deeper intentions.

Certainly, as a reader and sometime writer, I hope to be able to find the bandwidth to read as extensively and deeply, and be as generous as Professor Koh in sharing the stories and wisdom that are found between the covers of the world's best books.

CHAPTER 16

Tommy Koh: A Faithful Friend to Artists

~∞~

JEREMY MONTEIRO

My First Encounter with Tommy

Around 1993, two years after the National Arts Council (NAC) was founded, I received an invitation to attend a thank-you reception for arts resource panel members and arts advisers of the NAC, hosted by Professor Tommy Koh. He was the NAC founding chairman, and the overseeing Minister at the time was George Yeo. I was still serving my first term as an arts resource panel member.

Since then, I continued to serve almost continuously on the resource panel and later as arts adviser at NAC until I was asked in 2006 to serve on the board for two terms.

At the thank-you dinner I joined a line of people entering the hotel ballroom and Prof. Koh greeted each one of us personally as we entered. As if this was not a kind enough personal gesture, he would ask after a particular project we were working on or congratulate us on a recent show or exhibition, many of which he had attended. I remember some of the people ahead of me were Som Said and KP Bhaskar. When it was my turn, Prof. Koh warmly shook my hand with two hands and asked, "How are you, Jeremy? I really like your recent album *Always In Love* with Charlie Haden and Ernie Watts. Congratulations!"

I was stunned and shyly muttered my thanks to him. How did this top diplomat in Singapore have the capacity to remember everyone attending this arts event (there were about 150 of us) and also be able to remember what each of us had worked on or was working on?

At that point I had not developed the social and people skills that I have since acquired. For example, I never would have had the gumption to ask Prof. Koh out to lunch. I had never reached out to a senior government official like that before. It was he who first invited me to lunch saying that he wanted to meet various artists in different genres to get to know us better on a personal basis, to learn about our dreams and difficulties.

My first lunch with him was at the Cricket Club if my memory serves me right. He greeted me warmly and I said, "It's such an honour and privilege to meet you, Ambassador Koh." He said, "Call me Tommy." And since then, other than when I am addressing him formally or at official events, I've called him Tommy.

Tommy's tenure at NAC from 1991–1996 under Minister Yeo really was a period of serious and visionary long-term planning for the arts in Singapore. Many important plans were laid. Prof. Koh credits Minister Yeo for this "renaissance of the arts" in Singapore, but his own role in creating traction to bring these policies and plans into fruition cannot be understated.

It was during this time that the idea to build the Esplanade Theatres by the Bay was mooted and eventually approved by the government. It was to be a huge undertaking.

The Esplanade, which was first referred to as The Arts Centre, cost $600 million to build, a humongous expense but well worth it. It is now a platform for local and international artists in various performing disciplines to showcase their talents, and is internationally acknowledged as one of the best performing arts centres in the world. It continues to enrich the lives of Singaporeans who flock there to enjoy diverse performances in music, theatre and dance all year round.

I am very privileged to have performed in the various venues within the Esplanade on more than 20 occasions, including my recent 40th Anniversary Concert on September 30, 2016, which was attended by President Tony Tan Keng Yam as well as Tommy.

Raising the Arts in the Eyes of Policymakers

I believe that together with Minister Yeo, Tommy helped to raise the standing of artists in Singapore in the eyes of the government. We were no longer viewed as loafers and unimportant for Singapore society.

The government started to recognise that besides sports, which are important for the morale of a nation, the arts had a role to play in invigorating the soul of the nation and strengthening social cohesion. The government also started to see that there was great potential for the arts, as an industry, to contribute to the economy, besides being something to enrich the cultural scene in Singapore.

Tommy also convinced the government that if Singapore was to attract the best and brightest brains in science, finance and business to live and work here, there had to be a rich enough cultural scene such as high-quality concerts and art exhibitions they could partake in.

Against the backdrop of all he was doing for the arts, Tommy still had to perform his duties as a diplomat and negotiator for the government. Tommy's warm and cordial disposition sometimes hides his tough and stubborn ability to defend and protect Singapore even as he gains the trust and respect of foreign officials.

What I am most grateful for is having Tommy as my friend and mentor. The skills I have learned from observing him have taught me how to conduct myself well as an artist, an arts entrepreneur and as a person.

Whenever he was honoured in public, he would graciously accept the accolade and then go on to send back the kind words of praise — not with false humility, but he would genuinely name positive aspects and accomplishments of the people recognising him and their accomplishments. He would also name members of his team.

At many of the events he attended where there were musicians performing, he would usually also go to the side of the stage and praise all the musicians and technical staff personally. He asked and often remembered their names.

I would sometimes get direct lessons from Tommy. I asked him once how he managed to deliver such powerful speeches that were always the right length. He said, "We always have many things we want to say during a speech, but think of three of the most important things that relate to the subject at hand and speak about these three things."

He also advised me, "Now that you sometimes have direct dialogue sessions with ministers who may want to hear your views on the arts in Singapore, even though you may have many things to raise with them, think about your one most important issue and raise that. Don't raise a multitude of issues, because none of them will get much attention. At most, if you must, raise two issues." So nowadays I am always as pithy and salient as possible in raising issues and in my responses to government ministers.

One day, after he showed me around the Ministry of Foreign Affairs when they first moved to the former Mindef premises at Dempsey, he gave me a history lesson over lunch. The four southernmost provinces of Thailand — Pattani, Yala, Songkhla and Narathiwat — were part of the Kingdom of Pattani more than a hundred years ago. Although they managed to slowly assimilate after becoming part of Thailand, there is still occasional friction in that region from time to time because of the differences in language and religion.

In 2001 I asked Tommy to consider nominating me for the Cultural Medallion, Singapore's pinnacle award in arts achievement. He told me that since leaving the NAC in 1996, he had not nominated anyone for the Cultural Medallion and would think about it. He came back a week later and said, "Jeremy, I would be honoured to nominate you for the Cultural Medallion. It might be a bit difficult to accomplish because there has been no Cultural Medallion award given to a non-classical or non-traditional musician. But if you were to receive the award, you might open the gates for them." In 2002, I received the Cultural Medallion, the only person to do so that year.

I am very touched that Tommy and his wife Siew Aing have attended many of my performances over the years. Except for one year when he had accepted an invitation to attend a theatre presentation before the date of my concert was announced, they have attended 10 out my 11 Jazzy Christmas concerts at the Esplanade Concert Hall.

At a recent lunch with Tommy at the Tanglin Club on September 26, 2016, I told him that together with three friends, Albert Chiu, EFG

Bank's Regional CEO; Susan Peh, Senior Director of Yeo, Leong & Peh; and Edmund Lam, CEO of the Composers & Authors Society of Singapore, we had founded the Singapore Jazz Foundation. I asked if he would do us the great honour of being its patron.

He grasped my hand in the same way that he did on our first encounter in 1992, looked me in the eyes and said, "Jeremy, for you, yes. You and I have been talking about ways to increase the engagement and excellence of jazz in Singapore as well as how Singapore needs to have a serious jazz orchestra. And since these are precisely the foundation's aims and because you are a dear and loyal friend, I am happy to help." I was so touched to be referred to by Tommy as a "dear and loyal friend".

A Staunch Supporter of Artists

Many artists have received and continue to receive warm support and strong encouragement from Tommy. He likes to help artists who like to help other artists.

He often speaks very highly about the Singaporean master potter, ceramist and cultural medallion recipient Iskandar Jalil whom he affectionately calls *cikgu*, or teacher. Mr Iskandar recently received an Honorary Doctorate of Letters from the Nanyang Technological University. On many occasions, whether to friends, colleagues and overseas visitors, Tommy would present lovely pots by Cikgu Iskandar, and I have been fortunate to receive two such exquisite Iskandar Jalil pots from Tommy.

Another person he often praised and supported is the late great Singaporean arranger, composer and conductor, Iskandar Ismail.

Recently, when Tommy was asked to be the Patron of the Musicians Guild of Singapore, despite his many responsibilities, he readily offered his support.

Tommy shows his support to artists he admires or wants to encourage by going to our performances or exhibitions. He believes that if you are involved in the arts as a supporter, administrator or journalist, you have to attend as many of the concerts, plays or exhibitions as possible to absorb and enjoy the essence of the artists in Singapore and their works.

I remember at one of the last exhibitions by the late eminent Singaporean artist Chua Ek Kay, who had a unique style of using Chinese ink on paper, I felt quite embarrassed that I knew very little about his work. Besides Mr Chua's famous style of ink on paper, he was also a master watercolour painter. Tommy walked round the exhibition with a few of us, pointing out his favourite works and telling us how much he loved Mr Chua's watercolour work.

Tommy truly loves art and artists and I believe that it is this love that drives him to champion all of us. He also truly feels at home in the company of artists and many of us consider him a friend.

His Long Service to Singapore

On social media, Singaporeans have often talked openly over many years about how Tommy Koh would be a great president of Singapore. But he himself has never asked for nor expressed an interest in the office. And although I agree that if he chose to run for President he would be a strong unifying force and help heal the rifts amongst people on various sides of the political discourse in Singapore, I do believe that Tommy is most useful to Singapore and is most powerful exactly where he is for at least three reasons I can think of.

First, he is free to take positions on various international issues concerning Singapore and is able to articulate this in a manner that does not annoy many people.

Second, he is one of the few members of the establishment who is able to speak his mind against certain government policies and philosophies. His opinions and his raising of issues resonate with the public in a way that few others can.

Third, he loves being able to move about freely through all levels of society and facets of life in Singapore, whether it's attending concerts, attending policy dialogues or representing Singapore in trade and diplomacy. He also greatly enjoys his family life and loves spending time with his wife, children and grandchildren, after having served Singapore and indeed the world with the things he has done on behalf of the United Nations.

At 80, he remains one of the most loved and respected Singaporeans. Over many meetings and meals we have shared together, I have enjoyed many stories, history lessons, lessons on diplomacy and learned many insights into Singapore politics.

I think of the many reasons that make me proud to be a Singaporean. Tommy Koh is one big reason that I am proud to be a Singaporean.

CHAPTER 17

Tommy Koh: A Champion of Heritage and Museums

❧

KENSON KWOK

Opening the Doors to Singapore's "New" Museums Age

In October 2002 when Prof. Tommy Koh became Chairman of the
National Heritage Board (NHB), the project to turn the old Empress
Place Building into the permanent home of the then-fledgling Asian
Civilisations Museum (ACM) was in its final stages. The much-enlarged
ACM was launched six months later by Prime Minister Goh Chok
Tong in the course of an evening event attended by close to a thousand
guests. As Chairman of NHB, Prof. Koh was the chief host at this grand
opening.

The new ACM — with its atmospheric galleries, thematically layered
and sensitively-lit displays, and innovative use of technology — was
soon hailed by visiting museum professionals as an exemplar of the
"new" museum. Prof. Koh was proud of what we had achieved, and
I feel sure he quietly steered many VIP visitors to us.

Our first VIP visitors came the day before the official opening; Prof.
Koh was on hand to join me to welcome their majesties, the Sultan and
Raja Isteri of Brunei. Thereafter we received a steady stream of crowned
heads, heads of state and prime ministers, crown princes and princesses,
and other dignitaries. Some — like the US Assistant Secretary of State
for East Asia and the Pacific — Prof. Koh would accompany personally
to the ACM. Where a VIP visit included a meal to be hosted by NHB, he

educated all of us on the finer points of restaurant and menu selection and seating plans, a legacy of his diplomatic life.

Five years later in 2008 we opened the Peranakan Museum and Prof. Koh was again on hand to participate in the celebrations. Throughout his tenure at NHB, Prof. Koh and Mrs Koh came to many of our exhibition openings. He usually arrived early, in order to familiarise himself with the exhibition so that when the function commenced, he could focus on being a solicitous host to our guests. We could always rely on him to thank those of our supporters who needed to be thanked, and he did so in the nicest possible way. He would also thank us, the staff, by acknowledging the role each of us had played in a particular project or exhibition.

While I had known Prof. Koh socially before his time at the NHB, it was only after he came to the NHB that I saw him in action in a work setting. Under his characteristic mild-mannered demeanour we would occasionally catch a glimpse of a formidable intellect, and a steely resolve to get around objections and get things done. When it came to giving his views on contentious issues, he did not mince his words, but was always fair.

Every now and then, an article from the *International Herald Tribune*, the *Asian Wall Street Journal* or elsewhere that he thought was relevant or interesting for ACM would land on my desk. I am sure this thoughtfulness was extended to all my colleagues at the NHB. He had a huge network of eminent contacts in different spheres — diplomacy, academia, politics, industry — which he happily used to promote NHB museums.

In 2008 he chaired the panel of judges to choose the winning competition entry for the commission of the National Gallery Singapore. We were closeted together for two days while deliberating our choice. One of the points of discussion was whether the commission should be awarded to a proposal that had incorporated some elements of local symbolism in its design; in the end, we all felt that a bolder and more timeless solution was preferable. Prof. Koh was an excellent moderator, and the superb National Gallery we know today is a testament to his wise leadership at that critical juncture.

Reaching out to ASEAN

From the very outset of his tenure at NHB, Prof. Koh had wanted to promote greater interaction between NHB, its museums and their counterparts in ASEAN. He initiated and, from 2004 onwards, led a series of study visits by NHB to the ASEAN countries. One outcome of these trips was the Cultural Festival organised around museum exhibitions originating from different ASEAN countries. Special programmes were organised by our hosts — a Ramayana performance by moonlight in the grounds of the royal palace in Luang Prabang, Laos was particularly memorable. During these trips, another Prof. Koh emerged — the foodie. Whenever we happened to have some free time he would ask about where we could sample a particular local dish, and take all of us there. One such street food adventure however, produced unwelcome results the next day. A more refined and much happier experience was a banquet of traditional food prepared for us by a celebrated restaurant owner in Hue in Vietnam.

Since my retirement, I meet Prof. Koh at functions from time to time. Over a recent lunch at NUS he regaled us with stories from his time in Washington. I am convinced his understated and humorous style of public speaking was honed at that time, through observation and contact with the luminaries of US society not least of whom was then President Ronald Reagan, a legendary speechmaker and joke teller.

Having attended a fair number of exhibition openings during my time at ACM, I tend to excuse myself these days, but I will go if Prof. Koh is the guest of honour. I never tire of his trademark three points, sometimes expanded to four. And I am delighted to see that he continues to champion the cause of our museums.

CHAPTER 18

Tommy Koh and "The Artist, The State and The Market"

❦

KWOK KIAN CHOW

Professor Tommy Koh must have thought through the order of the words in the title of his 2013 article, "The Artist, the State and the Market", which was originally published in *The Straits Times*. The artist came first, as is with most of the other articles anthologised in the Art, Culture and Heritage section of *The Tommy Koh Reader: Favourite Essays and Lectures* (2013)[1] — all have the artist as the central focus.

To Tommy Koh, the human person and his or her vision and diligence in the arts are larger than Koh's personal preference in genres and styles of art. It is the triumph of the human spirit that comes through in these essays.

In the 2013 article, Tommy Koh also reflected on the many roles he himself played in culture and the arts, from the founding chairman of the National Arts Council (NAC) from 1991 to 1996, to the chairman of the National Heritage Board (NHB) from 2002 to 2011.

I was the Director of the Singapore Art Museum from 1993 to 2009. I was also Director and Senior Advisor of the National Gallery from 2009 to 2015. He was my chairman in the NHB; the Singapore Art Museum as well as the gestation and early years of the National Gallery development that came under NHB. Beyond the museums, the

---

1 Tommy Koh, *The Tommy Koh Reader: Favourite Essays and Lectures* (Singapore: World Scientific, 2013).

National Arts Council was the lead governmental agency overseeing the broader visual arts sector.

The two decades of 1991 to 2011 coincided with the realisation of the Singapore Art Museum, which was inaugurated in 1996. Later, in 2006, the then Minister for Information, Communications and the Arts, Dr Lee Boon Yang, formally announced the development of the National Gallery. Tommy Koh chaired the gallery's architectural design competition, one that attracted over 100 entries from some 30 countries. In 2008, Studio Milou was announced as the winner of the competition.

The Artist

These were significant infrastructural and institutional developments that Koh was involved in. More importantly, in my view, Tommy Koh supported the artists. This helped us see a parallel trajectory, that is, the organic growth in the content and practices of the arts.

Tommy Koh has a deep respect for the artists, and has written passionately about Ong Kim Seng, Lee Hock Moh, Kuo Pao Kun, Tan Swie Hian, Dr Earl Lu (as an artist and also the founding chairman of the Singapore Art Museum), Anthony Poon, Goh Choo San, Iskandar Jalil and Joanna Wong.

While a history of the arts in Singapore would witness multiple trajectories, voices and contributions, Tommy Koh's support for The Necessary Stage at a critical moment will always serve as an inspiration and reminder on the need to secure a larger space for expressions and engagements in the arts.

Koh wrote in the same news article above: "[W]hen an attempt was made to stigmatise forum theatre and The Necessary Stage, I wrote to this newspaper [*The Straits Times*] to defend them; if I had not done so, my narrative that the chairman of NAC is a patron and champion of our artists would have been shown to be just empty talk."[2]

As I pen these notes on Tommy Koh's contributions to the arts, the Nominated Member of Parliament (NMP), Kok Heng Leun, who directed forum theatre productions such as *Trick or Threat!* (2007),

---

2 *The Tommy Koh Reader*, 450.

is this week meeting many arts practitioners as a part of his Substation residency programme, in a dialogue project titled *Statements*, to discuss selected public statements by senior officials as a way to analyse official discourse in the arts and culture here. In this project, Heng Leun is assisted by Alvin Tan, the co-founder of The Necessary Stage.[3]

There is a linkage, a correspondence, between the earlier forum theatre moments and that continuing organic evolvement of the human spirit in the arts.[4] Tommy Koh's defence of the artists serves again and again as a reminder of our responsibilities in the arts.

Tommy Koh's close relations with artists were also extended to collectors. The latter include Pak Suteja Neka and Ibu Gusti Made Srimin, known for their enterprise in developing Neka Museum, the private museum that is now widely recognised for having the most comprehensive collection of Balinese art. "It is one thing to have a vision; it is quite another thing to bring the vision into reality,"[5] wrote Tommy Koh in his tribute to Pak Neka in the foreword to *Art Museum in Modern Balinese History: Art and the Passage of Time,* by Garrett Kam. Pak Neka was also appointed to the board of SAM in 2006.

The State

Among the curators and directors of different museums in NHB, there was understandably a degree of competition for resources, programming opportunities and collections. Given the privilege of the multiple museums in the NHB family, the diversity could have provided a basis for interdisciplinary conversations and cross programming. Yet we were curiously caught up with protecting our own disciplines, such as art, history, periods, collection ownership, at times to the extent that protectionism itself became the reason for disciplinary boundaries.

Tommy Koh's inclusive interest in culture and the arts, what he termed "culture-loving", encouraged expansive perspectives on culture.

3 "At Unique Sessions, NMP Kok Heng Leun Seeks Input From Artists", *Today*, September 30, 2016.
4 Kok Heng Leun's efforts in engaging the arts and audience community have been singled out by the Australian arts policy commentator, Professor Julian Meyrick, who noted that the Singapore NMP system is a version of the significant Chief Artist role in a country, who advises the political leadership and communicates to the society at large the essential cultural purposes of the arts.
5 *The Tommy Koh Reader*, 473.

As chairman of NHB, Tommy Koh repeatedly encouraged NHB staff to look at cultures and art in the region around us. He personally led NHB delegations to visit the museums and cultural institutions in Southeast Asia. This augmented well the SAM's collection focus in the Southeast Asia region. From the point of the establishment of SAM until around 2011, the number of art works in its collection grew some six-fold. Through the trips the curators, including myself, gained a broader perspective of history and politics as we considered the modern and contemporary art of Southeast Asia in broader historical, social and even geopolitical contexts. The Southeast Asia field trips led by Tommy Koh also became cross-disciplinary study missions for us.

In the timeline of the National Gallery, the year 2011 when Tommy Koh stepped down as chairman of NHB was about the halfway point of the Gallery's development. The institution eventually opened in November 2015. Tommy Koh wanted all the institutions, new and old, to be part of NHB, treating corporatisation as an organisation structural issue within NHB, that is, corporatised under NHB.

The course of the organisational changes had not been very clear to me as I had relinquished my National Gallery directorship in 2011 to take on the senior advisory role (which I later relinquished in 2015). There is much concern currently about the division of the National Gallery and SAM as separate entities. The structural issue may not be as important as the division between "modern" and "contemporary" art, constraining both institutions to advance curatorship and programming based on contemporary reflections on art trajectories in *longue durée*.

In retrospect, the inclusive approach of the then NHB could have led to a more considered structural arrangement driven by strategic interdisciplinarity rather than some other organisational rationale. The hardening of the division of "modern" and "contemporary" categories does not facilitate curatorial and programmatic innovation.

The Market

As for Tommy Koh's taste in art, it appears to also resonate with interests in the persons who created the art. In *The Tommy Koh Reader*, he writes in an essay entitled "The Joy of Collecting" about his friendship with the pioneer artists Cheong Soo Pieng, Chen Wen Hsi and Georgette Chen as well as the second-generation artists Wee Beng Chong, Tay Bak Koi, Tay Chee Toh and Quek Wee Chew.[6]

Tommy Koh's taste in art may also be related to his views on three other perspectives. In the same aforementioned article, he states, "[In] recent years, we may have… veered too much towards what I would not call elitist, but the cutting edge or experimental… the curators should include more works which are accessible and fewer works which are comprehensible only to experts in contemporary art."[7]

This first perspective above is interposed with a second, that of the focus on Southeast Asia: "[O]ur comparative advantage is in presenting South-east Asian art to the world."[8] The third is about reception: "The pendulum should come back to the centre and not swing to the other extreme. We should not dumb down the activities of NAC and NHB. We should not underestimate our citizens."[9]

My take on this is that one's taste in art may only be discussed in relation to other cultural and societal concerns. On the other hand, it does not mean that one does not have a strong personal liking for specific styles and expressions. Tommy Koh has his own taste in the arts, and he allowed himself the pleasure of talking about his own collection.

However, those other articulations about culture and the arts have to be contextualised in the broader realm of times, geographies, institutions and policy directions. It is to remind us that those other issues are larger than a personal taste, but one loses oneself if he or she does not on the other hand have personal preferences.

---

6 *The Tommy Koh Reader*, 453–454.
7 Ibid., 451.
8 Ibid.
9 Ibid.

CHAPTER 19

My "Historical" Encounters with Professor Tommy Koh

※

TAN TAI YONG

First Encounter

In July 1997, I appeared on a television discussion panel with Professor Tommy Koh. He was chairing the discussion for the programme, *Perspectives*, on who should be writing Singapore's history, and how we should understand our past. We debated the importance of history, the lessons it holds for the present, and the manner in which history has been written and presented in Singapore. I had only known Tommy Koh by reputation and wondered to myself as I prepared for the panel discussion: Would he, as a senior public figure who was closely associated with the establishment, take a firm position on the need to defend a state-endorsed national narrative? And would he, as a diplomat, fend off interpretations of history that were at odds with the version that Singaporeans were taught in schools? I did not know what to expect, but by the end of the programme, not only was I not disappointed with the level of discussion that had taken place, my admiration for Tommy Koh as an open-minded and historically conscious intellectual was sealed.

Not unexpectedly, he was extremely knowledgeable about Singapore's recent political past — he was, after all, a participant observer of key events in Singapore's political history since the 1950s, but what struck me most was his openness to the view that history's real value lies in not telling us what to think, but, rather, how to think. He understood that history is a contested terrain and that both the victors and vanquished would have their respective versions of the past; he was also aware that understanding history from only one perspective would be limiting. That evening was momentous for me on two counts: It was my first substantive appearance on national television, and my first happy introduction to Tommy Koh. He was someone with whom I would have, on many subsequent occasions, several interesting conversations on the history of Singapore and Asia.

The National Museum

I must have left an impression on Tommy Koh that evening because a few years later our paths crossed again when I was appointed to chair the National History Museum Board. This was, of course, Tommy Koh's doing. In 2002, he was appointed Chairman of the National Heritage Board, in which capacity he would oversee the museums, heritage centres, national monuments and historic sites in Singapore. This was a big remit, but it was clear that Tommy Koh was especially suited for his new role. Drawing on his extensive travels and appreciation of world cultures, he knew that history and culture had critical roles to play in the making of a successful city, and in transforming ordinary cities into great ones. He understood that Singapore's rapid transformation into a world city had been achieved at a cost to its historical and cultural heritage. Since becoming independent in 1965, Singapore had devoted the first 25 years of nation building to economic development and the building of a world-class infrastructure.

But, even as our small city-state became known for its economic success, it came to be regarded as something of a cultural desert. In the subsequent 25 years, there was a growing realisation that as important as economic growth is for any city, attention should also be given to social-cultural issues and improving the quality of life. The arts and heritage had much to contribute in this area. Singapore rightly added three more ambitions to its national agenda, "to improve the city's liveability and quality of life, to harness the power of culture and the arts, and to make Singapore a global city of distinction."[1]

Under Tommy Koh's 10-year stewardship of the NHB, plans were put in place for a major expansion and rejuvenation of the local museum landscape. The emphasis was on investing in museums as part of nation-building efforts to represent national history and accumulate cultural capital. The oldest museum in Singapore, the National Museum, was reconstituted into three specialised museums: the Asian Civilisations Museum, the Singapore History Museum, and the Singapore Art Museum. This was to allow the individual museums to cater more specifically to different interests and better represent the diversity behind Singapore's multicultural heritage. In that same period, the NHB also started conserving what remained of Singapore's built heritage. The record has been impressive: at present, over 7,000 buildings have been conserved and more than 70 national monuments are protected by law.

A year into Tommy Koh's appointment as NHB Chairman, the iconic National Museum building in which the Singapore History Museum was housed underwent a major revamp. After extensive renovations lasting three years, the prominent historical landmark was opened in 2006 and rebranded as the National Museum of Singapore. The old neoclassical building had been beautifully restored, and it now boasted a modern new wing. With a history dating back to the 19th century, the National Museum was strategically placed to tell Singapore's pre-colonial, colonial and modern history. In guiding its re-development, the chairman's brief was clear: He wanted the National Museum to bring to life the events and people who helped shape modern Singapore. He insisted on making the museum accessible to all Singaporeans by making the Singapore story compelling, the storytelling appealing, and the location inviting.

To give richness and depth to the Singapore story, the curators developed a permanent Singapore History gallery based on a narrative that went back 700 years to the 14th century. It was an attempt to show that Singapore's history did not only start in 1819 with the arrival of

---

1 Tommy Koh, "History, Culture and the Making of a Successful City," Keynote Address at World Cities Summit, Singapore, July 8–12, 2016.

the British, and that Singapore had existed as a trading settlement long before the arrival of the Europeans to Southeast Asia. The aim and challenge was to highlight in an engaging manner the underlying themes of the Singapore story, some of which remain relevant today — the island's maritime connection and its role (going as far back as the pre-colonial period) as a port-city plugged into Arab, Chinese, Indian and Southeast Asian trade networks; and the cultural exchanges and influences that came with such connectivity.

One of the so-called KPIs (key performance indicators) that was constantly talked about during our museum board meetings was "visitorship" — the number of people who visited the museums each year. Tommy Koh spared no effort in making history and heritage accessible to the public and to students through initiatives such as the Heritage Festival, which led to greater numbers of people visiting the various museums. At that time, I must admit that I was not convinced that "bean-counting" or number crunching was an effective way of measuring a museum's appeal and success; I thought it was a crass way of quantifying the worth of cultural institutions. But, I was wrong and, on reflection, the Chairman's instincts were correct. Museums were largely pointless if it did not bring in people. It was not sufficient that the exhibitions and shows appealed only to a small group of cultural elites or only to curious tourists.

The revamp of the Grand Old Dame marked a shift in the role and approach of national museums in Singapore. The National Museum of Singapore needed to play a role in nation-building and it had to have mass appeal; and while its curation and exhibitions had to be authoritative, built on study, research and interpretation, its packaging had to be accessible. So, to ensure that the Museum did not remain an exotic place appealing only to a small group of culturally-minded Singaporeans, Tommy Koh suggested that the museum develop exhibits that would allow the public to relate history to their everyday lives.

In response, the National Museum introduced four Singapore Living galleries, which focused on the cultural themes of food, fashion, film and fashion. With the aid of technology and multimedia, the four galleries showed how we have evolved as a society through the food we eat, the clothes we wear, and the ways we preserve memory. These galleries not only reflected the colour and flavour of our multi-ethnic society, it also showcased our uniqueness as Singaporeans.

Cultural Diplomacy

In all his time leading the NHB, the diplomat in Tommy Koh never really took a back seat. Years in the diplomatic service had taught him the value of historical and cultural awareness when it came to diplomatic negotiations. He was a firm advocate of cultural diplomacy, which he practised in his own inimitable style and with the most consummate skill. Tommy Koh considered the soft power of heritage and culture to be as integral to foreign policy and diplomacy as the hard power of troops and trade: "To negotiate successfully with another country, a good negotiator should study that country's history, culture and negotiating style. In other words, in addition to IQ and EQ, a good negotiator should also cultivate his cultural intelligence. [...] I am always astonished by the fact that ministries of foreign affairs pay so little attention to historians and cultural anthropologists."[2]

Applying the same beliefs while he was at NHB, he insisted that our heritage agencies engaged the region, and he personally led several visits to museums, archives and heritage agencies in the region. In a bid to build "cultural capital" and raise Singapore's international profile, exhibitions of works by Singaporean and Southeast Asian artists were held overseas regularly. There were also collaborations with cultural institutions in India, China, Japan, Korea and ASEAN countries in efforts to deepen existing relations and create new partnerships. This outward-looking strategy dovetailed with the Renaissance City Plan (RCP) initiative that was launched by the government in 2000 to make Singapore a global arts city. Not only did the local arts and heritage scene benefit from substantial funding channelled to NHB for the development of museum and heritage-related programmes, the RCP initiative also enabled Singapore's heritage and culture to be promoted on the international level.

---

2 Tommy Koh, "Eight Lessons on Negotiations," in *The Tommy Koh Reader: Favourite Essays and Lectures*, ed. Tommy Koh (Singapore: World Scientific, 2013), 236.

The role of culture in the making of a successful city is an enduring one. The theme at a session in the recent World Cities Summit, held in Singapore in July 2016, was "Culture — Should Cities Care?" Tommy Koh, who was invited to deliver the keynote address, summed up the extent to which arts and culture have become a part of Singapore's nation-building efforts:

I am also happy to report that, after many years of investment and effort, we have overcome the old perception that Singapore was a cultural desert. Today, Singapore is a cultural oasis in the heart of Southeast Asia. The arts have blossomed. The busy arts calendar includes the Singapore International Festival of Arts, the Singapore Night Festival and the Singapore Biennale. The annual Heritage Festival celebrates our rituals, traditions and food. The opening of the Esplanade, the centre for performing arts, in 2001, was an important milestone in our cultural journey. The opening of the National Gallery, in 2015, was another milestone. The journey continues. In the years ahead, we will have to focus on developing the soft aspects of our cultural assets, namely, our talent pool, our cultural capital and our acceptance of diversity. We are heading in the right direction and I am very optimistic about our future.[3]

I was fortunate to have served as Chairman of the National Museum Board when Tommy Koh was leading the national effort to preserve and promote Singapore's heritage and history. As an historian, it was a privilege to have been part of a vision to promote and sustain the arts, culture and heritage in Singapore. In that effort, Tommy Koh has been a tremendous team leader. He was effective, in his urbane and gentle style, in leading a team of diverse talents to make Singapore a city with a deep sense of history and culture. Greater public consciousness on the need for heritage conservation and the growth of a thriving museum scene in Singapore are outcomes of Tommy Koh's successful years at the helm of the National Heritage Board.

---

3 Tommy Koh, "History, Culture and the Making of a Successful City," Keynote Address at World Cities Summit, Singapore, July 8–12, 2016.

CHAPTER 20

Best Chairman, Cultural Diplomat and Heritage Champion

—— ❧ ——

MICHAEL KOH

Being well trained by Tommy, I will make three points:

First: Tommy, the Best Chairman of the National Heritage Board

Unifying leader

Tommy chaired the National Heritage Board (NHB) from 2002 to 2011. As chairman he strove for diversity and inclusivity, and built a board comprising 24 members at its largest. He made sure that women had a strong presence on the board, along with members of the community and media. NHB probably still holds the record as having the largest board overseeing a statutory board. Many would baulk at having such a large board that was like a mini United Nations with many diverse views. However, with Tommy's expert chairmanship, he always helmed the board with gentlemanly steerage, commanding the respect of all members. He expertly translated diverse views with diplomatic aplomb and always succeeded in obtaining consensus on the direction to proceed. Diverse opinions were translated into strong proposals and the management always had clear guidance to follow-up. Tommy set high standards, increasing targets year on year and always gently supported the management behind the scenes, giving useful directions and advice.

Visionary

Tommy had a vision for a NHB family of museums of art and heritage that were independent but still very much part of the MICA[1] family. His benchmark was the Smithsonian family of museums in the United States. He felt strongly that the museum scene in Singapore was too small to have many autonomous museums. The museum sector was not a greenfield site and there would be cannibalisation of resources.

This principle guided the NHB family to greater heights during Tommy's term, with each museum also having their own expert boards. However, when he stepped down NHB museums faced the prospect of corporatisation. Today the visual art cluster is corporatised and no longer part of the NHB family. Fortunately under the new Ministry's[2] leadership, the rest of the NHB museums remain as part of it and continue with Tommy's legacy of pursuing successful community programmes and high-quality exhibitions for the people, working as one NHB family.

Fundraiser extraordinaire

NHB was always big on ideas and short of funds to bring them to fruition. Tommy mooted the annual Heritage Gala, targeted S$1 million to be raised and was determined to raise the funds to supplement NHB's budget. He united all of NHB's fundraising efforts under one major event instead of having individual museums directly source for private funds. He made personal appeals, cajoled the board members, charmed friends and companies into giving to the NHB cause. It is hard to turn down Tommy's charm. And being a gourmet advocate of Singapore food, he always took charge of the menu. The best of chefs go all the way to meet Tommy's gastronomic standards and created the best for every Gala dinner.

On one occasion, Tommy arranged a lunch meeting for me to make a pitch to businessman Kwek Leng Beng for a donation to the new ACM extension. I asked for S$1 million. Tommy looked at me and said it was

---

1 Ministry of Information, Communications and the Arts
2 Ministry of Culture, Community and Youth

too low. Prompted, Mr Kwek then asked, how about S$5 million? With this generous donation from the Hong Leong Foundation and with the matching government top-up, NHB managed to build a whole new extension to the ACM, named as the Kwek Hong Png Gallery, after Mr Kwek's father. Tommy taught us never to be afraid to ask.

Raising the bar

Tommy always challenged us to financially break even, while raising targets of visitorship and exhibition quality annually. Management did not fail him, except for one year when we had to fork out S$1 million from the meagre NHB reserves to pay for the Peranakan Museum renovations that had gone over budget.

He challenged us to produce a world-class magazine to surpass the Smithsonian magazine. NHB rose to the occasion and *BeMUSE* magazine was born. Generous benefactors like Shangri-La and Pontiac Land gave generously and in return we distributed *BeMUSE* to hotel rooms and gained instant international mindshare. More importantly, because we increased the number of copies produced, the overall costs went down and we were able to cross-subsidise and provide free copies for the public. *BeMUSE* was critically well received by foreign museums and the local community. It also gave an opportunity for our young curators to be published and be known through the good quality of the magazine.

Stalwart defender

In 2010, the valuation of the Tan donation to the Peranakan Museum embroiled NHB in controversy and NHB's valuation systems were crucified in the local press. Tommy stood up for NHB when no one else dared to, and wrote a succinct letter to *The Straits Times*' Forum page, making a strong defence of NHB, whilst saying NHB's systems could also be reinforced further. At Tommy's invitation, Mrs Lee Suet Fern stepped forward to take over the chair of ACM and Mr Baey Yam Keng joined the ACM Board. NHB will be ever grateful for them showing their steadfast support and belief in ACM and NHB at that critical time.

Tommy was a beloved chairman, well respected and often deferred to. When news broke that he would be stepping down, some board members quietly asked me how the board would be managed without his strong yet benevolent leadership. How could the diverse board be held together, without a man of his stature in the Chairman's seat? He truly led NHB through its golden years, setting higher and higher targets with the trust and confidence that management would deliver, which we did as we could never let down Prof. Tommy Koh, the best chairman ever!

Second: Tommy, the Cultural Diplomat

ASEAN knight

Tommy insisted on visiting the ASEAN countries with management and board members who might be interested. Some of the management did not like these trips, and even felt that some ASEAN countries would not have sufficient heritage assets to exhibit. Tommy knew this scepticism and deliberately orchestrated these visits to counter such views. In so doing, he exposed board members and management, opened up doors and also imparted a profound respect for other cultures. The first visit was to Laos, then to Vietnam, the Philippines, Myanmar, Brunei, etc. I am sure he was disappointed that NHB did not cover all ASEAN countries before he stepped down, and that such visits did not continue after his term.

However, he did leave much follow-up in the wake of his cultural diplomacy efforts. His inspiration rubbed off on management and we presented the ASEAN festivals such as Vietnam, the Philippines, Indonesia and Thailand, amongst others. NHB was rewarded in these various efforts as working in tandem with the Ministry of Foreign Affairs, Tommy managed always to secure top officials from these countries to grace the exhibitions. One of the most moving was when then President Gloria Arroyo made the effort to come straight from the airport to open the Philippines festival, even before checking in for the APEC Summit she was attending. She was originally meant to stay 15 minutes but ended up staying for over one hour.

Making friends

Tommy mooted the idea of the "Friends to Our Shores" programme, in which Singapore through NHB would recognise important leaders or national heroes of foreign countries who had visited Singapore. Markers with a short history accompanied by a bust are placed around ACM Green. Such heroes as Jose Rizal, Ho Chi Minh, Deng Xiaoping, Jawaharlal Nehru are honoured here. Jose Rizal for example spent two weeks in Singapore en-route to Spain where he was being trained as a doctor, and then sadly onboard a prison ship in the harbour on the way back to the Philippines to meet his imminent death at the hands of Spanish colonialists. These markers are often ceremoniously visited by heads of states, with some laying wreaths at these markers during official visits. They are pleased that Singapore has accorded honour and recognition to their national heroes.

Tommy had the intellect, profound knowledge of history and connected all the dots together, internationally and locally. Through his cultural diplomacy efforts, he made NHB museums a hub for cultural heritage for ASEAN and a staging point to create more awareness in the diversity of ASEAN and our region. His efforts gave Singapore a link in the hearts and minds of visitors and forged stronger people-to-people ties.

Third: Tommy, the Heritage Champion

Cultural exposure

Tommy backed the management fully to work with foreign museums to bring in blockbuster shows that educated and exposed the Singapore public to world culture and heritage. He opened up doors and together with then Minster for Foreign Affairs George Yeo and then Singapore's Ambassador to France Burhan Gafoor, mooted the idea of cultural cooperation with France. This was the catalyst that launched many cultural exchanges, bringing famous French works of art and heritage to Singapore and also giving us the opportunity to exhibit our collection and bring our heritage to many renowned French museums.

A taxi driver once told me that he was so glad that NHB was bringing the world to Singapore, as he could have never afforded to travel the distance to see these exhibits of artefacts and art. He was grateful that his children got to learn from them and be exposed. Tommy thus effectively levelled the playing field.

Fostering greater awareness

Tommy strongly supported the idea that NHB should curate and manage the Malay Heritage Centre, Sun Yat Sen Nanyang Memorial Hall and Indian Heritage Centre. He felt that integrating them within the NHB family would better enable these smaller heritage institutions to tap a larger audience base and create greater awareness of our ethnic heritage. In this way we could foster a better understanding of one another amongst our communities. The compelling stories, the many programmes and diverse exhibitions that these institutions have held are a testimony to his efforts.

Tommy was a friend to many Singapore artists, taking the time to visit each personally and being the guest of honour at their exhibitions, despite his busy schedule. He was in touch with our diverse communities and made it a point to be the heritage champion of Singapore.

In Conclusion: Thank You, Tommy!

On a personal note, Tommy brought me out of a safe zone and an established career path in urban planning. He challenged me and gave me exposure that I would have never known about. He also gave me the opportunity to build on the foundation of the NHB family to bring it to greater heights. He put to full use my architectural training in conceptualising, designing and implementing 8Q SAM, Indian Heritage Centre, Malay Heritage Centre, Sun Yat Sen Nanyang Memorial Hall, National Art Gallery and setting the future for the ACM extension. Life at NHB with Tommy was always exciting, with his drive and vision. It was never a bed of roses with so many challenges, but to have the honour and privilege of serving under Tommy's expert chairmanship effectively wiped away the heartaches, tense moments, sleepless nights and productive fights that were inherent in my job.

So, my heartfelt message to him:

Dear Tommy, wishing you a happy 80th birthday with many more blessed and fabulous years to come. You were the greatest chairman, the cultural diplomat extraordinaire, and the heritage champion of Singapore. Your vision and ideas moulded and shaped NHB and much of the arts and heritage scene. You have left a lasting legacy for all of us and continue to inspire many now and in the future.

Thank you!

CHAPTER 21

Tommy Koh: A Reader
and a Gentleman

ELAINE NG

A Tireless Champion of Literature

The name Tommy Koh may be synonymous with our foreign service, but it is his love for reading that endears him to staff at the National Library Board (NLB), Singapore.

Professor Koh's — or "Prof.", as NLB staff fondly call him — formidable intellect and his finely honed skills as an orator, diplomat and strategist are widely known. Perhaps less well known is the fact that it is literature and the arts that sustain his inner life and being. In an essay on "The Joy of Collecting" in 1998, he wrote: "Literature, music and painting are the three art forms which are my daily companions. They bring me much happiness." He has credited the study of literature at secondary school as one of the best investments he has ever made in terms of broadening his mind and in helping him to think, write and speak clearly.

In a book review for *Today* newspaper on May 28, 2003, Prof. wrote: "The main benefit of reading a novel is to gain greater and deeper insights into the human condition, about the mysteries of life and of the human heart." More recently in 2012, he was moved to respond to a Gallup survey which concluded that Singaporeans were an unhappy lot. In a riposte written for *The Straits Times* on December 29, 2012, he recommended 10 rules — in his usual practical and no-nonsense manner — that could help make one a happy person. And this remains one of my favourite Tommy Koh takeaways until this day.

One of the rules — Rule No. 8 specifically — is "Read books and listen to music." Prof. explains further: "Books keep me company when I am alone. Books transport me to another country, another culture, another time and into the lives of other people. Reading is an endless source of happiness." To that I would add, "Reading is free", given the easy access to the public library system in Singapore.

In an interview with *Today* newspaper on February 24, 2003, Prof. shared that he was an active library user in Singapore as well as during his diplomatic postings in New York and Washington. His wife and children regularly visited public libraries in the United States, spending hours at a time and lugging home plastic bags full of books. Prof. had hopes that Singaporean parents too would bring their children to the library and encourage them to read, especially since, in his estimation, we have some of the world's best libraries.

Early on, Prof. had observed that "Singapore has become a literate but not literary society." In another article in *The Straits Times*, titled "The Joy of Reading" published on July 25, 1982, he wrote: "Schools in Singapore do an excellent job in preparing their students for examinations. They do not, however inculcate in their students a love for books and the good habit of reading…. Singaporeans often complain that they can't find the time to read. I find this a lame excuse for not reading. One can always find the time if one is interested in reading."

Tommy Koh and NLB's Read! Singapore

His affinity for books would lead him into forging a close relationship with the NLB. Prof. had the vision of setting up a city-wide community reading programme — taking inspiration from the "One City, One Book" initiative he had observed in American cities during his time in the US. In time, the campaign, which tries to get everyone in the city to read and discuss one book, had crossed the seas to Brisbane in Australia. As an advocate for reading, Prof. liked the idea as it encouraged both reading and community bonding in one fell swoop. By creating an opportunity for people to rediscover the joy of reading and subsequently sharing what they have read on various platforms, social and community ties could be forged in the process.

With Prof. as the patron, NLB's READ! Singapore was launched on May 28, 2005. Instead of one book, the inaugural READ! Singapore offered 12 works of fiction, three each in English, Chinese, Malay and Tamil, and all curated along the theme "Coming of Age".

The English books on the list included Harper Lee's classic *To Kill a Mockingbird*, Mark Haddon's Whitbread prize-winning *The Strange Incident of the Dog in the Night-Time*, and Singaporean author Colin Cheong's *Tangerine*, which Prof. had read three times over the years, each time gaining "new insights and new pleasures" from this 1996 Singapore Literature Prize winner. The vernacular book titles included Han Han's *7-Eleven Kuang Xiang Qu* (*Love at the Convenience Store*), Isa Kamari's *Satu Bumi* (*One Earth*) and D. Jeyakanthan's *Sila Nerangalil Sila Manithargal* (*Some People at Some Moments*).

The 10-week programme included an array of ancillary activities: meet-the-author sessions, book discussions, a 12-hour reading marathon, film screenings and performances. In his speech at the closing ceremony of READ! Singapore on August 6, 2005, Prof. said that the initiative was important in helping Singapore "achieve one of our new ambitions. The ambition is to be a culturally developed society." It was appropriate that Prof. would come up with the tagline, "A Nation of Readers", which perfectly encapsulates the two campaign aims of reading and nation building.

To make reading fiction even easier for time-pressured Singaporeans, short stories were included in subsequent years. Cross-translations, i.e., translating a Chinese story into Tamil and vice versa, allowed all the selected works to be available in the four official languages, with a view towards promoting inter-racial understanding. Selected stories were later made available in audio format for people with physical and visual disabilities and for senior citizens with failing eyesight. In 2011, MobileRead, a free mobile phone application was developed for readers to download the stories onto their tablets and smartphones.

By the time READ! Singapore celebrated its 10-year run in 2014, the campaign had drawn the active participation of more than 1 million members of the public through book discussions and related activities. The campaign spawned almost 90 independent reading clubs in government ministries and statutory boards, schools and tertiary institutions, community clubs, private companies and other organisations, some of which are still going strong.

I am very grateful to Prof. for working so tirelessly with NLB staff, the Steering Committee and various programme partners. Mrs Koh-Kiang Lai Lin, our former Director of Reading Initiatives, expresses how all of us at NLB feel when she says that READ! Singapore would never have taken off without the support of Prof.: "As the project grew in scope, Professor Koh became involved in every step along the way, from using his contacts to raise funds from the private sector to being interviewed by the media on radio and television, and one year, even helping to secure rights to a short story called *The Stars* by the late Cabinet Minister S. Rajaratnam."

Guiding NLB on the World Stage

In 2012, the Library of Congress in Washington DC invited NLB as a partner in hosting the International Summit of the Book, an annual conference to discuss and debate the role of books and reading in culture and society as well as issues relating to publishing. Prof.'s strong network of contacts in the US and his close ties with Dr Samuel H. Billington, then Librarian of Congress, helped pave the way for Singapore to host the 2nd International Summit of the Book in August 2013.

Prof. and I, together with a few NLB librarians, attended this inaugural event at the start of a Washington DC winter in December 2012. Over the two days of the Summit, held at the Coolidge Auditorium at the Library of Congress, an international panel of thought leaders from academia, libraries, culture and technology engaged in spirited discussions about the book as one of the most powerful forms of information transmittal.

Washington DC was obviously familiar territory for Prof., having spent six years in the city as Singapore's Ambassador to the US. He recognised familiar faces everywhere we went, and at some of the restaurants we dined at, he knew staff members by name. It's clear that Prof. is still a well-respected figure among the local and international communities in DC, despite having left the US more than two decades ago.

For Prof., the opportunity to host the International Summit of the Book in Singapore was a coup in cultural diplomacy, a chance to position our country in the international discourse on books, reading and literacy.

Back in Singapore, Prof. graciously chaired our Steering Committee and personally invited many of the speakers, both in Singapore and overseas, to take part in the Summit. As a result of his involvement, we were able to secure several illustrious names from academia, libraries and the publishing world to be moderators and speakers in the panel discussions.

On the day of the event, topics such as the meaning of the book in civilisation as well as the future of the book and that of the library were aired and roundly debated by scholars and thinkers such as Professors Kishore Mahbubani and Wang Gungwu from Singapore; Dr Ismail Serageldin, Director of Bibliotheca Alexandrina in Egypt; Professor Cathy Davidson, the American scholar of cultural history and technology; and Ken Wissoker, Editorial Director of Duke University Press, among others.

Our celebratory dinner event at Raffles Hotel that same evening was likewise meticulously put together under Prof.'s supervision. He thought it would be meaningful to have Singaporean writers such as Catherine Lim, Suchen Christine Lim and Edwin Thumboo read excerpts from their works in between courses. Even the carefully planned dinner menu did not escape Prof.'s attention.

Few people who attended the Summit were aware that Prof. was running a fever on that day. Yet he bravely soldiered on, delivering his opening and closing remarks at the Summit in his usual disarming fashion and pushed on to attend the dinner. I am sure Prof. must have heaved a big sigh of relief when he eventually went to bed that night, but looking at him in action throughout the day, no one would have known that he had been feeling poorly. His dedication is truly remarkable.

The Singapore Story in Print

Barely three months later, in November 2013, we had to prevail upon Prof. yet again when NLB commissioned the official SG50 book in celebration of Singapore's Jubilee Year. Without hesitation, he agreed to helm the Editorial Advisory Committee.

Over the course of the following year, Prof. worked closely with members of the committee — people drawn from a varied spectrum of society, including business, law, social work, architecture, sport, the arts and heritage preservation. He knew that the committee's diverse views were important in shaping a book that would tell the story of Singapore over the 50 years since Independence. Given the large number of commemoratory books flooding the market in 2015, he wanted a book that would stand out from the crowd.

With typical clear-eyed vision, he knew the book had to be pictorial in content and accompanied by narratives that should be engaging, balanced and thoughtful — inspirational but not espousing propaganda. Above all, these narratives should tell the larger story of Singapore, the story of a people overcoming the odds together to build a nation. He wanted a book that people would read and keep, not just use it to decorate a bookshelf.

It was a tall order for a book, and Prof. had to manage the different expectations of the editorial committee, the team of writers and editors from *The Straits Times*, including prominent journalists such as Han Fook Kwang and Cheong Suk Wai, as well as the overarching objectives of the SG50 Committee led by Minister Heng Swee Keat, the national-level agency supervising all the anniversary celebrations.

In the end we produced a coffee table book that received a warm reception from the press as well as the public. It captured the personal recollections of 58 people from all walks of life, both movers and shakers such as architect and urban planner Liu Thai Ker and former SIA Chairman J. Y. Pillay, as well as a bus driver, a nurse, a fire fighter and other ordinary folk. It was a book "about the people of Singapore" as Prof. so succinctly described it at the launch event on May 20, 2015.

The first print run of 10,000 copies of *Living the Singapore Story: Celebrating Our 50 Years 1965–2015* sold out quickly — which is quite a feat by local publishing standards — and the book went into a second reprint soon after.

More Than a Man of Letters

Seeing Prof. in action at various meetings has been a learning experience for us at NLB: he deftly answers multiple questions, poses difficult issues for people to deliberate on, and considers alternative suggestions, but always, at the same time, staying focused on the important issues at hand. Nothing seems to ruffle his feathers, no problem or issue ever seems insurmountable, and his meetings are always liberally peppered with humour to diffuse any potentially tense situations.

Prof. has the uncanny knack of making you feel like you're the most important person in the room when he speaks to you. People just take to him, which means half the battle is won even before the serious negotiations begin.

When Prof. launched his book *The Tommy Koh Reader: Favourite Essays and Lectures* on October 20, 2013 at NLB, I described him as a "man of letters" and a "man of warmth" in my speech. He is an intellectual, a scholar as well as a generous and kind-hearted gentleman who is fiercely committed to service. I can think of no better way to describe him.

It's no exaggeration to say that Prof. lights up a room when he walks into it. When you see him smiling warmly and pausing to say hello to familiar faces or waving to someone in recognition, you don't get the sense that he is working the crowd. He is just genuinely happy to see people.

Prof. has been a familiar face at NLB during the time that I've been CEO here. Whether it's a request to be the Patron of READ! Singapore or to chair the committees of the many NLB-led initiatives, our numerous invitations to him to grace a book launch or an event as guest of honour, or to moderate a panel discussion (the list goes on), he has never once declined. Although Prof. will tell you in jest that he works for me — this is what he tells me when I ask for his help — it is actually we who need him, and will gladly work for him.

Prof. has attributed the success of his term as Ambassador to the US to his wife, Siew Aing, whom he calls his "secret weapon". We here at NLB think of Professor Tommy Koh as *our* secret weapon. Many of the ambitious initiatives we've rolled out over the years would not have seen the light of day if not for the good Professor's enlightened leadership, generous gift of his time and wise counsel. We remain forever indebted to him.

CHAPTER 22

A Master Himself

Danny Yeo

Beginnings of a Delightful Food Journey

My food journey and friendship with Professor Tommy Koh started all but six years ago, thanks to an article in *The Straits Times*.

The food editor then and current *Life!* editor Tan Hsueh Yun wrote an article, "Celebrate Our Hawkers with Culinary Medallion," on September 14, 2010, in which she mooted lauding our local hawkers with National Day Awards. The hope was that by giving the best ones official national recognition, hawkers in general would be encouraged to keep food standards high. The move would also, she argued, "make parents more accepting of alternative routes to success — in the kitchen rather than in a boardroom or clinic."

This article caught the attention of Alan Chan, Chief Executive Officer of Singapore Press Holdings (SPH), who is known to relish his hawker food. He tasked its marketing division to carry out a nationwide search for top hawkers and suggested a few possible judges, including Professor Koh, who is known to champion hawker fare, especially since he returned to Singapore in 1990. This task eventually fell on my lap and in early October that year, planning for the first-ever Singapore Hawker Masters search began.

Initially, I was not too sure if I should contact Professor Koh directly or go through someone higher in the SPH echelons. Would he respond to someone in middle management like myself, I wondered. After all, the man is no less than a household name, having among his many achievements taken on roles such as Singapore's Permanent Representative to the United Nations and Ambassador-At-Large at the Ministry of Foreign Affairs. I figured that a man of his stature might not have the time or patience to go around nibbling on prata and slurping up laksa with us.

After some deliberation, I dropped him an email and soon realised that all my fears were unfounded. Not only did Professor Koh respond promptly, he added that it would be an honour to serve on the judging panel. This would be the first of many good impressions he left me with.

Taking the Show on the Road

The inaugural Singapore Hawker Masters meeting was held over lunch sometime in mid-October 2010 at the Imperial Treasure restaurant in Great World City. As the person in charge of the project, I thought I should get there earlier, before all the judges. I arrived about half an hour before the agreed time, only to see Professor Koh already there, chatting animatedly with the restaurant staff. When I introduced myself, he greeted me with so much warmth that I felt instantly at ease. Throughout the meeting, Professor Koh was notably humble. While he was forthcoming with his opinions, he also listened attentively to the views of the other judges. Perhaps it was his candour and affable demeanour, but it took only this meeting for me to feel comfortable calling him "Prof.", the same way his friends and close associates do.

It was at this meeting where we decided that the inaugural Singapore Hawker Masters search would start in November that year. It would eventually become the most stringent annual search for the country's top hawkers. Each year, masters of six dishes would be picked through three stages. First, readers of *The Straits Times* and *Lianhe Zaobao*, which presented the event, were asked to nominate their favourite hawkers. Three hawkers for each dish with the most number of nominations, along with three others picked by the judges, were then listed in the two newspapers for readers to vote. Finally, the judges would visit the three hawkers of each dish with the most number of votes and crown the best masters.

Ever the Congenial Diplomat

During our time together, I could not help but notice many of Prof.'s admirable traits. One of it was his penchant for punctuality. For every judging session, when the shuttle bus pulled up at his office at the Ministry of Foreign Affairs at Sherwood Road, he would always already be waiting at the front porch. Another was the humble way in which he managed his celebrity. Now, I knew Prof. was famous, but our food sprees proved that he is truly recognisable in practically every corner of Singapore. At almost every judging stop, members of the public and hawkers would greet him, with many coming forward to shake his hand. Such was his popularity that it was at times not easy for the judges to taste the food incognito. For their own reasons, many Singaporeans associated Prof. with the government and the ruling party. I remember we were making our rounds at the Albert Centre Market & Food Centre one afternoon, when an elderly man came up to ask him, "Election coming huh?" In his usual calm way, he said smilingly, "No, we are just here to eat."

At the hawker centres, Prof. had no airs about him and always thought about others. He would talk to the hawkers whenever possible, either while waiting for our food or after eating. He probed into the history of their stalls and dishes, the working hours and then some. When judging sessions ended around noon, Prof. would "tar pau" or buy takeaway meals from the finalists' stalls for his personal assistant and colleagues to try. He even gathered their feedback and shared them with me. He also honed his secret skill of taking nice photos of the hawkers and food with his iPad, often posting them on Facebook.

Although Prof. lived in the United States for many years, there was no doubt that he still knew his hawker fare like a true blue Singaporean. Most of his preferences coincided with the majority of the judges, although I sensed that his wife, Dr Poh Siew Aing, has some influence on his tastebuds. In situations where some of her favourite stalls were among the finalists, Prof. would vote for them. There were occasions when the judges had a hard time picking a master between two finalists. Ever the diplomatic at heart, Prof. would suggest declaring them as joint-winners. Unfortunately that was not an option, as we wanted Singapore Hawker Masters to be a prestigious award with only one master for each food category. Prof. could have argued harder for joint-winners and we may well have just relented, but not once did he try to assert his influence in that fashion. At the food table, he was a team player. As usual, he would give his views but always went along with the majority. He keenly understood what is probably the oldest philosophy when it comes to food — that one man's meat is simply another man's poison.

I recall another display of his selflessness in 2014, when one of the judging sessions was scheduled for November 12. While planning the dates, our team had not known that it was Prof's birthday. I later told Prof. that he could skip this session, as he would probably want to spend time with his family. But he refused to do so. Instead, he chose to give us a few hours of his time that day to join the judging session — a testament to his passion in supporting local hawkers. We did a simple cake-cutting at the SPH News Centre lobby before setting off. It was a modest gesture, but Prof. nonetheless seemed appreciative and touched.

After the second year, we had difficulty getting ministers to be the guest of honour at the Singapore Hawker Masters awards ceremony. Then it dawned on me suddenly that we had a perfect candidate in Prof. all along. High-profile and recognisable? Check. Likeable? Check. Someone whom hawkers love to snap photos with? Triple check! Still, as someone humble who prefers avoiding the spotlight where possible, Prof. needed much persuasion to take on the title. "Let someone else take the limelight," he said. Eventually he agreed, albeit reluctantly. But everyone else knew he was the best man for the role. Thereafter, Prof. became our "resident GOH".

There is standard protocol surrounding guests of honour at events, including assembling a welcome party to greet them. The award ceremonies for Singapore Hawker Masters were no exception. However, in both 2013 and 2014, Prof. arrived way ahead of his scheduled appearance, surprising everyone by showing up inside the hall and talking to the Hawker Masters. In his typical gregarious and down-to-earth fashion, he made sure he knew the names of all the hawkers and their dishes.

It goes without saying that Prof's fellow judges for Hawker Masters, including culinary doyenne, Violet Oon, and the president of Far East

Food Concepts, Chia Boon Pin, all enjoyed having Prof. on the panel, and are quick to sing his praises. One of the judges, *The Straits Times* food critic Wong Ah Yoke, noted: "During our marathon food tasting sessions for the Hawker Masters and throughout the judging process, Professor Tommy Koh struck me as a person who thinks of others before himself. He was never flustered, was always the perfect gentleman and was particularly careful that no one feels uncomfortable or slighted in any way." Fellow judge Dennis Wee, Chairman of Dennis Wee Group, described working with Prof. on the panel as a "pleasure". He told me: "[Prof.] was always very calm and made us feel very much at ease. I am surprised that he still remembers the old-school taste of local dishes despite being away from Singapore for so many years."

Spurring Our Culinary Heritage

It is a pity that after I retired in 2015, SPH discontinued the Singapore Hawker Masters search. It definitely helped to increase public aware-ness of good hawkers who still use original, old-school recipes passed down through generations. This is apparent from the long queues at the Masters' stalls and the online buzz surrounding them. On many occasions when I returned to these stalls to eat, other customers would tell me they were there to check out the food because the hawkers were conferred Master status. Some even brought their children along to acquaint their young tastebuds with "authentic" Singapore dishes.

I suspect Singapore Hawker Masters could have drawn Michelin's attention to the fact that our hawker food are deserving of their awards. I am glad that two Masters made it to the Singapore Michelin Bib Gour-mand Guide 2016 — Balestier Road Hoover Rojak at Whampoa Market Place and Tian Tian Chicken Rice at Maxwell Food Centre. I am sure if their search were more comprehensive, most, if not all, of the Masters would be listed too.

But Singapore Hawker Masters was only beginning to achieve its other objective of spurring more people, especially the young, to step into the kitchen and preserve our culinary heritage. We hear of more young people setting up hawker stalls these days, but many of them whip up dishes that stray from original recipes and are tweaked to suit a more modern palate. I know of at least two Masters who have called it a day — the owners of Selera Kita at New Upper Changi Road and Song Kee Fishball Noodle at Upper Serangoon Road. Zahara Abu Bakar, who sold mee rebus at Selera Kita, had a nagging pain in her hands which her doctor attributed to the routine stirring of gravy. Her children are not keen to take over her business, she told me. Over at Song Kee Fishball Noodle, the Chua brothers, Soo Meng, Soo Chai and Poh Seng, handed over the business to their cousin, citing manpower shortage and long hours as reasons for throwing in the towel.

I know I am not alone in wanting to revive Singapore Hawker Masters. When Prof. and I had lunch together in July 2016, he mused about bringing it back. Who knows if that will ever happen, but for now, I am just thankful that some of the things it stood for continue to live on — tasty and affordable hawker food, the dedicated people who cook it, and hungry Singaporeans like Prof.

From the bottom of my tummy, I thank Prof. for lending his time to this meaningful project, and for giving all of us on the team the opportunity to know him over countless bowls of wanton noodles and plates of chicken rice. He may have helped to crown many hawker masters over the years, but in my eyes, Prof., with his calm affability, selfless humility and astute taste buds, is a master in his own right.

Tommy Koh, Singapore's new Permanent Representative to the United Nations (UN), presenting his credential to UN Secretary-General U Thant at UN Headquarters, 1968. (Photo courtesy of United Nations. From *The Tommy Koh Reader: Favourite Essays and Lectures*, Singapore: World Scientific, 2013)

With Singapore's first foreign minister, S. Rajaratnam at UN General Assembly, 1974. (Photo courtesy of United Nations. From *The Tommy Koh Reader*)

Singapore Prime Minister Lee Kuan Yew on his 1985 state visit to the United States (US), with US President Ronald Reagan and Chief of Protocol Selwa Roosevelt. Mrs Koh is behind Tommy Koh. (From *The Tommy Koh Reader*)

Members of the Singapore's first Censorship Review Committee (1991–1992). Koh Buck Song is fifth from the right in the back row. (Photo courtesy of MITA)

The National Arts Council team in 1991. Khor Kok Wah is second from the right.
(From *The Tommy Koh Reader*)

The ASEF management team in 2000. Peggy Kek is second from the right (front row).
(From *The Tommy Koh Reader*)

Closing ceremony of the Rio Conference, June 1992. Tommy Koh is second from the right. (Photo courtesy of United Nations)

Launch of Mobil Oil's Singapore Environmental Heritage Series, "A Guide to the Bukit Timah Nature Reserve", October 1992. From left to right: Tommy Koh, Tan Cheng Guan of Mobil Oil, Prof. Wee Yeow Chin, and Nature Society (Singapore) activist, the late Dr Clive Briffett. (Photo courtesy of Ilsa Sharp)

With Prof. Wee Yeow Chin and Mrs Elizabeth Chan at the launch of *Private Lives: An Exposé of Singapore's Rainforest* and the Digital Nature Archives of Singapore in July 2012. (Photo courtesy of Chua Ee Kiam)

Joint conference organised by the Asia Society, Institute of Policy Studies, Institute of Southeast Asian Studies and Singapore International Foundation, January 1993. Prof. Chan Heng Chee is on the far right. (Photo courtesy of Institute of Policy Studies)

ASEF Board of Governors Meeting in Luxembourg, October 1997. (Photo courtesy of Anouk Antony)

The Institute of Policy Studies marked its 10th anniversary in November 1997. Arun Mahizhnan is on the far left, last row. (Photo courtesy of Institute of Policy Studies)

Keynote address at the APEC Business Advisory Council (ABAC) Meeting in Brunei, February 1999. (Photo courtesy of APEC Secretariat)

Tommy Koh making his welcome remarks as Co-Chairman at the UNITAR-IPS-JIIA Conference, April 2001. (Photo courtesy of Institute of Policy Studies)

Prime Minister Goh Chok Tong (third from right) officiating the opening of the Asian Civilisations Museum in 2003. George Yeo is to his left and beside him is Kenson Kwok. (Photo courtesy of the Asian Civilisations Museum)

Tommy Koh with Chua Mui Hoong (right, back row) and her family at the launch of her book, *A Defining Moment: How Singapore Beat SARS* in July 2004. (Photo courtesy of Chua Mui Hoong)

Signing of the Settlement Agreement of the Case Concerning Land Reclamation by Singapore in and around the Straits of Johor, April 2005. (Photo courtesy of Ministry of Foreign Affairs)

Prime Minister Lee Hsien Loong officiating the opening of the Peranakan Museum in March 2008. Kenson Kwok is on the far right and Michael Koh second from the left. (Photo courtesy of Peranakan Museum)

Launch of the Butterfly Trail @ Orchard at Nassim Green in June 2010. In the back row, to Tommy Koh's right is Dr Geh Min. (Photo courtesy of Nature Society (Singapore))

With fellow judges of the Singapore Hawker Masters in 2012. Danny Yeo is second from right in the back row. (Photo courtesy of Danny Yeo)

Receiving the 2014 Great Negotiator Award from Prof. James K. Sebenius, Harvard Law School, April 2014. (Photo courtesy of Tom Fitzsimmons)

Board members and staff of the Guide Dogs Association of the Blind at the inauguration ceremony of its third guide dog team in December 2012, with Patron Tommy Koh, Director Dr Francis Seow-Choen (third from the right) and Guests of Honour Ms Ho Ching (fifth from left) and High Commissioner of Australia to Singapore, His Excellency Philip Green (fifth from right). (Photo courtesy of Guide Dogs Singapore)

From left to right: Tommy Koh, NLB Chief Executive Elaine Ng, Founding Director of Bibliotheca Alexandrina Ismail Serageldin, NLB Board Member John Koh and NLB Deputy Chief Executive Tay Ai Cheng, October 2013. (Photo courtesy of National Library Board)

Tommy Koh with Simon Tay, November 2013. (Photo courtesy of SIIA)

With Jeremy Monteiro, May 2016. (Photo courtesy of Jeremy Monteiro)

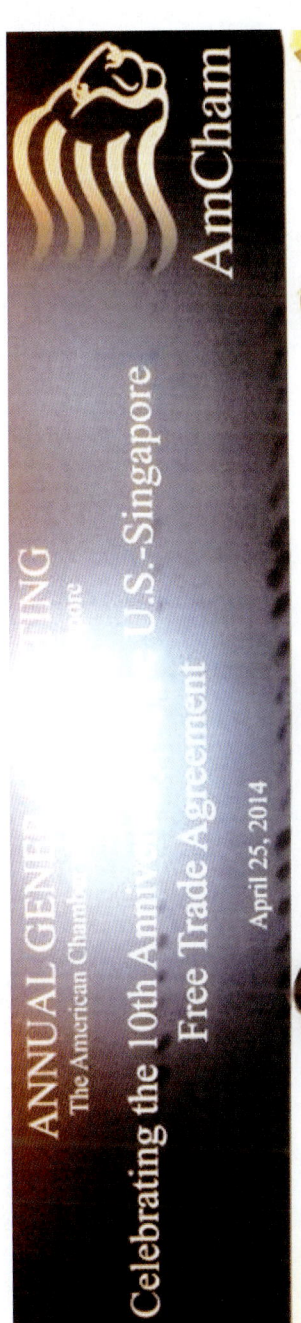

Celebrating the 10th anniversary of the US-Singapore Free Trade Agreement with (from left) Daren Tang, Ong Ye Kung and Ambassador Frank Lavin, April 2014. (Photo courtesy of Tommy Koh)

Members of the International Advisory Panel on Transboundary Pollution, May 2014. Front row (left to right): Judge Abdul Koroma, Prof. Edith Brown Weiss, Dr Vivian Balakrishnan, Prof. S Jayakumar and Judge Paik Jin Hyun. Back row (left to right): Prof. Nicholas Robinson, Rod Bundy and Tommy Koh. (Photo courtesy of Tommy Koh)

Speaking at the launch of *Living the Singapore Story* in May 2015. (Photo courtesy of National Library Board)

At the David Marshall Lecture on "Building the Rules-Based ASEAN Community: Strengthening the Centre" held by the Centre for International Law (CIL), National University of Singapore, November 2015. From left to right: George Yeo, Walter Woon, Simon Chesterman, Tommy Koh, S Jayakumar and Robert Beckman. (Photo courtesy of National University of Singapore)

The Singaporean secretariat and delegation to the 11th Japan-Singapore Symposium at the Garden of Hotel New Otani, April 2016. (Photo courtesy of Institute of Policy Studies)

With (left to right) Simon Chesterman; Irene Lye Lin-Heng; Desmond Lee, Senior Minister of State, Ministry of Home Affairs & Ministry of National Development; and Koh Kheng-Lian at the Conference on Attaining the Sustainable Development Goals — Environmental Law, Policy and Management, November 2016. (Photo courtesy of National University of Singapore)

At the CIL International Conference on "The South China Sea Award: The Legal Dimension" in January 2017 in Singapore. (Photo courtesy of National University of Singapore)

An early birthday celebration at the IPS Singapore Perspectives Conference, January 2017. Prof. Wang Gungwu welcoming Tommy Koh into the "80s club." Ambassador Ong Keng Yong is behind Tommy Koh.

With Associate Prof. Gregory Clancey (on Tommy Koh's left), and students of Tembusu College, National University of Singapore, March 2017. (Photo courtesy of Tembusu College, National University of Singapore)

Opening Session of the 12th China-Singapore Forum held in Beijing, May 2017. (Photo courtesy of James Tan, East Asian Institute)

Tommy Koh with his family, December 2016. Standing, from left to right: Mrs Alice Tan Gek Siang, Su-Lyn Tan, Aun Koh, Joycelyn Shu, Wei Koh and Mrs Koh Siew Aing. Seated, from left to right: Mr Albert Tan Hock Lim, Toby Koh and Tara Koh. (Photo courtesy of Erwin Tan)

The co-editors of this book celebrating Tommy Koh's 70th birthday in 2007, Singapore: Chang Li Lin (second row, first from left), Gillian Koh (second row, third from left), Yeo Lay Hwee (to the left of Mrs Koh), and Peggy Kek (first row, third from right). (Photo courtesy of Institute of Policy Studies)

Section III

Progressive Society

CHAPTER 23

Progressive Society:
Tommy Koh's Imprints

GILLIAN KOH

Introduction

This section discusses Professor (Prof.) Tommy Koh's contributions in developing a progressive society in Singapore in a range of areas — education and policy research, the environment, social inclusion of special needs persons, philanthropy and more generally, the development of civil society.

There is one other significant area of contribution by him towards making Singapore a socially conscious, inclusive, gracious and creative community — arts and heritage — which we decided demands special focus and its own section. That precedes this one.

Even then, we are conscious that the two sections by no means do justice to the depth and breadth of how Prof. Koh has helped to shape the soul and spirit of Singapore. This is not just our opinion but that of many contributors in this section who say that a proper accounting and analysis of what Prof. Koh has done in their specific areas of endeavour would require a book each.

Nonetheless, we have in this section, personal testimonies of those who have worked directly with him, which provide ample evidence of his progressive value system, his character as an authentic civic leader, and the true social change he has catalysed by his active and dedicated service in the non-government as well as intellectual spaces of our country.

So what makes Tommy Koh tick? What drives him? How has he effected this lasting impact on the people he has worked with and on our society?

A Life-Long Commitment to Nation-Building

Prof. Koh was born in colonial Singapore and was very much a part of the pioneer generation of Singaporeans. In his essay, "The Singapore of My Dreams", he lists as the first of his schoolboy dreams a Singapore ruled by its people, having caught the anti-colonial, nationalist bug from similar movements that were taking place in the rest of Asia as well as Africa at the time.[1] As an undergraduate and a progressive, independent-minded young scholar, he was noticed for his views on the future of Singapore. In 1968, he was recruited into the Foreign Service to be Singapore's Permanent Representative at the United Nations (UN); an act he described as being "helicoptered to the top of the ladder at a comparatively young age."[2]

It was surely a recognition of his intellect, his temperament and commitment to the country's interests, but there were those who wondered if this was government "co-optation" of someone who would otherwise be a political troublemaker at home. The sharp question is whether that is true? Would anyone, looking at his track record since, believe that to be the case? This essay should provide you with the answer. It will draw on what Prof. Koh himself has said about his dreams for the country and society, suggest how he has followed through on them, and point you to the essays that flesh out how he did that.

Rule of law and good governance

Prof. Koh was very much part of the young idealists of his generation who wanted self-determination for Singapore. His schoolboy dreams were accompanied by grown-up sensibilities of what that would

1 Tommy Koh, *The Tommy Koh Reader: Favourite Essays and Lectures* (Singapore: World Scientific, 2013), 137–145.
2 Tommy Koh, "Can Any Country Afford a Moral Foreign Policy?" in *The Quest for World Order: Perspectives from a Pragmatic Idealist* (Singapore: Marshall Cavendish Academic, 1997), 1.

entail — strong rule of law and good governance. He hoped "the law would be just and that people did not fear either the gangsters or the police."[3]

The young Koh penned an article in his secondary school's magazine, *The Rafflesian*, expressing his indignation at the sight of the police arresting hawkers making their living, and asked if it was possible for the government to create places for hawkers to ply their trade. Think now of our iconic "hawker centre" today that answers that need. Even if it is not clear whether Prof. Koh had a hand bringing it to fruition, what is clear is that Prof. Koh's involvement in a newspaper-sponsored, annual national competition to find the country's best hawkers called the "Hawker Masters Awards" supports the trade and promotes Singapore's heritage food. This is discussed in Chua Mui Hoong's essay in this section as well as Danny Yeo's essay in the Arts and Heritage section.

Anyway, you will not find the article in the archives of Raffles Institution (RI), his school, because, as Prof. Koh describes: "I suffered my first experience of censorship by the British Director of Education and was told that my article could not be published."[4] With that, Prof. Koh had become familiar early in life with the risk of going against the grain in sharing his views about the country. He would continue to argue with courage, as a public intellectual for the sort of Singapore he envisaged.

Along with those two dreams were two others — that "all families would earn enough income to enable them to live decently" and that "all Singaporeans would have access to good housing, clean water and modern sanitation."[5]

He chose an education that would allow him to contribute directly to ensuring the rule of law and good governance. Indeed, he was in such a hurry to see that dream come true that as an undergraduate and President of the University of Malaya Students Law Society in 1960 to 1961, he advocated the establishment of an ombudsman in Singapore so that complaints of what he called "maladministration" that could occur even under a generally honest government could be lodged, investigated and remedied. This is of course an idea that he is still very much associated with today.

---

3 Tommy Koh, *The Tommy Koh Reader*, 138.
4 Ibid.
5 Ibid., 137–138.

It is clear however that the starting point of his commitment to the rule of law is that it should serve the creation of a moral and compassionate society in addition to a safe and orderly one. This is found in his appeal for a greater accent on the rehabilitation of criminals than the use of the cane where possible in discussing the country's penal code. He was rewarded for his appeal with criticism from government minister Lim Kim San, who said Prof. Koh had been too kind-hearted and ruined by the Boy Scout Movement.

In any case, as the other sections of the book will have set out, it has been his life's work to try to strengthen the rule of law at home but also at the international level, having been integral to the promulgation of the United Nations Convention on the Law of the Sea (UNCLOS) in 1982.

Growth with equity

As a young adult, along with the dream of an independent Singapore that could take pride of place in the international community, Prof. Koh's schoolboy dreams morphed into greater sophistication. He dreamt of a Singapore that had a thriving economy providing good jobs for the unemployed and the young, and more importantly, that the fruits of that progress would be distributed such that there would be "growth with equity".

This is a *leitmotiv* of Prof. Koh's social outlook through the years. It has driven him to encourage the government to mind any widening of the income and wealth gap, as well as to prevent the formation of an underclass. He has done this through his opinion essays, as Donald Low and Chua highlight in theirs in this section, urging the government to do more in this regard and even consider instituting a minimum wage policy if the other policies it has tried prove not to work.

What has not been captured much is the fact that whenever Prof. Koh has had the opportunity to sit on corporate boards, he has sought to encourage the business elites to play their part too in fostering an equitable society. He has mentioned to this editor and colleagues that first, he would urge them to see that it is desirable to keep the ratio of the salaries at the top management rungs to the rank-and-file workers within a reasonable range and not allow for runaway inequality; second, that where possible, they should try to find meaningful ways to give back directly to society. Melissa Kwee shares in her essay that Prof. Koh is an advocate of the "1% Club" — the challenging idea that businesses commit to give 1% of their profits towards meaningful social projects, which was first promoted publicly by Emeritus Senior Minister Goh Chok Tong when he was prime minister. Prof. Koh has also promoted the idea of setting up corporate foundations. When he has had the opportunity to sit on their boards, he has led many initiatives to fund the arts, heritage conservation and other grant-making activities. As Kwee sets out, Prof. Koh has tried to persuade the wealth-generators in the country to act in their enlightened self-interest by supporting the community.

Rigorous policy thinking

Even as a young man, Prof. Koh had already expressed his wish that the country's progress and urban redevelopment should not be at the expense of its built heritage. In the "Dreams" essay referred to earlier, he stated he was part of a group of "idealistic young men called Singapore Planning and Urban Research group, or SPUR"[6] that lobbied the government to conserve landmark buildings, historic neighbourhoods and streets. SPUR was a ground-up think-tank of young intellectuals and architects that some of us know of because of the apocryphal story that government security agents had raided the office of one of its members presumably to check if the group was seditious. (There is an interesting factual story of a similar "courtesy call" in the essay by Prof. Wee Yeow Chin in this section.) SPUR's ideas and methods must have raised some suspicion within government quarters. It was registered as a society in 1966 and held many policy discussions and supported the move of the airport from Paya Lebar to Changi before eventually de-registering in 1975. Arun Mahizhnan's essay on Prof. Koh's contribution to the work of the national think-tank, the Institute of Policy Studies (IPS), suggests that the former might have been a sort of dress rehearsal for shaping an impactful policy research centre. Of

---

6 Koh, Tommy, *The Tommy Koh Reader*, 139–140.

course there could be no doubt that Prof. Koh would also have been inspired by the more established practices and think-tank culture he discovered in his time in the United States (US) before being tasked to run IPS after he returned.

Deliberation and consensus, not contention

Prof. Koh acted on his convictions, spoke up for what he believed in even in those early days; yet he did so in a way that was consistent with his belief in the rule of law and the democratic spirit. What was clear however was that he chose to avoid being directly involved in polarising political activism. What is the evidence for that? (Perhaps this is the puzzle that those who wonder if he had been co-opted have in their minds: Why didn't he take his progressive ideas to the ballot box? To this day, many ask if he would or could put himself forward to serve the country as its elected president. Would that ever be likely?)

Tommy Koh was a member of the University Socialist Club (USC) when he was an undergraduate at the University of Malaya between 1957 and 1961. Now, we know that a good many who were associated with the club went on to form the core of the People's Action Party (PAP) under Lee Kuan Yew, who was part of the legal counsel that successfully defended members of the USC in a sedition trial because of the anti-colonial article that they published in the Club's newspaper, *Fajar*. The article was called "Aggression in Asia?" and the trial took place in August 1954. Those young members were the vanguard of the nationalist movement and eventually, some of them formed the PAP breakaway group called the Barisan Sosialis, touting their more authentic socialist affinities and credentials.

Prof. Koh was described years later by one of the presidents of the USC, Jayaraj Rajarao, as a member who "offered novel ideas to make the club cohesive and challenging."[7] Rajarao said that Prof.

---

7 Jeyaraj C. Rajarao, "The Legacy of the Socialist Club of the University of Malaya: Influences and Reminiscences" in *The Fajar Generation: the University Socialist Club and the Politics of Postwar Malaya and Singapore*, ed. Poh Soon Kai, Tan Jing Quee, & Koh Kay Yew (Selangor: Strategic Information and Research Development Centre), 69.

Koh's "conviction to support legitimate activities was uncompromising but he was unimpressed with the seeming froth of the ebbing
tide of fascism and tyranny and the hidden roles of reactionaries.
He was cautious but not constrained in expressing his views. He was
articulate, precise and logical."[8] He stated, "Intellectually, I would rate
Tommy as the most outstanding."[9] Prof. Koh mentioned to the editor
that he published two articles in *Fajar* at that time, and argued in one
of them his preference that Singapore work towards independence
rather than merger. So it is clear that while he would have enjoyed
close association with those political activists, he was not tempted to
join them as he quite easily might have.

Although this editor is privileged to be acquainted with Prof.
Koh only in the past two decades, there has been occasion enough to
learn that he is, by nature, a consensus- and bridge-builder. Not for
him is the win-lose game of politics. I have often heard him say that
if given the choice, he would prefer that disputes are settled without
going to court, something that might be surprising given our usual
perception of lawyers! The reason: There is only one outcome — that
someone will win and someone else will lose. Prof. Koh prefers the
processes of mediation and arbitration and he is very good at it, even
though he seems to prevail in all circumstances as amply demonstrated in the case of the Pedra Branca dispute with Malaysia that
went before the International Court of Justice in 2008, as well as the
arbitrated settlement of the Singapore-Malaysia Land Reclamation
dispute brought before the International Tribunal of the Law of the
Sea in 2002.

If Prof. Koh had ever joined partisan party politics, he would likely
have redefined it altogether. Here is a funny tale to explain why: When
he was a law student, some friends managed to persuade him to contest
for a seat on the council of the students' union. Instead of the usual
practice of running down his opponent, a Mr Subramaniam, he praised
him. The outcome? Prof. Koh won!

---

8 Ibid.
9 Ibid.

Multiracial, multicultural haven

Tommy Koh has also said that another part of his dream as a young man was that "mutual understanding, peace and harmony would continue to prevail among Singaporeans of different races, religions, languages and cultures."[10] We can probably take the liberty of adding "social class" in that list given what we know of him. Prof. Koh has attributed this to the strong imprint from his days at RI; his exposure to its multiracial faculty and student body, as well as the fact that RI admitted students solely on the basis of merit which meant that most of his classmates were from working-class homes.

In an essay reflecting on what RI taught him, Prof. Koh said that it was difficult to hold a prejudice against any colour or creed when Malays and Indians were outstanding teachers as was also the case with his close friends; among them, the hero of the class, the school's soccer star Mr Wan Hussin Zoohri, who has an essay in this volume. Prof. Koh states with such clarity, "the qualities of a man's mind and heart have nothing to do with his race, colour or creed."[11]

In what he calls an "Old Man's Dream", emphasising that he has not stopped dreaming, he hopes Singapore can become a cultural hub of Southeast Asia and even, the home city of the Asian cultural renaissance. Essays in the Arts section of this volume testify to his efforts towards making that happen.

Tommy Koh also envisions Singapore as the Geneva of the East where people of all nations would find warm hospitality and a secure meeting place even for representatives of adversaries in international disputes. This is much like Switzerland that is viewed as a neutral space where international organisations are hosted and international negotiations over the world's most challenging issues can take place. People here have to be known as peace-lovers, bridge-builders and trusted brokers. He also envisioned the country as a Venice of the 21st century, a place where the talented from across the world can live and work. He has written about how some of his best friends today are

---

10 Tommy Koh, *The Tommy Koh Reader*, 140.
11 Ibid., 42.

new Singaporeans[12] and in his essay "Reflections on Immigration",[13] he urges Singaporeans to be open-hearted and broad-minded to welcome immigrants. After all, he says he is a third-generation Singaporean on his father's side and second-generation one on his mother's side. Given how fair he is, that essay ends with an appeal to immigrants to make the effort to fit in and live by the values and norms of Singapore. His crisp definition of these is a classic and deserves to be replicated on the back of every MRT card!

Sustainable development, the preservation of natural heritage

So much of the international work that Prof. Koh is associated with in the past decades is in the area of sustainable development, the management of the world's natural resources, and the Law of the Sea. Much of this is covered in the other sections of this volume. Suffice it to say here that Prof. Koh's legacy in the local arena is just as rich and valuable. We have two essays in this section, the one by Prof. Wee and another by Dr Geh Min that capture just that. Dr Gregory Clancey shares in his essay how Prof. Koh actively instills the importance of the earth's natural heritage in young undergraduates as Rector of Tembusu College. In his "old man's dreams" for Singapore, Prof. Koh envisions Singapore as Asia's "greenest city" not just in the physical sense but more broadly in terms of physical infrastructure to manage water, sanitation, pollution, land use, as well as energy. Singapore, he says, must be a role model for sustainable development, for Asia and the world.

Progress Through Knowledge-Creation and Questioning Conventional Wisdom

Prof. Koh is not just a learned person himself but is committed to scholarship. He has published books to ensure that present and future scholars, and also policymakers can learn from the experiences of negotiation and diplomacy that he has gathered from say, concluding the

---

12 Ibid., 191.
13 Ibid., 173–174.

ASEAN Charter, the United States-Singapore Free Trade Agreement and resolving Singapore's disputes with Malaysia. He is devoted to the public documentation of ideas and developments in our country and encourages all of us to publish, publish, publish. He welcomes open scrutiny and critical analysis of everything; he believes in that discipline.

Chua and Prof. Simon Chesterman speak of him as someone who generates thoughtful and on many occasions, courageous material where he questions the mainstream or establishment view on various policy matters and international relations. Mahizhnan shares how Prof. Koh has given support for the publications of IPS. Prof. Wee's essay provides a good illustration of how Prof. Koh aided the conservation cause with not just his published endorsement of Malayan Nature Society (Singapore Branch)'s petition to save the Lower Peirce Forest but because Prof. Koh was already a champion for sustainable development globally and wielded that soft influence to good effect. Donald Low highlights in his essay how Prof. Koh has spoken up about that challenging area of achieving growth with equity.

Prof. Koh once said that a lesson that he had learnt from none other than Dr Goh Keng Swee, one of Singapore's pioneer political leaders, is that one should be prepared to "defy conventional wisdom":

> ... we should think for ourselves and not be a slavish follower of conventional wisdom and fashionable theories. Dr Goh was a rebel. For example, he was not afraid to deviate from Keynesian economics and the Western ideological bias against industrial policy. He would insist on thorough homework, study the experiences of others, but, in the end, adopt a solution which fits our circumstances and works.[14]

Again, it is a frame of mind that was already evident in Prof. Koh's youth. He explained in his essay "Memories of My Father" that his father instilled in him "a reverence for learning and the good habit of reading."[15] The senior Koh loved to read and the home was replete with magazines and books. He went to the extent of "opening an account"

---

14 Ibid., 23.
15 Ibid., 5.

for his son at what was then the City Book Store for him to get any book he wanted.

Prof. Koh has also described how his father stood up to a thug who was trying to steal a smaller man's bicycle. This, Prof. Koh says, taught him courage, "the courage to stand up to bullies and to defend the weak."[16]

Learning right from wrong, upholding the rule of law and integrity, winning the debate through rigorous argumentation, finding win-win solutions to unlock disputes — these are not easy things to achieve and achieve consistently. These are what make Prof. Koh a progressive leader and explain his special imprint on our society. The essays in this section provide details on how Prof. Koh does this.

Debunking the Co-Optation Theory

Some may ask if this is just too rosy or platitudinous an image of the subject of this book. Prof. Koh is well aware of the realities of politics, diplomacy, of political and social reform. This is reflected in his essay, "Can Any Country Afford a Moral Foreign Policy?" In what can be applied to the international as well as domestic community he says that while we live in an imperfect world, thankfully, it is not a "lawless world".

Prof. Koh recognises that individuals and states do act in their own self-interest. There may be situations, he explains in his essay, that hopefully are rare on the international platform, when national interest or the interest of a broader common good conflicts with "fidelity to law and morality". This can also be the case in the domestic setting — when a policy decision is caught between having to consider the common interest of the broad majority, or two forms of public good that are somehow mutually exclusive.

How would Prof. Koh resolve this? Has he been able to get it right every time? He counts himself as a "pragmatic idealist" and says that if a government were caught in such a dilemma, the politician or diplomat

---

16 Ibid., 7.

should bear the full brunt of a bad conscience and declare the damage done for the sake of a more critical goal, "so that the moral values will survive their violation."[17]

Has Prof. Koh ever had to face such challenging scenarios in his time as a civic leader, a pioneer in the arts and heritage space, a change agent in the green space, as someone who has had to argue against the policy paradigms of the duly-elected government from his own position within the establishment? Has he ever had to uphold the policy stance of the government and government agencies he was associated with, knowing that it will bring disappointment to civic actors on the other side of the fence? How did he feel on the occasions when fellow public intellectuals and academics, artists, activists have had to face the brunt of public castigation from political leaders or state prosecution because of their points of view or actions?

It is a balancing act for the "pragmatic idealist" to stand by his principles and process and yet recognise the authority of state institutions and the duly-elected government leaders.

Day-in, day-out however, perhaps because he recognises the "imperfect world", these have not led him to be cynical or disillusioned but to work hard to foster mutual understanding and trust between the government and civil society. Chua's essay illustrates how he's managed this balancing act, or rather, "confessed" to failing to save a controversial artist from prosecution. Low emphasises how being a liberal, progressive thinker as Prof. Koh can sometimes open one to being thought of as naïve in a what Low calls a "culturally conservative" milieu. What Low probably means is that it is a politically conservative one. Recall the epithet earlier of being a "soft-headed Western-educated liberal". Low explains that Prof. Koh's influence stems not just from his knowledge or the positions he has held in his career but also from his moral authority — being liberal and progressive not only in his views but in his temperament. Prof. Koh Tai Ann, his dear friend, explained once how challenging it can be to argue against the state and its policy positions. Low, a member of the younger set of public intellectuals draws strength as do many from what they see — Prof. Koh acting on the courage of his

---

17 Tommy Koh, "Can Any Country Afford a Moral Foreign Policy?", 1.

convictions. This leads us to the next section, the inspirational way that Prof. Koh has lived and led.

Servant Leader, Team Leader, a Leader of Leaders

One more thing about living the way he started, Prof. Koh also says he learnt important values about service and leadership from the Boy Scout Movement at RI:

> *I learnt it is good to be altruistic, to want to do good deeds for others, especially for those in need of help. I learnt that one must take care of those over whom one exercises authority. I also learnt that one can lead others, not by instilling fear in them, as Machiavelli taught the prince to do, but by inspiring them with one's example and through teamwork.*[18]

All the contributors to this section speak of this inimitable quality that they have found in Prof. Koh as a leader. Dr Francis Seow-Choen's essay testifies to how Prof. Koh gets directly involved in the causes he supports; Dr Clancey shares warmly about how Prof. Koh adds his personal touch to activities at the Tembusu College, and Kwee shares about Prof. Koh's habit of giving of himself to the promotion of philanthropy in Singapore.

Prof. Koh nurtures and trains leaders. Dr Geh provides a personal account of how Prof. Koh is a true mentor. He helps people rise above what they think are their limitations; he opens doors to resources and collaboration, to connections and opportunities for growth. The story of the Very Special Arts group he is associated with, found in Kwee's essay, is further illustration of that.

Conclusion

Without a shadow of a doubt, Prof. Koh has been consistent in both form and substance to his own set of ideals, and has taken responsibility as far as he could to achieve his schoolboy and young adult dreams. He

---

18 Tommy Koh, *The Tommy Koh Reader*, 42.

has not become cynical nor has he lost the faith, but he continues his advocacy for a progressive Singapore as a pragmatic idealist who effects social change, one person at a time, one organisation at a time, and yet with the capacity to impact many public policy areas all at one time. He adopts effective evidence-driven advocacy. There are many smart people inhabiting the centres of authority and influence in Singapore but sometimes you notice that their intellectual faculties and activities are dimmed by cynicism. Not so with Prof. Koh.

Prof. Koh has a sense of fun and wonder, and he often asks the question of "Why not?" when you go to him with an idea for a new project or cause. The glass is always half full or as Dr Geh states in her essay, he would summarily act to fill it. She also adds that he does not just think out of the box because for him there should be no boxes in the first place. That spirit is best captured in the oft-quoted words of Robert Kennedy, an advocate of the civil rights movement who took on the mafia in the US. as well: "There are those that look at things the way they are, and ask why? I dream of things that never were, and ask, 'Why not?'"

The wonderful thing is that Prof. Koh has that sort of ambition for Singapore. His is a pioneering, progressive spirit. He is more than willing to go against the grain to help build a compassionate, moral, vibrant society. Those who are not yet associated with him would probably love to be; and those who already are, just cannot get enough. He is a centripetal force for good, attracting allies where they can be found, to make Singapore and the world a better place. Please do not take this editor's word for it. Read it in the essays that follow.

CHAPTER 24

Against the Tide

DONALD LOW

Power, as my former boss in the Singapore civil service used to tell his staff, is the combination of positional power and knowledge power. Each time he mentions this dictum, I would be reminded of Tommy Koh. Not because Tommy possesses both in abundance, but because of the way in which Tommy has been able to wield moral authority and influence in spite of the fact that he has not always possessed a great deal of positional power. While Tommy has held important positions in public service, his ability to influence the views of decision-makers did not rely on those positions.

Tommy's extraordinary 50-year career in public service spanned a variety of roles, any one of which would have been remarkable on its own. Tommy was a distinguished law professor, one of Singapore's most capable diplomats, a beloved patron of the arts, and a widely respected public intellectual and think-tank chief. All these gave him considerable knowledge power that he could apply to the wide range of issues or problems facing Singapore.

His moral authority is also based on the huge respect that peers, colleagues and collaborators — even those who disagree with him — have for Tommy. This respect is not just a function of his positional or even knowledge power. Instead, it has more to do with his personality and temperament. Tommy is always considerate and respectful of others, regardless of their rank or station in life, and regardless of whether they agree with him. Tommy is not just a liberal in the substantive sense (in that he values liberty and equality), but he is also a liberal by temperament (in that he is always tolerant and open-minded). This is reflected in the incredibly diverse interpersonal relationships that he has cultivated, and the admiration and affection that everyone who has worked with or for Tommy has for him.

In my areas of research and advocacy — on inequality, social policy reform, and democracy and governance in Singapore — Tommy has been a vocal and consistent champion of liberal ideals. Working on these areas in Singapore can be a lonely endeavour. Not only is one sometimes castigated and marginalised by the (mostly) conservative elite, but he or she also risks offending the powers that be with a less than perfectly substantiated argument, or a less than respectful tone.

It is also not uncommon for the ruling elites here to label liberals and progressives in Singapore as "extreme", "unbalanced", "lacking in realism", "populist", "champagne socialist", and much more. What is seldom acknowledged is that those who espouse liberal ideals and progressive causes in Singapore are doing so in a social milieu that is culturally conservative, that is quite agnostic about inequality, and that views the liberal ideals of equality and freedom as impractical in Singapore given our vulnerabilities and constraints. They are therefore, often, swimming against the tide of popular opinion in Singapore.

Questioning Received Wisdom

That one of the roles of liberals in Singapore is to question long-held received wisdoms was perhaps best exemplified in the opinion essay that Tommy wrote for *The Straits Times* on May 19, 2012, titled "What Singapore Can Learn from Europe". To understand why this article is worth highlighting, one also needs to understand its context.

Europe, in the minds of many in the Singapore establishment, represents a complacent, self-indulgent continent that is headed for irrelevance. To the extent that Singapore has anything to learn from Europe, it is mainly to avoid the mistakes that most western European countries have committed — minimum wage, pay-as-you-go pension systems that become unsustainable as populations age, bloated welfare states, myopia and the inability of their political systems to take the long view. The Eurozone crisis, the continent's inability to integrate its immigrants and ethnic minorities, and the rise of populist far right parties in recent years have all lent credence to the widely-held view in Singapore that Europe is in terminal decline.

In "What Singapore Can Learn from Europe", Tommy presents a few surprising facts about Singapore and four northern European countries that are as, if not more, prosperous than Singapore:

	Per capita income (2010) in S$	Inequality, Gini coefficient (2010)	Average monthly wage of a cleaner	Average monthly wage of a bus driver	Total fertility rate (2010)
Singapore	59,813	0.46	800	1,800	1.2
Denmark	69,249	0.27	5,502	6,193	1.87
Finland	54,584	0.25	2,085	3,910	1.87
Norway	105,096	0.24	5,470	6,260	1.95
Sweden	60,613	0.24	3,667	4,480	1.98

In unsentimental and unvarnished prose, Tommy makes the following observations:

First, Singapore's per capita income is roughly similar to those of Denmark, Finland and Sweden.

Second, the four Nordic countries are much more equitable than Singapore. This is reflected in their Gini coefficients as well as the average monthly wages earned by the cleaner and the bus driver.

Third, some Nordic countries have a minimum wage and some, such as Denmark, do not. The minimum wage is, therefore, a means but not the only means to ensure that workers earn a living wage.

Fourth, the argument that the only way to raise the wages of low-wage workers is through productivity increase is not persuasive. I would like to know, for example, how the two women who clean my office can be more productive than they already are in order to deserve higher wages? I would like to know how the Singapore bus driver can be more productive so that his income will approximate those of his Nordic counterparts?[1]

---

1 Tommy Koh, *The Tommy Koh Reader: Favourite Essays and Lectures* (Singapore: World Scientific, 2013), 166–172.

On Tommy's last point in particular — how the Singapore government often points out that wages should rise only when they are justified by productivity improvements — it is worth highlighting that for much of the last decade (2000–2010), wage increases have in fact *lagged behind* productivity growth (see Chart 1). While labour productivity rose by about 20% between 2000 and 2010, real median wages rose by just over 10%. Although there were a few years in which real median income growth exceeded productivity growth, this reflects the fact that wages tend to be sticky while productivity growth can be quite volatile (especially during periods of economic contraction when output drops significantly but the median income does not fall by as much).

It is also not uncommon to hear that the problem of low-wage stagnation is due to low productivity: low-wage workers are paid poorly because they lack technical skills and, consequently, are not productive. This view ignores the wage-depressive effects of lax immigration and foreign labour policies.

That a loose immigration policy can depress the wages in the host economy is not an illiberal perspective; it is basic economics. It is also

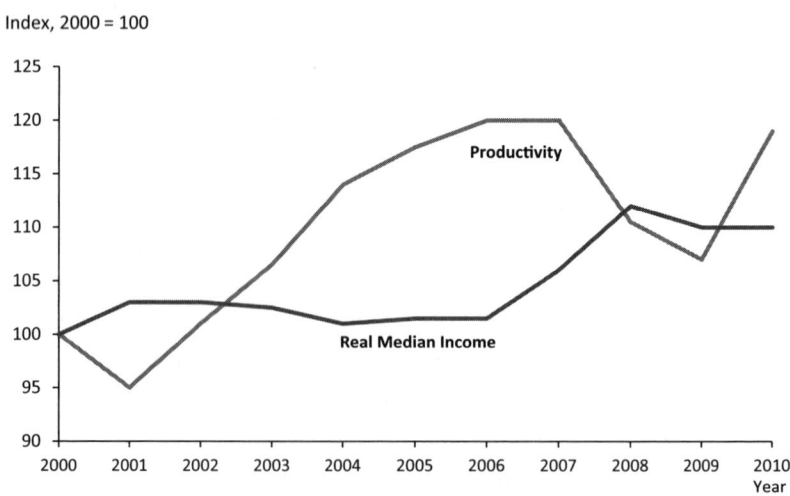

Chart 1:   Real labour productivity and real median wage growth, 2000–2010
Source: "Feature Article on Productivity and Wage Growth in Singapore," *Annual Economic Survey 2011* (Singapore: MTI, 2012), retrieved from https://www.mti.gov.sg.

supported by the simple observation that a bus driver in Sweden earns roughly 20 times what his Indian counterpart earns despite the fact that the Indian driver is just as, if not more, skilled. Neither is it the case that the bus driver in Sweden has much more capital or labour-saving technologies at his disposal. His superior earning power is due largely to the fact that the *supply* of bus drivers in Sweden is more constrained than it is in India.

Reflections on Inequality in Singapore

In Singapore's context, not only have loose foreign labour policies for much of the 2000s kept a lid on upward wage pressures at the bottom end, but they may also have contributed to a culture that views menial jobs as undesirable. The country's growing inequality of incomes may have mutated into an inequality of people's status. Certain jobs are perceived as low status ones that offer few prospects of advancement for the workers holding them.

Second, low-wage stagnation and society's perceptions of certain jobs as undesirable are not just the result of loose foreign labour policies. Social norms are also an important factor driving the increase in wage differentials. In the United States (US) for instance, we have witnessed over the last three decades, a rapid erosion of the unspoken norm that executive pay in a company should be no more than a few times higher than that of rank-and-file workers. This has been particularly so in the financial services industry, where the culture and compensation practices of traders have become increasingly dominant. The erosion of norms that kept wage differentials within a relatively narrow band previously, has led to skyrocketing compensation for top executives, even as the wages of median and low-income workers have stagnated. All this was occurring even though productivity growth was relatively high. The US experience again suggests that there is no necessary relationship between productivity and wage growth.

Third, ours is a society that is increasingly characterised by large power distances — or the expectation and acceptance of large power and income differentials between those at the top and those at the bottom. This, I contend, is what is most corrosive about inequality — it leads to a hardening of status and income differentials, which in the long run concentrates wealth and privilege, entrenches class identities and social hierarchies, and reduces social mobility.

Contrary to what many policymakers assume, a more equal distribution of incomes *promotes* opportunity and social mobility. One can think of income distribution as a giant ladder where the different income levels are the rungs, and social mobility as the ease with which people move up and down the ladder. When income inequality is high, the rungs are spaced far apart and it is much harder for people to climb the income ladder. This has also been the experience internationally: more equal societies like the Nordic countries enjoy significantly higher levels of intergenerational mobility than less equal ones like the US and the United Kingdom.

Accepting the diagnosis that rising inequality and low-wage stagnation are at least partly the result of domestic policies, power differentials and social norms may lead us to quite a different set of policy prescriptions from what the government has pursued so far. As Tommy has argued, it is more fundamentally a question of the kind of society we want to be. Do we want to be a Dubai or a Denmark, a London or a Copenhagen? And we have to choose. It is simply not tenable for Singapore — a city-state — to try to be all things to all people. For Tommy and me, the choice is obvious. But we are also probably in the minority. It is perhaps not surprising that the majority of Singaporeans does not believe that the state should take aggressive steps to reduce inequality, or that it should be concerned about inequality in the first place.

CHAPTER 25

Professor Tommy Koh and the Nature Society (Singapore) (1990–1995)

～⁂～

WEE YEOW CHIN

Introduction

The Malayan Nature Society (Singapore Branch), or MNS(S), was formed in 1954. Its main activity was nature education, such as giving talks and conducting nature walks. Whenever an opportunity arose, members contributed articles on local nature to the local print media, as in *The Straits Times* of August 9, 1982, in the article titled, "More Than a Spot of Nature in the City". Members have also authored books on aspects of local nature[1] and actively participated in producing the Singapore Science Centre's series of booklets[2] on our local flora and fauna.

Environmental Advocacy

Around the second half of 1980s, members found themselves thrust into the role of environmental advocacy.[3] This happened when birdwatcher

---

1 See D. H. Murphy and Kwan Hun, *An Eye on Nature* (Singapore: Maruzen Asia, 1983); and Wee Yeow-Chin, *Common Ferns and Fern-Allies of Singapore* (Singapore: Malayan Nature Society, 1984).
2 See Wee Yeow Chin, *A Guide to the Ferns of Singapore* (Singapore: Singapore Science Centre, 1983); Choo-Toh Get Ten, C. J. Hails, Bernard Harrison, Wee Yeow Chin and Wong Yew Kwan, *A Guide to the Bukit Timah Nature Reserve* (Singapore: Singapore Science Centre, 1985); Clive Briffett, *A Guide to the Common Birds of Singapore* (Singapore: Singapore Science Centre, 1986); and Wee Yeow Chin, *A Guide to the Wayside Trees of Singapore* (Singapore: Singapore Science Centre, 1989).
3 Cherian George, "The Nature of Politics and the Politics of Nature," in *Singapore: The Air-Conditioned Nation*, ed. Cherian George (Singapore: Landmark Books, 2003), 139–143.

Richard Hale, then Chairman of the MNS(S) Conservation Committee, stumbled upon a patch of degraded mangroves teeming with migratory birds. A conservation proposal[4] was prepared and, working behind the scenes, Richard succeeded in persuading the government to develop the area into a bird sanctuary.[5] This sanctuary was to become the Sungei Buloh Wetland Reserve, the first reserve to be created since Singapore's independence.

Encouraged by this success, a masterplan for the conservation of nature areas in Singapore was quickly compiled.[6] The government subsequently endorsed the document as reported in *The Straits Times* on April 8, 1991, in an article titled, "Back Masterplan by Nature Group, Mattar Tells Authorities"[7].

Enter Professor Tommy Koh as Patron

I have known Professor Tommy Koh since our days as students in Raffles Institution. We even shared a room in the then Dunearn Road Hostel when we were undergraduates at the University of Malaya in Singapore, the predecessor of what is known today as the National University of Singapore.

After graduating, we lost touch with each other until 1990. That was the year Tommy returned to Singapore after a successful tour as the country's Permanent Representative to the United Nations and Ambassador to the United States. In that same year, he was invited to be Patron of the Society, which he accepted.

I had, by then, been Secretary of the Society for more than a decade. When the incumbent chairman, Professor P N Avadhani was due for a sabbatical, the chairmanship was thrust onto me.

Tommy wasted no time in getting involved with the Society's efforts in nature conservation. In *The Straits Times* of April 23, 1991, Tommy's

---

4 See R. E. Hale, R. Subharaj, R. Ngim, Ho Hua Chew, C. Briffett and C. J. Hails, *A Proposal for a Nature Conservation Area at Sungei Buloh* (Singapore: Malayan Nature Society [Singapore Branch], 1987).

5 Y. C. Wee and R. Hale, "The Nature Society (Singapore) and the Struggle to Conserve Singapore's Natural Areas," in *Nature in Singapore* 1 (2008): 41–49.

6 P. N. Avadhani, Wee Yeow Chin, Chou Loke Ming, Clive Briffett, Richard Hale, Ho Hua Chew, Kelvin Lim, Lim Kim Keang and R. Subaraj, *Master Plan for the Conservation of Nature in Singapore* (Singapore: Malayan Nature Society [Singapore Branch], 1990).

7 "Mattar" refers to Dr Ahmad Mattar, who was then Minister for the Environment.

message on Earth Day appeared in the paper's "Talking Point" column, where he stated: "Firstly, I would like the Government to take a serious look at the recommendations of the Malayan Nature Society for conserving Singapore's natural habitats." He had no qualms in openly giving the Society his unstinting support and its policy positions his endorsement, if he truly agreed with them.

The Society's activists were, at the time, somewhat triumphant from their successful advocacy on saving Sungei Buloh. Led by locals who were new to the conservation agenda, they were full of enthusiasm but totally naive. As they lacked government contacts, they took their lobbying efforts directly to the mass media.[8] They also failed to realise that the much-touted masterplan included many areas that were teeming with bird life, which could easily be replicated within a few years. These included grasslands, groves of trees and newly reclaimed areas.

The ensuing media confrontation did not endear the Society to the government, and eventually, most of the areas that members lobbied to conserve ended up being developed.

Subsequently, when there were insinuations that the Society took orders from a foreign government, Tommy suggested that it was best that we made a total break from the parent society, which had been based in Malaysia. We took Tommy's suggestion and in October 1991, the Nature Society (Singapore), or NSS, was formed with myself as its Founding President.

Battle to Save Lower Peirce Forest

The move to cut ties with MNS was timely. Within a year, NSS was to embark on its major confrontation with the government over a proposal to clear a large tract of the Lower Peirce forest for a 36-hole golf course. The forest was over 80 years old and teeming with wildlife. Besides, it was part of the larger Central Catchment Nature Reserve that serves as a water catchment area. Replacing the forest with a golf course would wipe out the wildlife, not to mention, pollute our water supply.

---

8 Y. C. Wee and R. Hale, The Nature Society (Singapore) and the Struggle to Conserve Singapore's Natural Areas, in *Nature in Singapore* 1 (2008): 41–49.

We consulted Tommy who suggested that we prepare a report on the area. The matter was passed on to the Society's Conservation Committee. Probably because the bird population in Lower Peirce was not as visual as those in grasslands and groves of trees, the Committee was not interested. So as President, I took full charge. Subaraj Rajathurai, an experienced birdwatcher, assisted in gathering field data with the help of others. These were compiled into what we called an "Environmental Impact Assessment"[9]. Tommy added a foreword, signing off as Chairman, Preparatory and Main Committees, United Nations Conference on Environment and Development (UNCED). This obviously gave the document added credibility.

The 80-page document was then sent to the political leaders. As no positive response was forthcoming, a signature campaign was organised that resulted in the collection of over 25,000 endorsements by ordinary Singaporeans.[10]

Amidst the media confrontations, two officers from the Internal Security Department (ISD) made a courtesy call on the President at his office in the then Department of Botany, National University of Singapore.[11] The officers were curious to know about NSS's agenda and future plans. The meeting was short and cordial. The visit however triggered a rumour that the President's office had been raided and the signatures, seized. Of course it was only a rumour — the signatures had already been sent to a vault in a bank for safekeeping.

Just before Tommy left for Rio de Janeiro for his duties as the Chairman of the Preparatory and Main Committees of the UNCED, I had an opportunity to meet him and share with him my encounter with the ISD. As is typical of him, he dismissed the visit as inconsequential. So we simply ignored it.

A television programme was also being produced at that time, with a pre-recorded segment with Tommy before he left for Rio. An interview

9   Wee Yeow Chin, *Proposed Golf Course at Lower Peirce Reservoir — An Environmental Impact Assessment* (Singapore: Nature Society [Singapore], 1992)
10 "Forward in Independence, 1991–2014: Action for Nature," *Nature Watch* 22 (2014): 34.
11 Maria Francesch-Huidobro, "Statutory Bodies, Land Use Planning and Conservation in Singapore: *Issues and Challenges for Governability*" in *Public* Organization *Review* 6(3) (2006): 277–288; Maria Francesch-Huidobro, *Governance, Politics and the Environment: A Singapore Study* (Singapore: Institute of Southeast Asian Studies, 2008).

with myself was also recorded at the Lower Peirce site. The programme was trailed on our local television channels for screening, but just before that was to finally happen, the programme was withdrawn, probably due to its controversial nature.[12]

The first hint that the government might hold back on developing the site into a golf course came from *The Straits Times*' report of June 7, 1992, titled "Don't Worry About Reservoir, Dhana Tells Nature Buffs". In it, then National Development Minister S Dhanabalan was reported as saying: "If it shows that great ecological damage will be done, then we will not approve it."

In due course, the government did indeed shelve the plan to build a golf course at Lower Peirce.

Conclusion

NSS's lobby against the golf course at Lower Peirce coincided with the UNCED[13] that Tommy was directly involved in. This obviously played a major role in the government's decision not to proceed with the project. Then there was Singapore's national report to the UNCED Preparatory Committee that specifically stated: "The existing 2,079 hectares of nature reserves will be preserved".[14]

Furthermore, Tommy's unqualified support can be seen in the final statement of his foreword to the NSS's environmental impact assessment:

Singapore has an excellent record of reconciling economic growth with the protection of the environment. Many other countries look up to Singapore as a model to emulate. The building of a golf course on a nature reserve and protected catchment forest would constitute a violation of an ethic which we have always professed to believe in and practise.

This provided another powerful reason why the government would have thought twice about proceeding with the project. This statement

---

12 Francesch-Huidobro, *Governance, Politics and the Environment*.
13 United Nations Conference on Environment and Development, also known as the Rio de Jeneiro Earth Summit of 1992.
14 *Singapore's National Report for the 1992 UN Conference on Environment and Development Preparatory Committee* (Singapore: Inter-Ministry Committee for the UNCED Preparatory Committee, 1991).

was also picked up by *The Straits Times* of October 1, 1992 "Nature Society Suggests Other Sites for Golf Course."

To date, the NSS has only had two major conservation successes. As Francesch-Huidobro put it succinctly, Sungei Buloh was the result of the power of persuasion while Lower Peirce, the result of the power of protestation — one in successfully persuading the government to conserve an area, the other in preventing the clearing of an area for a golf course.[15]

It was indeed fortunate that NSS had Tommy as Patron to guide the Society through this difficult phase of its history.

---

15 Francesch-Huidobro, *Governance, Politics and the Environment.*

CHAPTER 26

Professor Tommy Koh's Green Legacy

~

GEH MIN

Tommy Koh, a Force for Good across Different Sectors

Many years ago, at an Institute of Policy Studies (IPS) conference on civil society, I asked whether civil servants could also be active members of civil society. It was popular then for politicians to speak of the "three Ps", that is, the public, private and people sectors, but there seemed to be a strict segregation between these, with limited interaction across the silos.

As president of a non-government organisation (NGO), I have often attended meetings or panel discussions where almost everyone else was either from the government or the private sector and I seemed to be the token representative from the people sector. Academics, in particular, seemed uncertain of which sector they belonged to. Also, in the period right after the Seattle IMF-World Bank years (think of the Seattle-World Trade Organization riots of 1999), the general feeling seemed to be that membership of civil society was not a badge that was worn with pride — at least not in Singapore.

After some hesitation and evasive replies from the distinguished panellists at that IPS conference in May 1998, Professor Tommy Koh stepped up and declared that of course it was possible. He himself was an academic, a government servant and an active member of civil society and stated that he had never any problems.

This incident represents for me, Tommy Koh to a T. He wears many hats simultaneously with panache and pride, juggles them skilfully, and selects them by his own criteria; not vanity, prestige or fashion.

Amongst the many hats that Tommy Koh wears is that of Patron of the Nature Society (Singapore), or NSS.

As a result of his popularity and wide interests, his patronage is, naturally, much sought after. He is probably patron to more organisations and societies than anyone else in Singapore except, perhaps, the President of the Republic. It may therefore come as a surprise to learn that he is in fact highly selective and turns down more requests to be associated with causes and social organisations than he accepts. Unknown, unrecognised, newly-fledged, struggling or even unpopular causes seem to be his preference; not prestigious or well-known organisations. For example, he has declined positions in many well-known international environmental NGOs despite his interest and reputation in that area globally. He is, in addition to his association with NSS, the Co-Chair of the Advisory Committee of the Asia-Pacific Centre for Environmental Law (APCEL). He has done much to establish and nurture these organisations through challenging times.

Guardian Angel to NSS

Being Patron of NSS is certainly no sinecure. Originally the Southern Branch of the Malayan Nature Society, a name change was thought expedient in 1991 as the organisation had increasingly come to be viewed as a "lobby" group, in addition to being a hobby group (see the chapter by Prof. Wee Yeow Chin on that). That was a result of the instances of its activism around certain proposed government plans that would intensify and escalate urbanisation in the 1980s and lead to the loss of many nature areas.

This transition was not an easy one for the Society and its members, and took the form of a long-drawn out and painful metamorphosis — with Tommy as guardian angel. Authorities and planners seemed to place little or no value on nature areas except as "open" or "spare" land and in the words of sociologist Professor Chua Beng Huat, "no space has been left to chance and even nature has to have the permission of the planning agencies to survive."[1]

---

1 Chua, Beng Huat, *Political Legitimacy and Housing. Stakeholding in Singapore* (London and New York: Routledge, 1997), 50.

Land use on such a small island has always been highly challenging and potentially controversial. While land for housing, transport and industry has always been in demand, it seemed to nature lovers that even golf courses had considerably more protection than biodiversity and nature. Environmental impact assessment (EIAs) for nature areas were not mandatory or performed. Even those areas with legal protection such as nature reserves could be bisected, fragmented or delisted.

At that time, no established channels of communication existed between NSS and the planners except by petition or through the reader feedback Forum Page of *The Straits Times*. This divide was deepened further by the apparently totally different language and values that the public and people sector operated in, at that time.

Consultation of the public, if any, certainly did not include NSS, which was viewed by many policymakers as "troublemakers". The first inkling of destruction of a nature area would be an announcement of a projected development or worse, the actual appearance of the dreaded bulldozers.

NSS members became very adept at spotting and interpreting early warning signs so that an appeal to the relevant government agency could be launched before it was too late. These almost always failed or disappeared into the black box of the state's confidential information.

The lack of meaningful dialogue or even feedback resulted in a division within NSS on the question of what was the best strategy to conserve nature. The moderate members felt that patient and persistent petitioning of the authorities was the only workable solution but many others felt that stronger and more proactive measures such as public petitions were necessary to raise public awareness and put greater pressure on policymakers to take heed of the concerns.

Tommy was always the champion of rational engagement and although rarely interfering with internal affairs in the Society, was always ready to open and re-open channels of communication, both externally and internally, after a clash of opinions. It was largely his moderating influence that held NSS together and prevented us from adopting the more radical measures of say, Greenpeace and other international environmental lobby groups. (Tommy prefers the term "advocacy" to "lobby" groups). It was also his legendary ability to see the glass as being half full rather than half empty that kept our spirits up after difficult engagements or discouraging failures like the loss of another nature area after countless, painstaking hours of data collection by volunteers to strengthen our case. That, especially after we had submitted the 1992 Singapore Green Plan which, though accepted and incorporated into Singapore's Concept Plan, seemed initially to have little impact on actual policy.

Tommy is not a mindless optimist but a meliorist. He believes in making things better by the three Cs of communication, cooperation and collaboration; of not just seeing the glass half full but of working together to fill it up!

Since he himself had achieved much by practising this, he was a convincing role model for us, especially as, despite his outstanding personal achievements, he is essentially a team player who believes in pluralism and the power of the many. His speeches and writing resonate with true empathy and active engagement rather than enforced diplomacy or passive tolerance. He is a persuasive and convincing speaker because he listens attentively to all views before giving his own. How else could he have achieved a diplomatic and legal milestone like getting agreement on the United Nations Convention on the Law of the Sea in 1992?

Many conservationists including those in NSS were uncompromising purists who only valued nature areas according to their authenticity and biodiversity — the more pristine the better — while Singapore policymakers then preferred "man-made" green, such as roadside trees, parks and golf courses. There also seemed to be a predilection for exotics over our natural biodiversity.

It took someone of Tommy's stature and skills to see the value of different points of view and convince both groups to accept that having a diversity of green areas, from the more managed to the more natural, was a viable compromise.

It was only after I became President of NSS in 2000 following a divisive internal conflict that I began to fully appreciate Tommy's commitment to NSS and how seriously he took his role as Patron.

Since I was extremely inexperienced, I also had the privilege of having him as a mentor. In neither of these roles was he prescriptive nor did he micro-manage our activities. He left us very much to our own devices; he let us get ourselves into trouble, but miraculously, he was always there to advise and help extricate us. He managed to combine maximum support with minimum interference. His diplomatic skills were much appreciated both in healing internal rifts and establishing links with policymakers.

Tommy worked particularly hard in giving us respectability and credibility outside the conservation community. Of course, his patronage was already an instant door-opener but he exposed us to areas outside our comfort zone whenever he could so as to help us open our minds, test our convictions, build connections and expand our influence. He was always inundated with requests to speak, write or represent the nature community and in my years as President of NSS, he would pass some of the requests to me. Standing in for someone of his stature was intimidating and humbling but the obvious disappointment of the audience in having me as a substitute to the illustrious and popular Professor Tommy Koh forced me to improve my public speaking and communication skills so as not to discredit him and the Society. In fact, there was no better way to learn those skills than to observe him closely. I would never have had the courage to stand as Nominated Member of Parliament in the year 2005 if it had not been for this invaluable training.

He believes in the importance of developing long-term trust and the ability to see the other side of the argument; to accept a constructive compromise rather than take a confrontational stance. Here again, he teaches by example, not prescription.

For Tommy Koh, it is not so much that he thinks out of the box but that there should not be boxes in the first place. His specialty is in building bridges, not erecting fences or walls.

Nature Conservationist, Extraordinaire

Tommy Koh's immense contribution to nature conservation and the natural environment extends far beyond NSS and Singapore to the whole world through far-sighted agreements and legal frameworks on sustainable development. He has achieved this not only by being a visionary thinker and effective implementer but also by the force of his personality. The stereotypical nature conservationist or "tree-hugger" is often depicted as an anti-establishment, anti-globalisation, over-emotional misanthrope. Clearly, Tommy Koh is none of these. In fact, he is the diametric opposite. How?

First, though passionately committed to nature conservation, his razor-sharp mind and impressive analytical skills have been unques-tionably proven by his diplomatic and legal achievements. He has demonstrated, beyond doubt, that environmental conservation involves both the head and heart.

Second, while "greenies" have often been perceived as social misfits, putting "bugs and slugs before people", this certainly does not apply to Tommy who is so obviously an outstanding "people's person". (His inimitable ability to enter a crowded room on a formal occasion and affably greet everyone as an old friend or, as a public speaker, start by acknowledging not just the very important persons there but half the audience by name with personalised thumbnail sketches thrown in, is awesome.) His hallmark trait is his generosity of spirit, which enables him to see people in the best light though by no means is he unaware of their shortcomings. Indeed, his ability to see the glass half full applies as much to people as it does to situations and challenges.

Third, many environmental conservationists have been accused of "representing a narrow interest group and not seeing the big picture." Tommy Koh shows us that it is possible to do both simultaneously; to be global as well as local; to be an architect of the Earth Charter as well as a champion for the conservation of the locally-endangered banded-leaf monkey. What is more, his vast and diverse network with the ground gives him perspectives and insights unknown to those with only a "heli-copter view".

These qualities have been tremendously valuable in promoting the cause and credibility of conservation and sustainable development movements both locally and globally.

Singapore's clean and green Garden City owes its existence to our visionary first Prime Minister, Mr Lee Kuan Yew but Tommy Koh has also made a valuable contribution to the greening of Singapore. Mr Lee saw Singapore's greening in largely socio-economic terms, as a stepping stone from "third to first world" and his approach was top-down and pragmatic with an emphasis on well-maintained parks, orderly road-side trees and manicured golf courses. He developed a Singapore model that is admired and emulated globally. Tommy Koh started as one of the international architects and implementers of sustainable development and environmental conservation. He promoted and supported these principles locally, in partnership with like-minded individuals and organisations.

That two men of such different personalities, styles of engagement, worldviews and methods of policy implementation have successfully evolved contrasting but compatible and even, ultimately, converging visions of Singapore's greening is our nation's great, good fortune.

CHAPTER 27

The Art of Making Institutions

ARUN MAHIZHNAN

There are those who are made by institutions and there are those who make the institutions. Professor Tommy Koh belongs to the latter tribe. One of the institutions he made is the Institute of Policy Studies (IPS). This is a short version of Koh's contribution to IPS. The full version would require a book.

When IPS was set up in 1988[1] as a "think-tank", that term was hardly known among Singaporeans. Singapore universities have had a number of research centres but they were academic in nature and theoretical in perspective. None had the tone, timbre and texture of a think-tank. I have often thought of the think-tank as the crucible where government policies forged in the heat of practical implementation are subjected to cold analytical rigour. There, policies are constructed, deconstructed or reconstructed with the aim of making them better — more sensible, more sensitive, more impactful. It is also a site where policymakers and policy beneficiaries come face to face for the purpose of dialogue and exchange. However, in the 1980s, it was not something Singaporeans were accustomed to.

Singapore had been ruled by the Lee Kuan Yew government since 1959, and rightly or wrongly, it had acquired a reputation for "knowing it all" — some would say that was indeed so and others would argue that was what the government made it out to be. Insiders knew then and it has lately been revealed to the public that Lee did indeed consult

---

1 It was officially incorporated as a public company limited by guarantee on December 29, 1987, with the status of an Institution of Public Character.

widely but discreetly and astutely. Be that as it may, few will deny that the Lee Kuan Yew government did what it did with minimum public scrutiny.

New Era, New Forum

Then came Goh Chok Tong as the successor prime minister in 1990, who was not and did not intend to be Lee Kuan Yew. Declaring Lee's shoes to be too big for him or, for that matter, anyone else, he preferred to "wear my own, and choose my own stride. I intend to be myself, and set my own style."[2] Later he defined what that style was: "I opted for a more consultative and participatory style of governance."[3]

His new style of governance found expression in a number of ways. One was the birth of IPS, which was actually conceived of and delivered in 1988, when he was still Deputy Prime Minister, waiting in the wings to be made prime minister.

At the opening of the Hon Sui Sen Memorial Library at the National University of Singapore (NUS), where IPS had its first home, Goh made public his intention to set up the think-tank and explained the rationale in the following way:

The Institute will have two major roles. Apart from imparting to the younger Singaporeans in public administration and managerial positions in the private sector, a good knowledge of Singapore's history, it will also provide a forum to stimulate lively discussions on Singapore's future. Younger Singaporeans want to play a role in shaping Singapore's destiny. This is healthy. We should encourage it. There is at present no regular forum for them to go to if they want to contribute their ideas, or to express their dissenting views. The Institute will provide a regular forum for them. They can brainstorm their ideas freely, frankly and without fear. It is a place where they can disagree agreeably. *The Institute will also undertake research studies.*[4]

---

2 Goh Chok Tong, "Speech for the Swearing-In Ceremony of the Prime Minister," Singapore, November 28, 1990.
3 Goh Chok Tong, "Keynote Address at the Wharton Global Alumni Forum," Singapore, May 27, 2005.
4 Goh Chok Tong, "Speech at the Official Opening of the Hon Sui Sen Memorial Library at the National University of Singapore," January 15, 1988; emphasis added.

The emphasis in the quote is added by me and I shall come to the reason soon. Before that, some preliminaries: When IPS opened its doors in 1988, its founding director was Professor Chan Heng Chee, an eminent political scientist from the Political Science Department of NUS, on secondment to IPS. She and her able Deputy Director, Associate Professor Jon Quah, also on secondment from the same department at NUS, laid out the first blueprint for IPS activities. These included a number of programmes aimed at informing and educating government and business elites about Singapore's past history, its political developments and the government's policymaking processes.

As luck would have it, within a year of IPS' founding, Chan was dispatched to the United Nations (UN) as Singapore's Permanent Representative. Quah took over as Acting Director but he too left a year later. Thus, in July 1990, just about 18 months after its inception, a new era began in IPS with the appointment of Tommy Koh as Director.

Koh was already an iconic figure in the firmament of the Singapore elite. As a student in the 1950s at the then University of Malaya in Singapore, he was an outspoken member of the Socialist Club, notorious for student political activism. He graduated top of his class in the law school with a First Class Honours, which no one obtained for another decade. He took a faculty position at the same school, spoke and wrote on several sensitive issues with extraordinary courage and independence, before becoming the Dean of the Law Faculty. Given his intellectual heft and a natural flair for diplomatic footwork, he was sent off to New York in 1968 as Singapore's Permanent Representative to the UN (the same post that Chan subsequently took). Some whispered at that time that this was a ploy "to get rid of a politically troublesome fellow" but no one could confirm it. In any case, Koh remained in the US for about 20 years in various diplomatic capacities and made waves both in the international arena and at home as a super-diplomat and an independent-minded Singaporean of great integrity. When he returned home in 1990, Goh, just about to be made prime minister in a few months, asked him to be Director of IPS. Goh knew what he was getting.

New Director, New Vision

Koh has always been a builder, not a destroyer — not even a creative destroyer as Schumpeter would have wished. So he strengthened the foundation laid by Chan and Quah, and expanded the scope and reach of IPS beyond what anyone had expected at that time. One of the earliest and smartest things he did was to bring in another star performer — Dr Lee Tsao Yuan — as Deputy Director. Lee, no relation to Lee Kuan Yew, was a President's Scholar with a PhD from Harvard. At that time, she was a Senior Lecturer in the Economics and Statistics Department of NUS. Unlike some leaders who feel that a fellow luminary would diminish their candescence, Koh relished having bright people around him. However, within a year of doing the smartest thing, Koh did the dumbest thing — he hired me in 1991. At least that was how it appeared to some as I had neither a PhD nor had I been a President's Scholar. Be that as it may, both Lee and I worked with Koh over many years as his deputies or surrogates, and helped him build IPS. Unmistakably, Koh was the master-builder. The image of IPS from 1990 to 2008, when it was merged with NUS, was that it was a Tommy Koh institution. It might as well have been called the Tommy Koh Institute of Policy Studies.

Let me share a few vignettes from the vantage point of a ringside seat as the Institute's former Deputy Director and Acting Director, why IPS was very much a Tommy Koh institution.

Even though Goh had declared his style as being consultative, the public wanted proof of it. The intelligentsia was watching IPS closely to see the manifestation of the forum where Singaporeans "can brainstorm their ideas freely, frankly and without fear." The emphasis I had added earlier to the Goh quote was to mark the operative words. Was IPS truly a place where free, frank and fearless discussions took place? That was the question on the minds of many. Indeed, it was on my own mind before I joined IPS. Let me cite one example that would help answer that all-important question.

Under Chan and Quah, IPS had already started a series called "Closed-Door Discussions (CDDs)". This series was open only to invited discussants and closed to the media and the public, hence its name. Such meetings were held under what is known as the Chatham House Rule, which means that reports of the discussions would be made without attribution to speakers' names or affiliations. The CDD was deliberately designed to sedate the pervasive fear of being on the wrong side of the government, which would deter people from sharing their frank views in policy discussions. More than any other activity that IPS engaged in at that time, the CDD was the canary in the mine — if the participants could breathe easy and share their views without looking over the shoulder, it would be a strong signal that Goh's hope of a free, frank, and fearless exchange of ideas would find a home in IPS, and IPS itself would survive government displeasure.

When I joined IPS in 1991, I experienced, at close range, the dynamics of CDDs. As IPS staff, I sat through most of them and came across many movers and shakers whom I had worked or interacted with in one capacity or another in my previous incarnations as a member of the civil service, private sector or media. I had known how guarded many were about their views on sensitive issues. In the early days of my tenure at IPS, I saw that the CDDs were nowhere as free, frank or fearless as I had hoped they would be. However, over time, I saw the thawing of the fear, the reserve, the reticence; never completely, but nevertheless noticeably. While there were other reasons, I believe the single most important reason for the change was the presence of Koh at IPS. Koh had a unique way of reassuring the participants that they were in a safe harbour and at liberty to express their views frankly and without fear of retribution, but in a *collegial* fashion. He emphasised that everyone was welcome to be critical, but was equally expected to be collegial. He often said the government needed critics but loving critics. He certainly was one himself. Though everyone knew him as a "government man" and that his top- and bottom-lines were to serve the government loyally, he was also seen as an *independent* Director or Chairman of IPS. Such was the aura he had acquired in the public mind. More than the Chatham House Rule, it was the Tommy Koh rule that made the CDDs valuable and meaningful to the participants, to IPS and, at the end of the day, to the government.

Beyond the CDDs, the way IPS conducted most of its programmes under Koh gave substance to the idea of the "think-tank" — where policies were analysed, where bridges were built among the various stakeholders of a policy area, and where the essence of research and analysis would be communicated to a wider audience to improve the quality of policymaking. Those roles of analysis, bridge-building and communication were collectively called the "ABC of IPS". Koh placed his imprint on each of these roles.

In 2001, when Singapore was facing dire economic prospects, the government appointed the Economic Review Committee (ERC) under then Deputy Prime Minister Lee Hsien Loong "to fundamentally review our development strategy and formulate a blueprint to restructure the economy."[5] This was a blue-ribbon committee comprising the best and the brightest who were tasked to look into and solve our problems. Under normal circumstances, no one would have ventured to set up an alternative committee. Koh did. He approached Lee and suggested that "this was an exceptionally important occasion for collective and collaborative contribution to national policymaking and add to ERC's own efforts,"[6] and IPS as a public policy think-tank could make such a contribution. Lee readily agreed. That in itself was a signal of his trust in Koh. A year later, when Koh presented the IPS Forum on Economic Restructuring (IFER) report with numerous alternative ideas and recommendations different from what his own ERC came up with, Lee not only listened patiently to the presentation but most unexpectedly, allowed Koh to publish the report. All of us involved in the development of the report had merely intended it as a "restricted circulation" document for government eyes only. We did not ever dream that it would be published for all and sundry to see. We were delighted — even if most of our recommendations were not, in the end, accepted. For it demonstrated, once again, that IPS was not a government mouthpiece, set up to justify government thinking and that even when it differed, it could only do so quietly behind closed doors. Lee made it possible but Koh gave him reason to do so.

---

5 Ministry of Information, Communication and the Arts, "Establishment of the Economic Review Committee," press release, December 3, 2001, retrieved from: http://www.nas.gov.sg/archivesonline/speeches/view-html?filename=2001120303.htm.

6 *The IFER Report: Restructuring Singapore Economy* (Singapore: Institute of Policy Studies & Times Academic Press, 2002), 1.

On another occasion, Koh tried to redress a "mistake" IPS had made earlier. As he had said in his preface to the book, *Impressions of the Goh Chok Tong Years in Singapore*:

> *When Singapore's first Prime Minister, Mr Lee Kuan Yew, stepped aside in 1990, the Institute of Policy Studies (IPS) missed an opportunity to publish a book assessing his 35 years as the first Prime Minister of Singapore and the impact of his administration on all aspects of life in Singapore. I was determined not to repeat the same mistake when the second Prime Minister, Mr Goh Chok Tong, passed the baton of leadership to Mr Lee Hsien Loong in 2004. I proposed to my IPS colleague, Arun Mahizhnan, that we co-edit a book assessing the 14 years of the Goh Administration.[7]*

In the event, the book was actually edited by Bridget Welsh, then with Singapore Management University, James Chin, then with Monash University, together with Tan Tarn How and myself from IPS. However, Koh was the guiding spirit throughout the development of the book.

As sometimes happens, despite best intentions, word went around that there were very sensitive articles in the book and that IPS would not only incur the wrath of Goh but attract defamation suits. Some highly placed individuals advised me that I should not proceed with the publication and if I did, I was on my own. Even Koh was cautioned but he was undeterred. He said he had read every chapter of the book and it was good to go. Though Koh had informed Goh of our book project, we were keen to demonstrate that the book was neither seen nor vetted by Goh or his nominees before its publication. This was unthinkable for many, but the unthinkable happened. Neither Goh nor his office vetted or previewed the book. Nor did any of us have to face the dreaded defamation suit. As the person most intimately involved in the production of this book, I believe till this day that the book would not have been published as it is if not for the personal assurance of Koh that it was good to go. To those who demand proof that IPS has indeed "done any

---

7 Bridget Welsh, James Chin, Tan Tarn How and Arun Mahizhnan, *Impressions of the Goh Chok Tong Years in Singapore* (Singapore: Institute of Policy Studies & NUS Press, 2009), xi.

independent stuff," I put forward the IFER Report and the Goh Chok Tong book. Made possible by Koh.

Rooted and Resilient

For those who play a major role in the public sphere in Singapore while at the same time serving within the Government of Singapore, it has never been an easy passage. One has to be sensitive and, at the same time, sensible. One has to have courage and, at the same time, the *nous* to compromise. One has to be exceptionally astute and adroit. Although I have never aspired to be one of them, I have always admired them. Koh is one of the few who have survived extraordinarily well in these perilous straits of our public sphere. I think one secret of his success is his ability to retain an inner core of values that remain rooted and resilient. He seems to have a special coating. Which is why I often refer to him as "Tommy Teflon Koh". Fondly.

Chapter 28

Tommy Koh: The Public Intellectual Who Speaks to a Nation's Spirit

―◈―

Chua Mui Hoong

Professor Tommy Koh Thong Bee wears many hats, has many interests and is a friend to many people across all social strata, professions and who live all around the globe.

In Singapore, he is known as the diplomat who served with distinction in New York as Singapore's Permanent Representative to the United Nations, and in Washington D.C. as the country's Ambassador to the United States.

He is a pioneer in many areas. He became the University of Singapore's Dean of the Law Faculty in 1971; the first Executive Director of the Asia-Europe Foundation (ASEF) from 1997 to 2000; the first Chairman of the National Arts Council from 1991 to 1996; and a member of the steering committee that conceptualised and oversaw the building of the Esplanade theatres. He was also Director of the think-tank, the Institute of Policy Studies.

He has a world-wide network of friends, as a cursory look at his Facebook page and photos there attest. In just one week in October 2016, as this article was written, the photos he posted included those of the former Ambassador of Denmark, Jørgen Møller, who has authored books on Europe; Professor Leo Tan, Singapore's botanical and scientific titan; and Professor Alan Henrikson whom Prof. Koh introduced in this way: "Alan taught for many years at the Fletcher School of Law and

Diplomacy at Tufts University. I was holding a book he edited entitled *Negotiating World Order* in which I have a chapter."

As for his interests, they are legion. Apart from his intellectual engagements in international law and diplomacy for which he is best known globally, his interests range from culture; to mental health; natural history and the environment; and a topic close to Singaporeans' heart, food — especially local street food, also known as "hawker food". He has been a judge on the Hawker Masters series — a contest organised by Singapore Press Holdings (SPH) newspapers to recognise the best hawker chefs — since its inception six years ago. Indeed, he was credited by SPH Chief Executive Officer, Alan Chan, as being the man who suggested having such Hawker Masters awards in the first place.

These days, despite his many hats, interests and accomplishments, most Singaporeans know him best for his regular commentaries in Singapore's most read English-language daily paper, *The Straits Times*. He writes monthly in the paper's Opinion, or op-ed pages.

In a way, writing to reach a mass public audience is a natural evolution for this former lawyer, diplomat and public figure. He has a keen intellect, a lively interest in issues social, political and cultural, and a certain activist's zeal to try to change things, or do things he believes are meaningful. And so he channels his considerable negotiating, writing and network-building skills into a role that is best described as that of a "public intellectual".

A Special "By Invitation Only" Public Intellectual

Prof. Koh is not a public intellectual in the mould of Noam Chomsky, who thinks that not only must an intellectual speak truth to power and expose lies; he or she should also not do so in the service of the state. For Chomsky and Edward Said, and others of a similar mind, the public intellectual is often a person defined by his or her opposition to the establishment or the state.

Tommy Koh is a public intellectual in a more modern sense of a person who speaks (or writes) to the public and for the public, on issues of public interest. His views carry weight because of his experience and who he is; and they matter because they touch on issues of public, political, and sometimes even spiritual significance. Despite his association with the government as a diplomat, Prof. Koh is energetic in his advocacy.

In the typology suggested by Massachusetts Institute of Technology professor Alan Lightman, a physicist who became an essayist and writer, there is a hierarchy of public intellectuals: Level I public intellectuals are experts who speak within their domain areas, like a cancer doctor who writes about cancer for a larger audience. Level II are experts who apply their domain knowledge within the larger social context of his or her field, like, say, a cancer doctor who writes on care-giving issues, or the public healthcare system. Then there are the Level III public intellectuals whom Prof. Lightman describes as "by invitation only".

> *The intellectual has become elevated to a symbol, a person that stands for something far larger than the discipline from which he or she originated. A Level III intellectual is asked to write and speak about a large range of public issues, not necessarily directly connected to their original field of expertise at all.*
>
> *After he became famous in 1919, Einstein was asked to give public addresses on religion, education, ethics, philosophy, and world politics. Einstein had become a symbol of gentle rationality and human nobility. Gloria Steinem has become a symbol of modern feminist thought. Lester Thurow has become a symbol of the global economy. Some other contemporary people I would place in this Level III category include: Noam Chomsky, Carl Sagan, E.O. Wilson, Steven Jay Gould, Susan Sontag, John Updike, Edward Said, Henry Louis Gates, Camille Paglia.[1]*

By that rubric, Prof. Koh is clearly a "by invitation" public intellectual in Singapore — and not only because he is on the panel of writers for *The Straits Times'* flagship column named, fortuitously, "By Invitation".

He has become a public figure that Singaporeans and people in the region look up to for his views on issues that go far beyond international law that is the realm of his professional discipline. This is as much due

---

1 Alan Lightman, "The Role of the Public Intellectual," (paper presented at the MIT Communications Forum, Cambridge, Massachusetts, December 2, 1999).

to the broad gauge of his intellect and his personality, as to the strength of his moral convictions.

For example, he has a natural penchant for negotiating, having won the Harvard University's Great Negotiator Award in 2014. As a peacemaker, he has the mediator's ability to get opposing sides to see, if not always to accept, the other's point of view, and to pursue common objectives amidst dissent. This tendency to find common ground amidst cacophony is manifested in his many essays on foreign policy and international relations, when he exercises his influence as a public intellectual with regional and global reach, for the sake of smoother international relations.

In fact, Prof. Koh has even entered into an intellectual defence of America several times: in 1994, amidst the rancorous Asian Values debate, he wrote, "There is plenty that's right with America" on September 10, 1994 in *The Straits Times*. When the American declinist school of thought was gaining traction, Prof. Koh weighed in with an essay about why America will still be No. 1 in 2039, published on October 7, 2009 in *The Straits Times*.

When much was said about President Barack Obama being a lame duck president, his foreign policy torn to shreds, Prof. Koh offered an essay in President Obama's defence:

> *A few years ago, the world's media and commentators adored United States President Barack Obama. They made him appear as if he could walk on water. The pendulum has, however, swung to the other extreme. The narrative today is that he is a weak and ineffective leader. In the past, Mr Obama could do no wrong. Today, it sometimes seems, he can do no right. I wish to restore some balance and objectivity to the evaluation of President Obama's foreign policy....*
>
> *President Obama has strengthened America's relations with its allies without creating an anti-China coalition. He has also improved America's relations with non-allies. He has played a positive role in the ASEAN Regional Forum and the East Asia Summit. He is energetically pushing the Trans-Pacific Partnership negotiations forward. President Obama has been good for East Asia.*[2]

---

2 Tommy Koh, "In Defence of Obama's Foreign Policy," *The Straits Times*, May 15, 2014.

He did likewise for United Nations Secretary-General Ban Ki-moon in the essay for *The Straits Times*, "The Misunderstood Asian Who Helms the UN" on August 27, 2016, highlighting Ban's contributions to facilitating peace in Gaza after 2008 and to addressing the issue of global warming.

As a natural mediator, he tries to get countries with a history of suspicion to view each other with amity. After a visit to Japan, a troubled Prof. Koh wrote an article, headlined "China and Japan: Frenemies?" Published on April 10, 2013, he urged Chinese and Japanese leaders to look back to the 1978 peace and friendship pact to heal their fraught ties.

He has argued eloquently the view that not only can rising China and India accommodate each other, but they can rekindle a sense of brotherhood, in the article published on June 15, 2013, titled "China and India: Hindi, Chini Bhai Bhai?"

Mediating Views, Bridging Divides

His is a voice of reason, wielding influence for the common good. In his essays, and in the many conversations he has had with diplomats, the lunches and dinners he organises or is invited to as a guest, and the multiple seminars, forums and meetings he is involved in, Prof. Koh is able to convince and influence people with his clear thinking and transparent, honest candour. His personality, as much as his views, is winsome.

In person, he is modest in demeanour, polite and personable. Over the years that I have known him, listening to him at seminars I covered as a journalist, and observing him at functions, I have seen the way he engages people. He has a real knack for remembering names and faces and understanding, viscerally, the web of connections that bind tiny Singapore together. He has a prodigious memory for events and dates, and a precise, lawyerly grasp of concepts and precepts. He has the gift of being able to distil into one or two simple sentences issues as complex as maritime law or the ins and outs of something like the arbitral tribunal ruling on the Philippines' case against China in the South China Sea in July 2016.

I was the author of a government-commissioned book on SARS in 2003, and saw how he chaired a meeting of senior civil servants convened to oversee the book project, to focus on the key issues and seek agreement on objectives. Not for him the blunderbuss style or the curt dismissals of a chairman who wants to hurry committee members along; instead, he was collegial yet efficient, encouraging progress by building consensus while giving space for dissent.

It is all too easy to mistake the mild-looking Professor with his trademark salt and pepper hair, round, black-rimmed glasses and wide smile, to be the kind of Chinese gentleman who might demur but not disagree. Until you actually engage him in conversation, that is.

Always up for an intellectual exchange, he once said that Singaporeans who are Western-educated like him, are game to engage and out-debate any Western critic. This was in the heyday of the debate over Western and Asian values referred to earlier, when he was fingered, alongside George Yeo, Kishore Mahbubani and Chan Heng Chee, as "little Lee Kuan Yews" espousing the latter's pushback against Western triumphalism.

Referring to himself, Mahbubani and Chan during that debate, he said in an interview:

> We are interested in the world of ideas, and we're comfortable with the cut and thrust of debate, because that's the milieu in which we grew up. And so we enjoy this. We're very at home in the West; we've lived there many years. We have no fear of disagreeing with our Western friends and out-debating them.[3]

He is most certainly not averse to rolling up his metaphorical sleeves to jump into the debating arena, even if it is with his peers and in public. For instance, in 2008, he disagreed with views by Barry Desker over the direction of ASEAN integration.

In 2010, he sparked a debate with economists by calling for Singapore to consider introducing a minimum wage to safeguard wages of

---

3 Cherian George, "Prof Tommy Koh: Why I Like to Debate the West," *The Straits Times*, October 15, 1994.

those at the bottom. This was in an article in *The Straits Times*, where he called for a review of existing measures such as Workfare that aim to raise wages for low-skilled workers. If these are not effective, he said:

> We should have a calm and rational discussion about the pros and cons of the minimum wage. Those who oppose the minimum wage have argued that it will increase unemployment, discourage foreign investment and reduce our competitiveness. I have reviewed the situations in Japan, South Korea and Taiwan, which adopted the minimum wage in 1959, 1988 and 1956, respectively. I have found no evidence in those three cases that the minimum wage has caused an increase in unemployment, reduced foreign investment or reduced competitiveness in those economies.[4]

That sparked a series of articles and rebuttals.

Prof. Koh also does not hesitate to take on establishment figures. On March 2, 2011, he wrote an article with the headline, "Disagreeing With Some Hard Truths", stating he disagreed with some of the views of Lee Kuan Yew in the just-published book, *Hard Truths*:

> We owe it to Mr Lee to take his views seriously. They are distilled from the experiences and reflections of an extraordinary man and leader. I agree with many of his hard truths. I agree with his assessment of the United States, of the historical importance of Deng Xiaoping and his deep belief in meritocracy and integrity.
>
> However, we also owe him the responsibility to contest his ideas if we disagree with them. It is in this spirit and with great respect that I wish to comment on the following three points.[5]

He challenged Mr Lee's views against inter-racial marriage, and the contention that Singapore was not ready for a non-Chinese prime minister. He also cited the examples of other small nations like Sweden, Finland and Belgium to refute Mr Lee's assertion that Singapore was too small and lacked the critical mass to produce world-class companies in manufacturing.

---

4 Tommy Koh, "Don't Knock Minimum Wage Yet," *The Straits Times*, November 11, 2010.
5 Tommy Koh, "Disagreeing With Some Hard Truths," *The Straits Times*, March 2, 2011.

In raising these issues, Prof. Koh was articulating the views of many in the intelligentsia at that time. In that sense, he was fulfilling one role of the public intellectual — to speak truth to power on behalf of the people.

Expanding the Bounds, Enriching Society

As a public intellectual, Prof. Koh traverses two worlds: he is both of the state, and outside it; an insider with long years of distinguished service in government and diplomacy; and an outsider who, equally, has "street cred" with the public at large, especially so in the arts and culture community and among nature and heritage lovers.

He has been particularly vocal in the area of the arts and culture. He once wrote:

> As the son of a book-loving father and an art-loving mother, I some-
> times think that I was fated to play a role in our country's cultural devel-
> opment in the past two decades.[6]

He was the founding chairman of the National Arts Council (NAC). In 1992, he chaired the Censorship Review Committee. He oversaw the development of the Esplanade theatres as mentioned earlier, and served on its board from 2000 to 2007. He chaired the National Heritage Board (NHB) from 2002 to 2011.

He has also been a champion for the arts and artistic freedom.

In 1994, controversy erupted when performance artist Josef Ng, during a New Year event organised by arts group 5th passage, stood facing a wall, stripped to his pants exposing his buttocks, and purportedly snipped his pubic hair. *The New Paper* published a report on the performance with the headline "Pub(l)ic Protest", a reference to Ng's protest against the arrest of 12 gay men for soliciting.

The NAC responded by pulling public funding for forum theatre and performance art, and banned Ng, and another artist involved, from public performances. The following month, *The Straits Times* ran an article saying that two founders of The Necessary Stage, which had put

---

6 Tommy Koh, "The Artist, the State and the Market," *The Straits Times*, February 6, 2013.

up forum theatre performances a year earlier, had trained at Marxist workshops.

Prof. Koh was NAC chairman at the time, and met artists to try to resolve the situation. He defended The Necessary Stage, writing in to *The Straits Times* to assert that:

> *TNS has a good track record and is one of the most promising theatre groups in Singapore.... The NAC will continue to support TNS as long as it keeps up its good work.... The only exception is that the NAC will not provide assistance to TNS to stage forum theatre.*[7]

The public statement of support by Prof. Koh as NAC chairman made a difference to TNS founders, one of whom, Alvin Tan, was reported to have spent sleepless nights wondering about the impact of the report alleging Marxist training on the group's future. NAC went on to grant TNS theatre space in the Marine Parade Community Centre under its arts housing programme, showing clearly that TNS was not under a cloud as far as the NAC was concerned.

As Prof. Koh noted on the incident later: "I failed, however, to protect performance artist Josef Ng from the wrath of law enforcement agencies."[8] Ng was charged with committing an obscene act in public, for which he pleaded guilty and was fined S$1,000.

As with making the intellectual case for the minimum wage, Prof. Koh uses the licence given him by his establishment credentials, to bring into the mainstream, a fringe idea, concept, performance, or group.

In so doing, he performs the duty of a public intellectual, in enlarging the scope of what is normal for public discourse and expanding the boundaries of what is permissible in a constrained society like Singapore.

In his writings, he has championed a range of noteworthy issues, such as local hawker food, nature and the environment, mental health issues, older workers, guide dogs for the blind, and the role of artists in the marketplace and society.

---

7 Tommy Koh, Letter to the Forum, *The Straits Times*, February 7, 1994.
8 Tommy Koh, "The Artist, the State and the Market," in *The Tommy Koh Reader: Favourite Essays and Lectures* (Singapore: World Scientific, 2013), 450.

As Singapore's most recognisable — and much loved — public intellectual, he has used his influence to urge Singaporeans to be gracious, to care for the environment, to care about the poor, the needy, the blind and the disadvantaged, and to strive for the non-material in the pursuit of happiness.

The best public intellectuals speak for a nation, and to a nation, to urge its denizens to go further, to strive for more, to go beyond the confines of today. By this yardstick, Prof. Koh does Singapore a service with his constant reminders, written and verbal, about what it means to be Singaporean, what it takes to be a better Singapore, and indeed, what it means to be human.

As he said at the opening of the visual arts museum National Gallery in November 2015:

> *We recognise that man cannot live by rice alone. We also need food to feed our hearts and our souls. To read, to sing, to dance, to love a great story and to be moved by a great work of art is to be human.*

Chapter 29

The Very Model of a Modern Practitioner-Scholar

Simon Chesterman

Tommy Koh epitomises the very best qualities of a practitioner-scholar. Deeply steeped in and committed to education, he was a member of the first cohort of law students at what was then the University of Malaya from 1957 to 1961. The only graduate to be awarded first class honours — an achievement not to be repeated for a decade — he joined the faculty the following year as an assistant lecturer at the renamed University of Singapore. By 1971 he had been awarded tenure and promoted to Dean. Today, he remains a full professor at what is now the National University of Singapore's (NUS) Faculty of Law.

Such a career would do many academics proud, and yet it speaks of only a fraction of Tommy's story. These academic milestones are but one strand of the rich tapestry documented in this volume, charting the many contributions that Tommy has made to his country and to the world. Before and after serving as Dean in the period 1971 to 1974, for example, Tommy was appointed Singapore's Permanent Representative to the United Nations (UN) in New York. He was given leave from the faculty that was extended and then extended again — as he took on roles as a diplomat, a lawyer and a supporter of countless important causes. Though records of the time are patchy, the last classes he taught appear to have been on the administration of criminal law and legal philosophy.

In the present essay, I am tasked with providing an account of Tommy as an educator and I begin with a puzzle: Why would a leading university like NUS keep an absconding professor like him on its books for more than four decades?

Dedication to the Development of the Academic Community

The first and most obvious reason is that Tommy has continued to serve the university — despite being on no-pay leave. As Dean, Tommy was well known for the care he took in mentoring and supporting his colleagues as well as his students. Contemporaries recall, in particular, his efforts to support them as academics but also as people, ranging from inviting them to home-cooked meals and on holidays, to even introducing at least one colleague to his future spouse.

Even while on leave from active employment, Tommy has been a source of counsel and support to NUS, through his stints as chair of the Faculty of Law's Advisory Board (2003–2011) and the Institute of Policy Studies (2004–2009), which became part of NUS in 2008; member of the Governing Board of the Lee Kuan Yew School of Public Policy; Chairman of the Centre for International Law (since 2009); and Rector of Tembusu College (since 2010). This is in addition to the many formal and informal ways he has helped NUS, from launching its Asia-Pacific Centre for Environmental Law in 1996 where he is Co-Chair of its Advisory Committee, to spearheading initiatives like the naming of a Chair at the Law Faculty after founding Dean Lionel A. Sheridan.

On a personal note, I can also attest to his ongoing affection and full-throated support for the faculty he graduated from and then led. Throughout my own tenure in the position he held well before me, his counsel has repeatedly been a source of wisdom and strength.

Commitment to Scholarship

The second reason it is appropriate to continue to regard Tommy as an educator, as well as a diplomat and a lawyer, is that he has repeatedly seized crucial moments of diplomatic or international law practice as opportunities to reflect on and to learn from the issues that are larger than the incident itself.

Many practitioners, upon completion of a big case, are content to pop a bottle of champagne and toast their victory. Tommy prefers to write a book to document what can be learnt from the episode. A good example is the publication of the volume, co-authored with another past Dean of NUS Law, Professor S Jayakumar, on the Pedra Branca dispute with Malaysia.[1] Published just over a year after the decision was handed down by the International Court of Justice, it is a first-hand account of the twists and turns of the dispute, as well as a thoughtful and thought-provoking examination of the possibilities and limitations of third-party dispute resolution more generally.[2]

Tommy has inspired others to ensure that lessons learned in the course of public service can be passed down to future generations also. Singapore diplomacy has been greatly enriched by his encouragement of the nation's diplomats to contribute to a book — *The Little Red Dot: Reflections by Singapore's Diplomats* — that began as a celebration of 40 years of independence but has since been extended into a series.[3]

This commitment to lifelong learning is also reflected in the "fireside chats" that he hosts, again with Prof. Jayakumar, under the auspices of the Centre for International Law. These and other activities are discussed further in Robert Beckman's essay in the present volume.

Public Intellectual

It would not be a book in honour of Tommy if one did not have a third reason for one's position. In this case, the reason it is appropriate that Tommy is known to so much of the world as "Prof. Koh" is that he plays

---

1 S Jayakumar and Tommy Koh, *Pedra Branca: The Road to the World Court* (Singapore: NUS Press, 2009).

2 Tommy repeated the effort in the wake of a successful defence of Singapore's land reclamation works against a challenge by Malaysia before the International Tribunal for the Law of the Sea: Cheong Koon Hean, Tommy Koh, Lionel Yee, *Malaysia & Singapore: The Land Reclamation Case — From Dispute to Settlement* (Singapore: Straits Times Press, 2013).

3 Tommy Koh and Chang Li Lin (eds.), *The Little Red Dot: Reflections by Singapore's Diplomats* (Singapore: World Scientific, 2005); Tommy Koh and Chang Li Lin (eds.), *The Little Red Dot: Reflections by Singapore's Diplomats, Vol. 2* (Singapore: World Scientific, 2009); Tommy Koh, Chang Li Lin and Joanna Koh (eds.), *The Little Red Dot: Reflections by Singapore's Diplomats, Vol. 3.* (Singapore: World Scientific, 2014).

a key role as a public intellectual. As tempers grew heated over the South China Sea in recent years for example, his was a voice of reason in mass media publications like *The Straits Times*. When UN Secretary-General Ban Ki-moon became a convenient whipping boy for Western media unhappy with the deficiencies of the UN, Tommy outlined the important if low-key role that Ban had played in advancing issues such as climate change, sustainable development, and gender equality.

Many of these essays are collected in *The Tommy Koh Reader*. A selection of his favourite essays and lectures, it begins with some of the tributes he has offered to family and friends over the years, before ranging across some of the areas in which he has had an impact: diplomacy, international law, culture and heritage, and the environment. An indication of the breadth of Tommy's output is that this collection of his "favourite" essays itself runs to more than 500 pages.

Speaking to the *Singapore Law Review* in 2012, Tommy described his years at law school as some of the happiest of his life.[4] It is a source of pride and inspiration that he continues to be such an example for our students and faculty through his support for the university, his commitment to lifelong learning, and his unstinting efforts to elevate the tone and the content of public debate on matters of national, regional, and global importance.

---

4 Tommy Koh, "In Conversation," *Singapore Law Review* 30 (2012): 19–22.

CHAPTER 30

Professor Koh as College Rector

—❦—

GREGORY CLANCEY

When the National University of Singapore (NUS) began founding residential colleges in 2010, one of its wisest innovations was to appoint prominent Singaporeans as their Rectors. While full-time academics were to serve as Masters, establishing practices and running things day-to-day, the Rectors would lend their significant reputations to the colleges and help set larger policies and agendas. As the founding Master of Tembusu College at NUS, I have been supremely lucky to serve with a founding Rector whose presence could not have given us more prestige, and whose policy experience could not be more valuable: Professor (Prof.) Tommy Koh.

Prof. Koh once shared that he only ever applied for one job in his life (the first one). He has been continually tapped on the shoulder for others ever since. When NUS called on him yet again in 2010, no one would have begrudged him had he politely turned down the request given his existing raft of responsibilities. I think he agreed to take on the extra job not only out of loyalty to NUS — though that clearly motivates him — but because he genuinely cares about the younger generation of Singaporeans. The College gives Prof. Koh a unique platform on which to share a lifetime of experience and wisdom, and the students here have been intensely responsive to his lessons and his presence. From the time we first met, at a lunch hosted by NUS Provost Tan Eng Chye and Vice Provost (now Yale-NUS President) Tan Tai Yong in 2010, it was clear that Prof. Koh saw rectorship as not just interacting with myself and the college fellows, but meeting and influencing students. It was his role to shape, and he has set the highest possible bar.

The Tembusu Forums

At one of our earliest formal dinners, Prof. Koh told the assembled fellows and students that his goal would be to "bring the world to Tembusu College, and bring Tembusu College to the world." He has more than kept that promise. Perhaps his signature contribution to college life has been the Tembusu Forums, which bring small panels of knowledgable individuals into debate or discussion before our predominantly undergraduate audience. Such events occur often on university campuses, but what makes ours special, and perhaps unique, is the audience and its dynamics. While we do not discourage professors and graduate students from attending, our target audience are students in their first and second years. And Prof. Koh makes it clear that these students are in control of the microphones during the question and answer sessions. As with most of what we do at the College, the purpose is sharpening the intellectual abilities and confidence of our students, as well as giving them insight into issues they might never consider in their regular degree programmes.

With Prof. Koh as both organiser and convenor, the Tembusu Forum has become the College's flagship event series, with 22 sessions (and counting) to its credit so far. It was launched in lively fashion in 2011 with a debate between the Ambassador of Israel and a young visiting American academic over the then current question: "Should the U.N. Recognize Palestine as a State?" Some forums have dealt with geopolitical questions as sharp as the initial one, such as "Will the U.S. Live in Peace with a Rising China?" (yes, the panel concluded), and "Will There be Another Sino-Japanese War" (no, was the consensus). Other times Prof. Koh has used the Forum to spur deeper historical reflection, as when we commemorated Holocaust Memorial Day, or the fall of the Berlin Wall and end of the Cold War. Still other times Prof. Koh assembled panels which provided insightful commentary on diplomatic relations between Singapore and its larger neighbours. Controversial domestic issues have not been ignored such as film censorship, racial harmony, human rights, and subsidising healthcare. Prof. Koh has twice used the Forums to hold debates and mock elections for the American presidency, with actual members of the two major political parties in America acting as surrogates. Some topics have attracted press attention, and panellists' views have often made news in the next day's papers.

Prof. Koh's skill and creativity are very much on display as he presides over these events. A year after the Great East Japan Earthquake, he invited the Japanese ambassador to come and take the podium by himself, under the theme of Japan's year of "trials, tribulations, and triumphs". The "triumph" referred to that year's surprise victory of the Japanese women's football team over its American rival. Prof. Koh arranged for a taped version of the highlights of the game to be played to the audience prior to the Ambassador's speech about his nation's disaster recovery efforts. This gesture struck me as a perfect illustration of Prof. Koh's instincts as a diplomat and as a person.

Dinners at the College

A second way Prof. Koh engages with students is through Rector's Dinners. He periodically invites groups of students with a particular interest to dine with him in the round, and engage in a directed conversation. On each occasion he also invites one or more prominent guests who share an identity or background with the group. Students interested in foreign policy, for example, dined with Prof. Koh and the Thai ambassador, while a group of design students were introduced to a prominent architect, and law students shared a meal with distinguished members of that profession, and so on. These conversations over meals have resulted in the sharing of real-world insights, while also allowing students to practise the all-important art of talking, listening, and eating at the same time.

Prof. Koh also takes a personal interest in our formal dinners, which occur at the beginning and end of each term, often selecting guests according to a particular theme. On one notable occasion he invited the ambassadors or senior diplomats of every country with at least one student at the College — a considerable number. Moreover, he had these guests seated among the students throughout the dining hall rather than seated together at the head table that might usually be the case at formal dinners with high-level visitors. At another dinner, the ASEAN ambassadors were our special guests.

Prof. Koh and Mrs Koh have never missed a dinner in the six years of his rectorship, and the students not only look forward to his addresses on such occasions, but corner him afterwards for "selfies" which invariably show up on their Facebook pages. In the last couple of years Prof. Koh has nearly beaten them at their own game however, being one of the most savvy users of social media in our college community.

Given that Prof. Koh brings so many prominent guests to the College, we even have a special group of students, called the "Tembusu Ambassadors", who act as their hosts or stewards (among many other tasks they perform). The group was founded, and is ably advised, by our student affairs manager Ms Sara Kuek. Applicants go through an interview and selection process to become an Ambassador, and the competition is keen.

Icons

Prof. Koh's patronage of a wide set of activities outside the College also creates opportunities for our students. As an environmental diplomat, he has always taken a deep interest in conservation, biodiversity and the welfare of animals. In 2012, Prof. Koh was the local patron of the Elephant Parade project, which saw dozens of artists, politicians, and other prominent Singaporeans paint elephant statues for a charity auction, where the purpose was to raise funds for the conservation of real elephants in India by then selling the decorated statues. On his initiative, Tembusu students were offered two of the statues to paint, and their sale on the auction block raised over $50,000 for the cause. In a subsequent act of generosity, the Tang family which had successfully bid for one of the elephants, donated it back to the College's young artists. Both elephants are displayed on our grounds to this day, and have become emblems of the College's continuing concern with animal welfare and species conservation.

In the same vein, Prof. Koh arranged for the College to participate in the Green Legacy Hiroshima Project that is affiliated to the United Nations. This is an initiative to disperse, for planting, seeds collected from trees close to "ground zero" in Hiroshima which had somehow survived the atomic bombing of 1945. Working with staff from the Singapore Botanical Gardens, our students painstakingly cultivated a camphor seed into a seedling, which was then planted on the College grounds (within sight of the elephants), and has now grown into a healthy tree. A plaque beside our camphor tree reminds students of the tragedy of war, the need for global peace, and the College's commitment to tree-planting for a sustainable environment — all causes which Prof. Koh has long championed.

The largest and most dramatic gift that has come our way through Prof. Koh's initiative are two pieces of the now-dismantled Berlin Wall. Donated to Singapore by a German collector, they were in turn loaned to NUS by the Ministry of Foreign Affairs as the first objects in our University Town Sculpture Garden which is shared by all the NUS colleges. In conjuction with dedicating the wall fragments in late 2016 — in the presence of the German Ambassador and Minister of Foreign Affairs — Prof. Koh convened a special Tembusu Forum on the Cold War, sharing his own experiences and teaching its relevance to a generation which has only known globalisation.

His Passions Have Become Our Own

Prof. Koh's passions have also found reflection in our classroom curriculum, in student interest groups, and myriad other aspects of college culture. Given his global recognition as a "great negotiator", it is only fitting that Tembusu's negotiation class (and separate master's classes on the same topic) are among our most popular. Our fellows also teach a senior seminar on climate change — which was the first of its kind at a Singapore tertiary institution — inspired by Prof. Koh's diplomatic leadership on that topic. In conjunction with the course, Prof. Koh organised a Tembusu Forum to commemorate the 30th Anniversary of the Earth Summit in Rio, which first put climate change on the global agenda, and which he was instrumental in convening. He organised a second forum last year to discuss the Paris Accords, featuring France's ambassador to Singapore among other speakers.

Prof. Koh's concern with biodiversity and animal conservation has also sunk deeply into our collective consciousness. Students voted in 2011 to name the College's five "houses" after endangered Asian animal species, and each year Prof. Koh passes the Rector's Shield to one house, which leads the others in raising funding and awareness for the plight of our "animal of the year". Some of the funding is used to mount a student expedition to the habitat of that year's species so they might better understand the problems surrounding its continued survival. The more committed students have formed a Tembusu Wildlife Association, and one member of our faculty teaches a summer school at the College on the theme of Animals and the City, which brings students from around the world to study the pressures facing species (and people) in our urbanising but still heavily-forested region.

Commitment and Charisma

Had I the space, I could pen many more pages about Prof. Koh's contributions to the College: his donations of paintings and other artwork, which form the bulk of our collection; his nearly monthly and sometimes weekly gifts of books and magazines to our reading room (many with attached personal notes about their contents, and often delivered in person); his taking the time to organise and personally lead students on field trips to museums; and his establishment of a Rector's Fund to provide bursaries for needy students, which is an oft-expressed concern of his. He seems to be thinking about the College all the time, looking out for us, and bringing us ideas and artifacts from wherever else he's been.

I could also write about the personal interest he takes in all members of the college staff. He works particularly closely with our Director of Programmes, Dr Margaret Tan, whose energy matches his own. Margaret is also an artist, and Prof. Koh's love and patronage of the arts, forms one of their common bonds. Their close cooperation on myriad projects guarantees that art, as much as conservation or diplomacy, looms large as a college theme.

Despite the familiarity which our students develop with Prof. Koh, he is still treated like a rock star whenever he appears among them. I recently had him to a Master's Tea, where he answered student questions for over an hour before retiring to the back of the room for cake and, of course, tea. These moments around the tea table are usually opportunities for even more questions by the students, but on this occasion, it was all about getting one's picture taken with Prof. Koh. His charisma has to do with his reputation, surely, but also with what students recognise as his genuine love for the College, and his gracious and caring attitude towards everyone he encounters, inside and outside our walls.

This essay would not be complete without a few words about Mrs Koh, whom we consider as much a patron of our College as her husband. Siew Aing does us the honour of regularly accompanying him to our events, interacting with students and staff, and taking a genuine interest in our community. She has also invited my family to share many meals with her own family and friends. When Mrs Koh hosts a gathering, it is quite apparent that she's an effective Singaporean diplomat in her own right. Prof. Koh's frequent references to "my wife" in his speeches, which often precede his self-deprecating humour, are illustrative of how very close and supportive of one another they are.

Prof. Koh has often said that, even before he became Rector of the College, the Tembusu was his favourite Singaporean tree. Given his record as an environmental diplomat and UN-designated "Champion of the Earth", the high crown and wide-spreading branches of the Tembusu tree are a fitting symbol for the College he presides over. Prof. Koh's giving nature, cheerful demeanour, and boundless energy exert a strong influence on myself and others here to make the College worthy of the loving attention he extends us.

CHAPTER 31

Professor Tommy Koh: Advocate for People with Special Needs

FRANCIS SEOW-CHOEN

International Lawyer, Eminent Diplomat, and Friend to the Man in Need

Professor Tommy Koh is a man of many talents and seemingly boundless energy.

Here is a man who has devoted his life to, and indeed has made his mark working for the betterment of the entire world! Inevitably, he is best known for his feats and heroics at an international stage; unifying global powers as one of the chief architects of the "Law of the Sea"; securing trade deals and raising Singapore's profile as an astute diplomat; and representing Singapore on a world stage as our Ambassador-at-Large. Not many can boast of peace at sea as one's legacy.

Lesser mortals enjoying such rarefied heights of professional success will almost certainly lack the motivation, time or energy to champion community projects of little or minimal profile.

Not so Professor Koh.

Indeed Tommy spends an inordinate amount of his life on projects and people that may not seem at all to be worth his while, at least to people who may not be so enlightened.

Tommy is not a businessman seeking the financially profitable. Neither is Tommy a politician seeking the appeal of the masses.

Nevertheless, in the course of an illustrious career marked by innumerable awards and honours, Tommy has consistently reached out to his fellow man — especially the people who might otherwise seem to be at the bottom rung of society — the suffering, the vulnerable, the uncared for. The ones that most of us know exist but for whom we do little or nothing.

A Worldview Shaped by Love for the Less Fortunate

Tommy is a man who "love[s] the world".[1] Evidently, this philosophy of life has painted not just his professional being but permeates his entire worldview.

A prolific author, Tommy's writings span esoteric and global topics ranging from "continental shelves" and "sovereignty rights" to domestic community issues on the unkind treatment of foreign labourers and maids, the abandonment of the elderly in Singapore[2] and the growing income disparity amongst Singaporeans.[3]

Tommy's championing of global issues while maintaining a strong voice for the local community and the downtrodden reveals a fundamental tenet he often emphasises in conversations with the author:

> We should all be fighting for what is right, while being kind to all, those in authority and subordinates alike.

Tommy has particular concern for those with special needs in our society. He is the patron of three societies for the disabled: the Singapore Association of the Visually Handicapped, the Very Special Arts (Singapore) and the Guide Dogs Association of the Blind, Singapore.

---

1 Tommy Koh, "Three Wishes for the New Year," *The Straits Times*, January 3, 2015.
2 Tommy Koh, "Are Singaporeans a Kind or Unkind People?" *IPSCommons*, November 26, 2012, retrieved from: http://www.ipscommons.sg/are-singaporeans-a-kind-or-unkind-people/
3 Tommy Koh, "Three Wishes for the New Year," *The Straits Times*, January 3, 2015.

Longstanding Support for the Blind

Back in 1988, Tommy who was then Singapore's Ambassador to the United States (US), observed "bureaucratic harassment and public indifference encountered by the disabled in their daily lives."[4]

He cited the story of his friend, Mr Kua Cheng Hock and Mr Kua's guide dog (named Stacy), which had to be sent back to Australia. This was because Stacy was consistently refused access into taxis and buses. Furthermore, the Ministry of Health did not allow Stacy into any of their clinics or hospitals when Mr Kua needed to visit these places. In 2005, Mr Kua approached Tommy regarding the establishment of an organisation dedicated to integrating guide dogs into Singapore.

Tommy quickly developed a plan to muster the support of government ministers, interested Members of Parliament, the relevant government regulators and authorities, as well as the Majlis Ugama Islam Singapura to buy into the idea of having guide dogs in Singapore. Without their support, Tommy said that the idea would not take-off.

With an ambitious plan in place, Tommy put his money where his mouth was; doing all the needed cajoling and soliciting to raise support for the initiative. The Guide Dogs Association of the Blind, Singapore was founded soon after, in 2006, with Tommy as its Founding Patron. Ten years later, Tommy remains as committed as ever, and is still the patron of the Association, leading it from strength to strength.

Tommy has always expressed his desire that Singapore should lead the way as the most disabled-friendly city in Asia. Working alongside other important personalities in Parliament, Tommy advocated for, and eventually succeeded in introducing legislation to permit the use of guide dog teams in all our forms of public transport. This legislative framework is now the bedrock for the Association's work and has proven essential in unlocking the full potential of every disabled person who is assisted by a working dog.

---

4 Cited in Mary Rose Gasmier, "Tommy Koh Calls for New Attitude to Disabled," *The Straits Times*, October 28, 1998, 27.

Not a man to rest on his laurels, Tommy has been at the forefront of advocacy for even greater and much needed protection and care for our disabled so that they are treated as important and equal members of our society.

At a keynote speech in 2012, Tommy voiced his distress at the lack of compulsory education for disabled children, the lack of employment opportunities for the disabled, and the problems of mobility and access for blind persons with guide dogs. Tommy noted that in the US, Australia, Brazil and South Korea, it was a crime to deny a guide dog team access to any public place. It was observed by Tommy that such refusal of access is still not a crime in Singapore.[5]

Regarding the attitude of able-bodied persons towards guide dogs and guide dog teams, Tommy always stood on the side of the less fortunate. For example, Tommy asked, "Is it too much for me to suggest that a sighted and able-bodied commuter should volunteer to offer his seat to the blind commuter?"[6]

Tommy was also concerned about access to eating places and other public places for our guide dog teams.[7] He appealed "to the owners and managers of our office buildings, shopping malls, hotels and food establishments to kindly consider allowing [guide dog teams] access to their premises." Tommy observed, "At the moment, there are still too many places in Singapore that do not allow entry to guide dogs."

His works and words inspire all of us to do more.

Work with the Association

Tommy's affinity for animals and nature coupled with his compassion and love for the disabled is truly something to be admired and emulated. In our 10 years of working together to enable guide dog teams to be successful here in Singapore, Tommy has been nothing short of amazing. It would take a book of its own to list all the boundaries Tommy has pushed to further the interests of the blind people supported by guide dogs in Singapore. Here I list but a few examples:

---

5 Tommy Koh, "Are Singaporeans a Kind or Unkind People?"
6 Tommy Koh, "Opening Eyes to Guide Dogs for the Blind," *The Straits Times*, January 15, 2012, 37.
7 Ibid.

Fundraising

In the early years of the Association's existence, funding was a major challenge. Funds were essential to run the Association and to help the blind work effectively with their guide dogs. Often, we turned to Tommy for counsel and advice. Unfailingly, Tommy raised funds for us from each and every way he could. From small contributions given to him for writing newspaper articles, to soliciting donations from parliamentarians, government ministers, businessmen and even bigger donations from banks and philanthropic foundations. No one was too low or too high for Tommy to approach for assistance.

Tommy earnestly believes that everyone can and should help someone in need, and that with privilege comes a higher duty to serve. In our early years, he connected the Association with HSBC Trust, which gave us access to more than $300,000 worth of funding over three years. Without that funding, we would probably have collapsed before we even started.

Using networks for good

One remarkable thing about Tommy (in a long list of remarkable things) is that he knows and remembers everyone. No one escapes his prodigious memory, while everyone is impressed by his down-to-earth affability and effortless charm.

Whether it was to organise a welcome for a new guide dog team or a fundraising dinner, all we needed to do was to have a chat with Tommy. We would know just the right people to invite thereafter. When we first collaborated with Guide Dogs for the Blind in Oregon in the US and were to sign our memorandum of understanding, Tommy got in touch with the Ambassador of the US here. Her Excellency attended the ceremony and witnessed the signing. When our third guide dog was brought into Singapore, Tommy reached out to Ms Ho Ching, the wife of Prime Minister Lee Hsien Loong to attend the welcome party as our Guest-of-Honour. These esteemed personalities brought much-needed press coverage and publicity for the Association and our work for the blind.

Inter-personal diplomacy

Tommy is an excellent negotiator. He is not just concerned with international diplomacy but also inter-personal diplomacy. On many occasions, I have witnessed how where others get ruffled and angry, Tommy would be composed and unflappable — capable of calming everyone down with just a few words. His deft touch deflates the aggressive behaviour of others and turns these people into friends.

Friend to the Nations, Champion of the People

In conclusion, in the years that I have come to know Tommy at a personal level, my respect and admiration for the man has grown tremendously. His is a top position in this land and indeed he is admired by many from other lands. His work in the international arena has meant that he has been bestowed with countless honours and the gratitude of countries, big and small. However, he is not one to stand on his pedestal high up in an ivory tower. He actively engages in all sorts of social projects to help people in need. His motto is always to show kindness which he deems to be "the greatest of virtues".

Tommy does not stop at doing what he should; rather, he is unselfish in doing all that he can. He believes in the goodness and value of all individuals and he is therefore ever ready to extend his hand of friendship and kindness to everyone. He has served and indeed continues to serve the world, the community of nations, the natural environment, his country, and our community.

We at the Guide Dogs Association of the Blind in Singapore along with many other associations both in and outside Singapore will be forever grateful to His Excellency Professor Tommy Koh.

Chapter 32

Building a Better World:
A Reflection on the Philanthropy
of Professor Tommy Koh

Melissa Kwee

I have always been driven by the wish to build a better world.

— Tommy Koh[1]

I first met Tommy Koh (whom I call "Prof.") when he was the Director at the Institute of Policy Studies (IPS). I was a fresh graduate running leadership programmes in secondary schools for girls. I had a long-standing interest in the area of peace and conflict studies and wanted to meet Singapore's most eminent yet accessible ambassador for advice. I too believed in building a better world, and that it is possible. Though terribly nervous at the time, I was calmed by his gracious and warm presence and soon felt like I was speaking to an old family friend. I was struck by his attentiveness and was surprised that he invited me soon after to a high-level conference linking senior Asian and American policy and social leaders. The Asia Society's Williamsburg Summit in 2003 gathered the who's who of the region and the American policy elite, and I was a young nobody. Prof. Koh's confidence in me — and his belief that a dive into the deep end would not cause me to drown — saved me. Kurt Hahn, the famous German educator and founder of the Outward

---

1 Tommy Koh, Jury Member, The Rolex Enterprise Awards, 2006, http://www.rolexawards.com/profiles/jury/tommy_koh, accessed March 3, 2017.

Bound movement's motto for youth was "*est plus en vous*" — "there is more in you than you think". We all need people who dare to believe in us. Without words, I received this from Prof. Koh and I am deeply grateful for it.

There are three themes I would like to draw upon as I reflect on the breadth of Prof. Koh's philanthropic contribution. Through these, I will elaborate on the characteristics of his service and what we can learn from him. The three themes are: the responsibility of power to serve; being a voice for the voiceless; and the idea of Singapore as our home and gift.

The Responsibility of Power to Serve

Prof. Koh could have ended up being a very different person. Educated in the world's leading academic institutions, appointed by the late Lee Kuan Yew to be Singapore's Permanent Representative to the United Nations (UN) at the age of 30, and the National University of Singapore's (NUS) youngest Dean of the Law School, he could have become an ivory tower bureaucrat with leisurely pursuits and enjoyed a comfortable retirement. Yet, as Stanley Tan, Chairman of Asia Philanthropy Circle shared with me about Prof., "he chose to be a great servant."

It is not every one of privilege and power who extends himself to take up causes and use his network of influence and intellect to solve problems that do not materially affect his own life. Prof. Koh's mentor, the late Deputy Prime Minister, S. Rajaratnam warned all of us that "Singaporeans should not become a people who know the price of everything and the value of nothing."[2] Value, Prof. Koh asserts, is created by developing strong and genuine relationships with family and neighbours, to be a true friend, to love one's country, to preserve personal integrity, to adopt meaningful social causes and serve others.[3]

One of Prof. Koh's most loved causes has been the promotion of the arts and our Southeast Asian heritage. He credits his mother for instilling this love of the arts in him. As the founding Chairman of

---

2 Koh, Tommy, *The Tommy Koh Reader: Favourite Essays and Lectures* (Singapore: World Scientific, 2013), 141.
3 Ibid, 141–142.

the National Arts Council (NAC) from 1991–1996 and the National Heritage Board (NHB) from 2002–2011, Prof. Koh shaped Singapore's cultural scene through these organisations. He did it with the vision that a nation's spirit is embodied in and shared through cultural art forms, and that creativity is at the heart of every nation's success. He has also always believed that businesses have an important role to play as patrons of the arts and can in turn benefit from being part of a more creative society that appreciates beauty and culture in its many forms. Michael Koh, then Chief Executive Officer (CEO) of the NHB, shares:

> *Prof. Koh holds all the credit for starting up philanthropic efforts in the arts and heritage sector whilst serving as Chairman of the NAC and thereafter Chairman of the NHB. He spent tireless efforts encouraging individuals and corporates to give generously behind the scenes. Many of them responded positively and with a smile, all thanks to Prof. Koh's gentle charm and convincing arguments to make the arts and heritage accessible to all.*[4]

During his tenure, Prof. also initiated the first cause-based credit card, the OCBC Arts Card, which is still the card of choice for regular arts patrons.

Responsibility is the consequence of power and influence. With greater power and influence, comes greater responsibility. Prof. Koh has always believed this to be true for wealthy individuals stewarding their gifts and achievements, and for corporations and government stewarding public resources and trust. Prof. Koh was a strong proponent of Emeritus Senior Minister Goh Chok Tong's idea of a "1% Club" where business leaders pledge 1% of the profits of their companies to charitable causes. His service on the board of corporate foundations like APB Foundation and on boards of companies like Singtel and DBS were opportunities for him to share his perspective and conviction about corporate social responsibility (CSR). CSR, Prof. reminds us, is good for the business's brand and the value proposition to employees to join and stay on at the firm; it enhances the morale and reputation

---

4 Michael Koh, email message to author, December 5, 2016.

of the corporate citizen to be recognised as a positive contributor to society in such ways.

Prof. Koh also encouraged corporate philanthropy through the establishment of corporate foundations. He advocated for and currently serves as the Chairman of Singapore's first private sector-sponsored community foundation, SymAsia Foundation, which was established as an umbrella, donor-advised fund to help connect donors to causes and thereby, create deep and lasting social impact. As the founding Chairman of the Board, Prof. Koh is credited by Bernard Fung, Deputy CEO of SymAsia Foundation, for creating the strategy and advising the management and board, by:

> *making wise recommendations based on skillsets, backgrounds and contributions, and drawing on his list of friends and contacts. Under his leadership, SymAsia has received well over S$120 million of dona-tions for national, regional and international causes; and has innovated in the philanthropic management of certain gifts comprising non-cash assets.*[5]

Beyond responsibility, Prof. Koh also confessed a great joy and personal satisfaction from philanthropic giving. In an article "How to be Happy," he enumerated 10 rules to help Singaporeans lead happier lives. Rule seven was:

> *Volunteer and support philanthropy … whether we are rich or poor, we should contribute to a cause of causes, close to our heart…. A wise man once said, "No man can be truly happy if he lives only for himself."*[6]

A Voice for the Voiceless

Prof. Koh's other passion that underpins a great deal of his service is a conviction to represent the under-represented and to be a voice for the voiceless. That is indeed what he has done for foreign domestic helpers, refugees, trafficking victims, persons with disabilities and children from

---

5 Bernard Fung, email message to author, December 5, 2016.
6 Tommy Koh, "How to be Happy," *The Straits Times*, December 29, 2012.

poor families. He has advocated for their rights and dignity, and sought to create opportunities for them to be counted and empowered. Prof. Koh has written publicly about the issues, the challenges and the needs. He has raised funds and volunteered for causes, served as patron, chairman, trustee and grantmaker for corporate foundations and private trusts.[7] In many cases, he stood for emergent or pioneering causes, or those without the initial endorsement of the great and the good. Prof. Koh is a giraffe; he sticks his neck out.

Prof. Koh possesses a rare gift of speaking plainly about difficult issues with anyone, including the guilty parties, without giving offence. It has enabled him to speak plainly about social justice despite the unpopularity of the topic. His winsome and genuine personal attention to the issues, and indeed, to the individual lives concerned, reflects an authenticity that goes beyond advocacy for the sake of making a point. Whether a family in vulnerable circumstances, or a disabled artist, Prof. Koh shows personal interest. When persons with disabilities were shunned and little public discourse or advocacy existed, Prof. Koh founded Very Special Arts to create and provide access and opportunities for people with disabilities through the arts. "Without the vision and generous intention of Professor Tommy Koh, VSA Singapore would not be here today," shares Maureen Goh, the Executive Director of VSA Singapore.[8] "For such a distinguished and well-known person in the government and the arts community, Professor Tommy Koh is ever so humble. He always showed concern for my progress as an artist and my personal health…. Professor Koh is such a generous and gracious man," shares Raymond Lau, a VSA artist with Tourette's Syndrome.[9] Prof. raised funds to help make it possible for Raymond to exhibit his art in New York in 1998. Raymond won the UOB Painting of the Year Award in 1993 and was conferred NAC's Young Artist Award in 2001.

---

7 Prof. Koh has served as patron for: Nature Society, Singapore; the Asia-Pacific Centre for Environmental Law; the Singapore Association for Environmental Companies; The Substation; the Singapore International Film Festival; Theatre of the Deaf called "Hi! Theatre"; VSA Singapore; SAVH; Rainbow Centre; and the Singapore Librarians' Association. He is a trustee of two educational trusts: Lee Wee Kheng Charitable Trust and Tan Chay Bing Education Trust, and served as chairman of the National Arts Council, National Heritage Board, Chinese Heritage Centre, and the Empress Place Museum.
8 Maureen Goh, email message to author, December 5, 2016.
9 Raymond Lau, email message to author, December 5, 2016.

Prof. Koh's passion, infectious enthusiasm and conviction, underpinned by intellectual reasoning, make him a natural philanthropist and influencer who inspires others. He is gentle and compelling in his advocacy, and does not make anyone feel as if they owe him or anyone else anything. It is the mark of a gifted fundraiser that no one thinks of him as such. In his own disarming way, Prof. simply shares his passion and vision and invites others to partake in the joy and excitement of being a contributor.

Last, but not least, Prof. Koh's sense of justice is not limited to sentient beings; he is an advocate for all creation and an environmentalist concerned for urban sustainability, sustainable development more generally, and the protection of natural habitats. His advocacy on environmental issues has also been a longstanding commitment ranging from local conservation issues to his Chairmanship of the UN Conference on the Law of the Sea and the 1992 Earth Summit in Rio which earned him the accolade of Champion of the Earth by the United Nations Environment Programme in 2006.

The Idea of Singapore as Our Home and Gift

Though a global citizen and true friend of both the West and East, Prof. Koh calls Singapore his home and is deeply loyal to his country. Says Prof. Koh,

> *My wife used to ask me: 'Where would you like to spend your retirement years?' I would reply that I wish to work until I die and would like to die in the land of my birth. I have spent my whole life working for Singapore and, although I have never signed a bond of service, I feel bonded to Singapore.... One of our founding fathers, Mr S. Rajaratnam, used to say that being a Singaporean is not a condition of one's birth but of one's conviction.*"[10]

His articulation of the convictions that bind him to Singapore are some of the clearest expressions of Singapore as a land of fiery ideals and not merely of efficacious pragmatism. Though often phrased as his

---

10 Tommy Koh, "7 Habits of a Singaporean," *The Straits Times*, September 11, 2013.

wishes for Singapore and Singaporeans, Prof. Koh continuously affirms his belief in Singapore's essential character as a multiracial, multireligious Southeast Asian nation that lives in peace and prosperity, values meritocracy and honest work, and operates with a good government that is willing to do what is right and not necessarily what is popular. His beliefs, like all ideals, hold Singapore and Singaporeans to a higher standard. He expresses what few others dare to — a moral imagination of Singapore.

> In our country, people of different races, colours and religions live in peace and harmony. We celebrate our diversity as a blessing and not a defect. We recognise and reward talent and merit and we dislike class, privilege and snobbery. We treat our women well and our talented women have helped to make Singapore the success that it is. We are admired for our integrity, reliability and competence. If I have another life to live, I would like to be born again in Singapore.[11]

As our actions are a reflection of who we are and determine what we shall become, Prof. Koh's living expression of our Singaporean identity is perhaps his greatest contribution. If Singapore is a kind, giving and competent country, it is because its people are likewise. It is because Singaporeans are kind and giving towards one another, using their competencies in service of others; striving to bring out the best in one another; the best in everyone. If that is who we are, then that is also what we have to offer, to one another, to Singapore, our neighbours and to the world. There are few who have done that better that our dear Prof. Koh.

---

11 Tommy Koh, "SG+50: Future Trends 2065; Letter to My Grandchildren in 2065," *The Straits Times*, August 3, 2015.

Section IV

International Law

Chapter 33

Tommy Koh: A Guardian of Singapore's Sovereignty

꧁

Pang Khang Chau

I first heard of the name "Tommy Koh" in the late 1970s, when I was a primary school student. That was an era when schoolchildren received their news from broadcast television instead of Facebook or Twitter.

Back then, Professor Tommy Koh was Singapore's Permanent Representative to the United Nations (UN) in New York. From time to time, the evening television news would report on the remarks and activities of Prof. Koh at the UN. I recall being thoroughly in awe of this larger-than-life figure who was out there, halfway around the world, flying Singapore's flag and defending tiny Singapore's interest in the midst of so many other countries much larger than ours.

My memory of the events and issues that gave rise to those news reports is now hazy. But the sense of awe I felt those many years ago has never faded.

The UN is a creature of international law. It owes its existence to an international treaty signed in 1945 in San Francisco, i.e., the Charter of the United Nations. The decisions of the principal organs of the UN such as the Security Council and the International Court of Justice are binding on member countries because of international law. The internal working procedures and decision-making rules of the UN are governed by international law.

Prof. Koh's role, as Singapore's Permanent Representat UN, was to work with and through these international law ru guard Singapore's interests. The importance of this role is evident from the following account by Professor S Jayakumar of his meeting with Mr Lee Kuan Yew before he proceeded to the UN to succeed Prof. Koh as Singapore's Permanent Representative:

> *After a long delay, Mr Lee returned to the room, visibly preoccupied. He said, "Look Jayakumar, let me tell you what's happening." He explained that there was a problem with Johor and the Water Agreements. Water was a matter of life and death for Singapore and should Malaysia renege on the Water Agreements, it could even lead to war. I might then have to bring it up in the UN Security Council. We arranged to have another meeting with Tommy when he returned and before I left for the UN.*
>
> *The next meeting, with Lee Kuan Yew and Tommy Koh, was in 1971 when Tommy had relinquished his UN post and before I went to New York to succeed him. Mr Lee again raised the issue of the Water Agreements. It was impressed upon me that I would have to be ready with all the arguments should we ever have a problem with Malaysia.*[1]

While Prof. Koh never had to raise the Water Agreements at the UN, much of what he did throughout his stint at the UN was to prepare for the day when Singapore needed to invoke international law to ensure that the Water Agreements were honoured and enforced. As the late Mr Lee Kuan Yew told Prof. Jayakumar: "Water was a matter of life and death for Singapore."

When Vietnam invaded Cambodia in 1978 and installed a puppet government there, an important principle of international law concerning the freedom of smaller states from aggression and interference by their larger neighbours was at stake. Prof. Koh worked skilfully to rally votes from countries at the UN and succeeded in ensuring that the puppet government installed by Vietnam in Cambodia did not receive recognition. This forestalled the creation of a bad precedent in international law which would have been detrimental to Singapore's interest.

The crowning achievement of Prof. Koh's stint as Singapore's Permanent Representative to the UN was the successful conclusion of the

---

1 S Jayakumar, *Be at the Table or Be on the Menu: A Singapore Memoir* (Singapore: Straits Times Press, 2015), 49.

10-year long negotiations over the UN Convention on the Law of the Sea (UNCLOS). Prof. Koh, together with his eminent colleagues on the Singapore delegation (Prof. Jayakumar, Chao Hick Tin and S Tiwari), safeguarded Singapore's interests by securing the freedom of navigation through certain straits that are used for international navigation, such as the Straits of Malacca and Singapore, thus ensuring that Singapore's lifeline through trade routes by sea remains always open. As Singapore is entirely surrounded by the territorial sea of neighbouring countries, Singapore did not stand to benefit much from the 200-mile exclusive economic zone (EEZ) newly recognised in UNCLOS.[2] It was therefore of significant consolation to Singapore that UNCLOS limits the rights of coastal states in their EEZs to the exploitation, regulation and safe-guarding of economic resources and does not allow coastal states to claim full sovereignty over their EEZs. This meant that the freedom for other states to navigate through and conduct other legitimate activities in these EEZs are preserved. Similarly, the creation of the International Seabed Authority to exploit and regulate resources on the international seabed ensures that countries without EEZs or without significant EEZs get the opportunity to participate in the exploitation of resources on the deep seabed.

Today, a Singapore company has been awarded a seabed exploration contract by the International Seabed Authority and a Singapore official is serving on the Legal and Technical Committee of the International Seabed Authority.

Prof. Koh's achievements at the UN, and in relation to UNCLOS specifically, are explored in detail in Justice Chao Hick Tin's first-person account: "Service to the UN: Tommy Koh and UNCLOS", which is the first in this section's essays concerning Prof. Koh's contributions in the area of international law. Justice Chao was the pioneer international lawyer in the Attorney-General's Chambers (AGC). He headed AGC's international law practice for many years until he was appointed a judi-cial commissioner of the Supreme Court bench in 1987. From 1974 to 1981, he worked closely with Prof. Koh as a member of the Singapore

---

2 While it may be possible for Singapore to claim a modest EEZ near Pedra Branca where the territo-rial sea generated by Pedra Branca opens into the South China Sea, it is not possible to claim an EEZ from the main island of Singapore given the proximity of Singapore's neighbours.

delegation at the UNCLOS negotiations. Justice Chao's essay highlights the critical role Prof. Koh played in narrowing the differences among delegations, and Prof. Koh's skilful chairmanship of the final session of the conference, which led to the successful adoption of UNCLOS.

I came to know Prof. Koh personally in early 2000s, when he was Singapore's Chief Negotiator for the United States-Singapore Free Trade Agreement (USSFTA). I was then working in the Ministry of Law and my role in relation to the USSFTA was to provide input to the negotiating team on policy areas concerning compulsory land acquisition and the liberalisation of the legal profession. The chief negotiator for a free trade agreement has to pull together the disparate, and sometimes contradictory, policy objectives of many different departments and agencies within the government, and to forge compromises among them. The role is often compared to the task of herding cats, and I happened to be one of the "cats" Prof. Koh had to herd towards the pot at the end of the USSFTA rainbow.

The conclusion of the USSFTA, which is a treaty binding in international law, gives Singapore legally enforceable rights of access to the US market. This is yet another example of how Prof. Koh has contributed to the promotion of Singapore's interests through international law. But Prof. Koh's achievements in the field of international trade law do not end there. Margaret Liang, formerly Singapore's Deputy Representative to the World Trade Organization (WTO) and Director of the International Economics Directorate of the Ministry of Foreign Affairs, outlines Prof. Koh's contributions to the WTO dispute settlement in her essay "WTO Dispute Settlement System: Singapore's Involvement". The dispute settlement system was described by the Director-General of the WTO at the first WTO Ministerial Conference in Singapore as "the heart of the WTO system."[3]

While still on the topic of dispute settlement, it was through Singapore's two major disputes with Malaysia in the international courts that I was eventually given the privilege of working directly and very closely with Prof. Koh. He served as the Agent of Singapore in both disputes.

---

3 John H. Jackson, *The World Trade Organization, Constitution and Jurisprudence* (New York: Routledge, 1998), 66.

The first dispute was the Land Reclamation case in 2003. Claiming that Singapore's reclamation works at Tuas and Pulau Tekong caused transboundary environmental damage to Malaysia and made it more difficult for ships to sail through the Johor Strait, Malaysia applied to the International Tribunal on the Law of the Sea (ITLOS) for an order to halt Singapore's reclamation works. My involvement was to assist with the preparations of the ITLOS proceedings and provide research and other support from Singapore as part of the AGC "home team" for the main team at ITLOS in Hamburg.[4] As I did not attend the hearing in Hamburg and ceased to be involved after ITLOS gave its decision, I can do no better than to commend to readers Mrs Cheong Koon Hean's first-person account of how Prof. Koh handled the Land Reclamation case in her essay "Malaysia and Singapore: The Reclamation Case — From Dispute to Settlement". Mrs Cheong, at the relevant time a Deputy Secretary in the Ministry of National Development, was a key member of the Singapore team who made a very persuasive presentation before ITLOS on the technical and engineering aspects of the case. She explains in her essay how Prof. Koh combined his knowledge of international law, his deep understanding of UNCLOS, his experience as a diplomat and master negotiator and his warm and likeable personality to achieve an outcome which was acceptable not just to Singapore, but to Malaysia as well.

The second dispute — the Pedra Branca case before the International Court of Justice (ICJ) — took me on a four-year adventure with Prof. Koh, an adventure that began in 2003 when I was a mid-level lawyer with only seven years' experience. Indeed, it was because of the Pedra Branca case that I was transferred to the International Affairs Division of AGC, thereby commencing my own fledgling career in international law.

In the course of those four years, I attended countless meetings with Prof. Koh during the preparations for the Pedra Branca case and exchanged views with him and other members of the team on drafts after drafts of Singapore's written pleadings and oral submissions. The

---

4 My involvement was limited to the provisional measures proceedings heard before ITLOS and I was not involved in the joint study and negotiation of a settlement which took place after the ITLOS decision. During the provisional measures proceedings, I headed the "home team" which was responsible for providing research and other support from Singapore for the main team attending the proceedings in Hamburg.

Singapore legal team benefited much from Prof. Koh's clarity of thought and expression as well as his keen insights on the relevant international personalities and events. Prof. Koh brought a diplomat's flair and nuance to the deliberation within the team, which I initially found jarring, given that I had previously done litigation only in the domestic courts. Over time, I came to appreciate that Prof. Koh's approach was borne out of a deep-seated belief that state-to-state litigation is but an extension of diplomacy and that, between close neighbours, we cannot avoid continuing to deal with each other on various fronts after the case is over. Prof. Koh therefore approached the case with a constant eye towards "the morning after". A detailed yet characteristically succinct account of Prof. Koh's role and contribution is given by a long-time friend of Prof. Koh, former Chief Justice and former Attorney-General Chan Sek Keong in his essay "Tommy Koh and Pedra Branca".

In both of these disputes, Prof. Koh brought his knowledge, expertise, experience and talents to bear in safeguarding Singapore's sovereignty and securing positive outcomes for Singapore through international law.

As a very small country, Singapore is vulnerable to adverse impacts on the environment arising from activities taking place in other countries. Singaporeans are reminded of this truism annually when Singapore is engulfed for several weeks each year in transboundary smoke haze from forest fires. Prof. Koh's successful chairmanship of the 1992 Earth Summit in Rio has made the world a safer place for Singapore, environmentally speaking. The Earth Summit adopted two major international treaties on environmental law — the Convention on Biodiversity and the UN Framework Convention on Climate Change. It also adopted the non-legally binding Forest Principles, which led eventually to the negotiation of a Convention on Desertification. More significantly, the Earth Summit adopted Agenda 21 — a comprehensive action plan for the 21st century on the environment — and the establishment of the UN Commission on Sustainable Development to review progress on the implementation of Agenda 21.

Most importantly from an international lawyer's perspective, the Earth Summit adopted the Rio Declaration on Environment and Development which led to the rapid development of international environment law over the past quarter of a century. As the *Max Planck Encyclopedia of Public International Law* explained:

> At the international level, it had great practical impact. In the after-
> math of Rio, virtually every major international convention concerning
> multilateral co-operation came to include environmental protection
> as one of the goals of State Parties. A spike in the number of treaties
> adopted after the Rio Conference demonstrates the impact of the meet-
> ing and its concluding texts. The legal work of the UNEP, first set forth in
> 1981 in the Montevideo Programme for the Development and Periodic
> Review of the Environmental Law, was revised in September 1992 on
> the basis of the UNCED[5] outcomes.
>
> The significance of the Rio Declaration also lies in the contents
> of the declaration. Sustainable development became the key organiz-
> ing concept with environmental protection seen as one of its three pil-
> lars. The emergence of new principles between the Stockholm and Rio
> Conferences is reflected in the texts and has been echoed in numerous
> instruments since 1992. Like the Stockholm Declaration, the Rio Decla-
> ration has shaped international and national environmental law.[6]

Koh Kheng-Lian and Irene Lye Lin-Heng, in their essay "Tommy Koh: The Earth Summit and Capacity Building for the Environment", comment on Prof. Koh's role in the Earth Summit process and docu-ment the role he played, following the successes attained at the Earth Summit, to develop the capacity to train up lawyers in environmental law locally and regionally. Koh Kheng-Lian and Irene Lye Lin-Heng are respectively the founding Director and current Director of the Asia-Pacific Centre for Environmental Law which was co-founded by Prof. Koh and his good friend, Dr Parvez Hussan, in order to jump-start environmental legal education in the Asia-Pacific region.

After being tapped by the UN for the law of the sea and environ-mental law, Prof. Koh was next approached for assistance in the area of international peacekeeping. For over a decade, Prof. Koh chaired a

---

5 "UNCED" stands for the UN Conference on Environment and Development, which is the formal name of the 1992 Earth Summit in Rio.
6 Dinah Shelton, *Stockholm Declaration (1972) and Rio Declaration (1992)*, in ed. R Wolfrum, *The Max Planck Encyclopedia of Public International Law* (Oxford University Press, 2008).

tripartite conference series that debriefed on UN peacekeeping missions that were ongoing or recently concluded so that lessons learned could be adapted for future missions. Nassrine Azimi and Chang Li Lin, who served in the secretariat of the conference series, describe in their essay "Peacekeeper and Peace-Builder" how Prof. Koh's deft chairmanship and international experience was brought to good use, especially when some of the observations required courage and integrity for a thorough review. The UN Lessons Learned Unit was one positive outcome of Prof. Koh's efforts and leadership.

Given Prof. Koh's outstanding contributions and immense international influence, some of us working within the Singapore government began thinking about how Singapore could maintain a pipeline of international law talents who could carry on the work and continue the legacy of Prof. Koh and other pioneer Singapore international lawyers of his generation. Various measures were adopted as part of this initiative to develop international law expertise in Singapore. Those of us working on this initiative referred to it half-jokingly as the "Where do we find the next Tommy Koh?" initiative. One key measure under this initiative was the establishment of the Centre for International Law at the National University of Singapore. Not only was the Centre geared towards enhancing the research, teaching and learning of international law in Singapore, it was also intended that the Centre would become the focal point of the common efforts of various Singapore stakeholders to build a hub in international law.[7]

When the Centre was established in 2009, there was clearly no better person to chair its Board of Governors than Prof. Koh himself. The founding Director of the Centre, Robert Beckman, provides in his essay — "Tommy Koh and the NUS Centre for International Law" — an insider's account of how Prof. Koh supported the Centre and created a synergy between his life's work and the important work of sharing the lessons learned with the new generation of international lawyers. Under Prof. Koh's leadership, the Centre has been an immense success. Consistent with Prof. Koh's global and cosmopolitan outlook, the Centre

---

7 Singapore Parliamentary Debates, Vol. 84, Col. 1083 (2 Feb 2008)

has become a hub for developing international law expertise not only for Singapore, but for countries in the region as well.

While this collection of essays does not cover the full breadth and depth of Prof. Koh's contributions, it is hoped that they will provide the reader with a sufficient flavour, from a variety of perspectives, of how Prof. Koh leveraged his wide range of talents to work with and through international law to safeguard Singapore's sovereignty and find new paths and solutions for difficult challenges, regionally and internationally.

As Prof. Koh wrote 16 years ago:

> *The reason which led me to study international law was my desire to help build a world ruled by law. The quest for a just world order would dominate my thinking for the rest of my life.*[8]

In my view, there is no doubt that Prof. Koh has, through his firm conviction and persistence over a distinguished career spanning more than half a century, achieved tremendous success towards this goal, much more than anyone could possibly imagine.

---

8 Tommy Koh, *My Adventure with International Law*, (2001) 5 Singapore Journal of International & Comparative Law, 277

CHAPTER 34

Service to the UN:
Tommy Koh and UNCLOS

❧

CHAO HICK TIN

I first ran into Tommy Koh in 1967, shortly before I joined the Singapore Legal Service in June that year. I recall that it was at an event I attended. I knew who Tommy was as his reputation had preceded him, not only as the top student of his cohort, but also as someone who would speak his mind. Our exchanges were limited to just some pleasantries. I had another fleeting encounter with Tommy in 1968, shortly before he left for New York to take up his appointment as Singapore's Permanent Representative to the United Nations (UN). From both those encounters, brief though they were, Tommy came across to me as someone warm and sociable.

My real interaction with Tommy started in 1970 when I was a member of the Singapore delegation to the 25th Session of the UN General Assembly. Throughout the three-month duration of that session of the General Assembly, the Singapore team worked closely with Tommy. It was then that I witnessed how he ran his mission, how he reasoned out his approach to issues and how he dealt with people. The delegation would meet at 9.00 a.m. every working morning, and even earlier if circumstances required it. The team members would report anything of significance that had occurred the day before, and go through the issues that were likely to arise from the various UN meetings scheduled for that day (including the meetings of the General Assembly and the various committees). We would discuss the stand that we should adopt, including the question of whether any intervention should be made at the respective meetings. Of course, in each case, our decision was always subject to any instructions, whether broad or specific, that we might receive from the Ministry of Foreign Affairs. Barring any particular needs, my general responsibility was to take charge of the Sixth Committee, which dealt with legal issues. The closest parallel I can think of to describe how Tommy managed his mission is someone who pilots a ship — systematic when working with different people doing different tasks, and always seeking to build a consensus in the event of any differences. That was Tommy's trademark working style. It gave newcomers to the world of diplomacy like myself a better understanding of the dynamics at play in multilateral negotiations. Tommy was calm and unflappable at all times, even under stressful circumstances. In every sense of the word, I received my first lesson in multilateral diplomacy from him. I realised then that the role of a lawyer was indeed very different from that of a diplomat in a multilateral setting. A lawyer advances his client's case to the court in the most convincing manner possible, whereas a diplomat does not do that. In multilateral negotiations, taking the bull by the horns is not likely to work; instead, persuasion and patience are the order of the day. This important attribute that I picked up from Tommy became very useful when I dealt later on with work relating to the Law of the Sea. Indeed, one of the major issues which was on the agenda of the General Assembly that year concerned the Law of the Sea.

Three years earlier, in the autumn of 1967, Dr Arvid Pardo, the Maltese Ambassador to the UN, had succeeded in asking the General Assembly to appoint an ad hoc committee to study issues relating to the peaceful uses of the seabed and the ocean floor. The result of that committee's three-year study was the adoption of a recommendation that there be a declaration by the UN that the seabed and the ocean floor beyond the limits of national jurisdiction, and their resources, should be the common heritage of mankind. This recommendation was approved and adopted by the General Assembly. The declaration adopted brought into focus the critical issue of determining where the limits of national jurisdiction were and how those limits were to be demarcated. The four Geneva Conventions of 1958, in particular the Continental Shelf

Convention, did not provide a clear answer to this question. The upshot of the General Assembly's deliberations was to expand the membership of this ad hoc committee and extend its mandate. Singapore became a member of the committee, and it was thereafter known as the "Seabed Committee". The Seabed Committee was tasked to prepare for a plenipotentiary conference in 1973 to consider the entire spectrum of issues relating to the Law of the Sea.

As events turned out, Tommy attended only the first session of the Seabed Committee, which was held in Geneva in March 1971. In mid-1971, having completed his three-year term as Singapore's Permanent Representative to the UN, Tommy returned to the Law Faculty of the National University of Singapore as its Dean, and Professor S Jayakumar succeeded him as our Permanent Representative in New York.

During the first session of the Seabed Committee, I saw clearly how well regarded Tommy was by other delegates. This was despite the fact that the broad coastline states were well aware that Singapore's position in many respects would be quite different from theirs. Personally, I believe it had all to do with Tommy's unique facility for making friends and instilling confidence in whomever he worked and interacted with. People sensed his warmth and sincerity, regardless of who they were in the diplomatic world. Rank was never a relevant or important consideration to Tommy. He would talk to a First or Second Secretary of another country in the same way as he would to its Ambassador. Equally important, he made it a point to remember people's names and address them by their first names. No matter how difficult a person he was dealing with, he never showed it.

In 1974, Tommy returned to New York as Singapore's Permanent Representative to the UN for a second time. That was also the year in which the Conference on the Law of the Sea was convened in Caracas, Venezuela where substantive issues were discussed. I should add that earlier in December 1973, the Conference was convened in New York to deal with certain procedural matters. That was regarded as the first session of the Conference. Tommy led the Singapore delegation to Caracas. Delegates were perhaps unrealistically optimistic that a convention could be adopted during the 10 weeks that the Caracas session of the Conference was scheduled to last, even though there was no existing draft convention for their consideration. The Caracas session of the Conference divided its work into three committees, with the first dealing with issues relating to the seabed beyond national jurisdiction; the second dealing with issues relating to the territorial sea, navigation through international straits, the archipelago concept, the economic zone and the continental shelf; and the third dealing with pollution and scientific research. It was obvious that the work of the Second Committee was more important to most delegates.

Right from the start, the Caracas session of the Conference was highly politicised, with many delegations espousing views advocating extreme positions. It soon became clear that there was no way in which the Conference could complete its task within the 10 weeks that it was scheduled to last. This was not helped by the fact that at the first session of the Conference held in New York in December 1973 it was decided that all substantive decisions of the Conference should be arrived at by consensus. At all previous UN conferences where a convention had been adopted within the time allotted for the conference, the conference delegates had always had before them a draft convention prepared by the International Law Commission, and differences on the text of the draft convention had been decided by the normal mechanism of voting. That, however, was not the case for Caracas. There was no common ground among the delegates. The positions taken by the various states were poles apart, and no agreement was possible. It was soon apparent that a consensus was some time away. Thereafter, the Conference convened once or twice a year, alternating between Geneva and New York.

From 1974 to 1981, I had the opportunity to witness at close range Tommy's trademark diplomatic skills being put to use as he worked tirelessly behind the scenes to narrow the differences among delegates at the Conference. Notwithstanding Singapore's position as a geographically disadvantaged state completely hemmed in by its neighbours, with hardly any real possibility of even extending its territorial sea up to the then likely limit of 12 nautical miles, Tommy was always the quintessential diplomat. While always conscious of the need to protect Singapore's vital interests, he was at the same time acutely aware that for a small state like Singapore, law and order on the oceans was vital. Thus, he never ceased, in collaboration with delegates from other states that held a more moderate position, to attempt to broker a consensus in relation to any issue that appeared to be developing into an impasse. There was also something about Tommy's demeanour, such that even opposing sides were willing to consider his suggestions, as they perceived him to be a fair and objective interlocutor.

Towards the close of the 1974 session of the Conference, it became apparent that the absence of a draft convention had to be addressed if the Conference were to end anytime soon and successfully. A great deal of informal consultations then took place. Tommy and other leaders at the 1974 session pursued this issue feverishly, and the question was eventually reduced to just this: who should be charged with this task of drawing up a draft convention? It did not take long for a consensus to emerge that in relation to the issues which fell within the purview of the Second Committee, Ambassador Satya Nandan from Fiji, a fair and well-regarded person who held balanced views on many of the issues which needed to be ironed out, was favoured. Tommy had a close personal and working relationship with Ambassador Nandan, and they both had great mutual respect and regard for each other. Both knew very well that to enable the Conference to eventually end successfully, moderation was the key. I had no doubt that the constant exchange of ideas between Tommy and Ambassador Nandan contributed to the text, which the latter subsequently drafted.

By the end of the 1975 session of the Conference, single negotiating texts relating to the respective issues dealt with by the three committees of the Conference had been presented. Two sessions of the Conference were held in 1976, with the spring session in New York and the summer session in Geneva.

At the two sessions of the Conference in 1976, the thrust of the discussions was directed at refining the three single negotiating texts. In 1977, the three were merged into one to form a composite single negotiating text. Tommy and other moderate delegates at the Conference continued to play their roles as conciliators and mediators.

The exchanges between delegates were often robust. I recall a particular meeting in 1976 where, out of the blue, after I had made an intervention, a delegate from a developed broad coastline state passed me a note asking me whether I was calling him a liar. In reply, I wrote him a note stating that the things that he had said during his intervention (he had spoken before me) were inconsistent with what he had stated earlier. I also pointed out that in my intervention, I had not in any way suggested that he had lied. He was not satisfied and threatened to take the matter up. After the meeting, to keep Tommy in the picture, I showed him the notes that I had exchanged with that delegate. In his characteristic manner, Tommy merely smiled. Thereafter, Tommy did not mention to me whether the matter was ever raised with him.

By the 1979 session of the Conference, a consensus was more or less on the table, with only some issues relating to the financial arrangements for the mining of the seabed beyond national jurisdiction still outstanding. In 1980, Tommy was tasked by the Chairman of the First Committee to spearhead small negotiating groups to iron out the differences between the main protagonists relating to the use of the seabed beyond national jurisdiction.

In December of that year, the then President of the Conference, Ambassador Hamilton Shirley Amerasinghe of Sri Lanka, passed away. Initially, candidates from two Asian countries were before the Conference but neither received clear support. A draft ensued and Tommy was eventually elected by acclamation. I believe this had all to do with his ability, leadership style and integrity; he was someone whom the delegates were comfortable with and they were convinced that he would discharge the office of President of the Conference with even-handedness and well-balanced consideration.

Upon Tommy assuming the Presidency of the Conference, a challenge came from an unexpected source — policy change in Washington as a result of the election of Ronald Reagan as President of the United States. His administration rejected the draft text that had been drawn up for the proposed convention, yet at the same time, in the words of an article published on the August 1, 1983 issue of *The New Yorker*, "they propose to take all the benefits to this country negotiated in it, but without paying the negotiated price." In that year, despite efforts to bring the US on board, the US delegation remained intransigent. Notwithstanding that, the Conference adopted the draft convention, now formally known as the United Nations Convention on the Law of the

Sea (UNCLOS), by an overwhelming majority. To this day, the US has neither signed nor ratified the UNCLOS.

In the words of the author of the above-mentioned article in *The New Yorker*, Tommy was "one of the most consulted and most hardworking men at the [C]onference," and his negotiations "tended to be scholarly". He was also referred to as having "more influence" than diplomats from much larger countries. I do not think anyone who saw Tommy in action during those years would disagree with these remarks.

The significance of having a convention to govern the uses of the oceans cannot be over-emphasised. The UNCLOS is vital for the maintenance of international peace and order. It provides a means of averting conflicting claims on matters such as the extent of a state's territorial sea, freedom of navigation through international waterways, and the extent of a coastal state's authority over fisheries, mineral resources and marine scientific research in its economic zone. Tommy's efforts throughout the many sessions of the Conference, both before and after his appointment as President of the Conference, strongly contributed to the rule of law, which is now in place over the oceans.

As a result, the UN has been able to build a more peaceful and equitable world. I need not say more in Tommy's honour than to quote the words of the former UN Secretary-General, Kofi Annan, who once described the UNCLOS as "… one of the [UN's] greatest achievements," as well as those of our Prime Minister Lee Hsien Loong who said, at the 8th S. Rajaratnam Lecture held in 2015, that "when the UN Convention on the Law of the Sea (UNCLOS) was being negotiated … in 1982 … Professor Tommy Koh … played a central role in the negotiations as President of the Third Conference on the Law of the Sea." These lines are a fitting tribute to a man who worked tirelessly and selflessly for many years towards putting in place a legal framework to govern the oceans of the world.

CHAPTER 35

Tommy Koh: The Earth Summit and Capacity Building for the Environment

~ω~

KOH KHENG-LIAN AND IRENE LYE LIN-HENG

In the 1990s Tommy was already internationally known as Singapore's diplomat, statesman and negotiator in the international world community for his many roles not least as chair of UNCLOS (UN Conference on Law of the Sea). However, he still took many participants by surprise when he chaired the Main Committee at the Earth Summit (known also as the United Nations Conference on Environment and Development, or UNCED) and also its Preparatory Committee (Prep Comm for short). A story is told: "Who is Tommy?" wondered some participants rather incredulously when he was nominated chair of the Earth Summit and its Prep Comm, and, to add to the surprise, Tommy was from the tiny island of Singapore, not always visible on the world map! Singapore was also not in the radar of things environment, let alone a sustainable city. In the years that followed Tommy proved his mettle as chair as he steered the complex negotiating process with his team into one of the most productive UN conferences on the environment.

"Who is Tommy?" was recently confirmed by Professor Emeritus Nicholas A. Robinson, former Deputy Chair of the International Union for Conservation of Nature (IUCN) Commission on Environmental

Law, who attended the Prep Comm meetings. He recalled when asked about Tommy's role at UNCED:

> I well remember Tommy at the Prep Comm meetings for the Rio Earth Summit, and at the Earth Summit itself. He was always unflappable. He moved the agendas along with grace and goodwill, and this was surely one of the reasons the 800 pages of the Agenda 21 could be agreed by consensus ... and all the square brackets deleted. When the Prep Comm began in 1990, delegates did not know Tommy, despite his essential role in concluding the UNCLOS negotiations ... I was upset that they were cold, and some even hostile, to his being named to chair the Prep Comm. They wondered, "Who is this guy?" Well, he won them over day by day and two years later had earned their praise and high regard. The pace was a forced march, gruelling, but ultimately successful. Without the Rio Principles — which he hammered out of the Prep Comm in 1971 and no one dared to change thereafter — and without the Agenda 21, we would not have the success of the adoption of the 2015 Sustainable Development Goals. Tommy set the stage for real global collaboration. We are all in his debt.[1]

It is not only Singapore but also the world that is indebted to Tommy, as he yet again discharged himself with distinction, this time at UNCED. He never spared his gavel and hammered it to one of the most productive and successful of UN environmental conferences. His negotiating style was much admired. He shared his reflections on negotiations in "The Art of Chairing Conferences: Lessons Learnt" and "The Earth Summit's Negotiating Process: Some Reflections on the Art and Science of Negotiation" in his book, *The Tommy Koh Reader: Favourite Essays and Lectures*.[2] Tommy was conferred the 2014 Great Negotiator Award by an inter-university consortium of Harvard, MIT, and Tufts, and Harvard's Future of Diplomacy Project. Tommy's style of negotiations is an important tool not only for the development of

---

1 Nicholas A. Robinson, personal conversation with Koh Kheng-Lian, March 10, 2017, Bonn, Germany. The authors would like to thank Professor Robinson for permitting the use of this quote.
2 Tommy Koh, *The Tommy Koh Reader: Favourite Essays and Lectures* (Singapore: World Scientific, 2013).

environmental law but it can enhance environmental education in many ways such as changing mindsets and is an aspect of behavioural science — to transform thinking among stakeholders. This is crucial in environmental education and capacity building that aim to be transformative for effective implementation of environmental laws.

The Asia-Pacific Centre for Environmental Law (APCEL)

When Agenda 21, which called for capacity building in environment, was adopted at UNCED, no one would have guessed that Tommy and his good friend, Dr Parvez Hassan, then Chair of IUCN Commission for Environmental Law (or IUCN-CEL, now IUCN World Commission on Environmental Law) would be the co-founders and co-chairs of the Asia-Pacific Centre for Environmental Law (APCEL), located at the Faculty of Law, National University of Singapore (NUS), Tommy's *alma mater*. It answered the call for capacity building in Agenda 21, making it the first implementation in the context of environmental law. APCEL's objectives, which include capacity building, research, exchange of information, cooperation and collaboration with law schools, institutes and centres are aligned with Agenda 21's capacity-building objectives.

At APCEL's 20th anniversary of its establishment, celebrated on November 10, 2016 at the National University of Singapore, Emeritus Professor Koh Kheng-Lian,[3] Honorary Director of APCEL, recounting the history of how APCEL came into existence, remarked that sometime in October 1992, Dr Parvez Hassan came to Singapore to discuss with Tommy his idea of establishing a regional environmental law centre in Singapore. She said, "Tommy *immediately* contacted me to connect Parvez with the then Dean Assoc. Prof. Chin Tet Yung, of the Law Faculty." When contacted, Dean Chin also approved of such a centre. Regarding the vision for the centre that both Parvez and Tommy had at this meeting, Parvez had this to say:

> When I approached Tommy, it was the clear objective to jump-start environmental legal education in the Asian and Pacific region; the challenges

---

3 Koh is the co-author of this essay.

included (1) very few, indeed, a handful, of law schools in the region included the teaching of environmental law; (2) UNCED had popularised and mainstreamed environment protection as a globally-accepted priority but the capacity to implement was lacking; (3) producing a cadre of environmental lawyers in each country was a pre-requisite for developing national legal frameworks and institutions; (4) APCEL was conceived to train lawyers and law teachers in the region and to provide them materials and a syllabus to start environmental law in their law schools on return and to develop the capacity to deal with environmental issues at the national levels; the dream played out well as APCEL plus 20 showed; Tommy and I went into APCEL with this clear vision.[4]

Looking back today, Tommy's approval to go ahead with the establishment of a regional centre at the Law Faculty was a leap of faith into the unknown, in that the regional centre had to start from literally zero. Back in the early 1990s, as Parvez said, hardly, if any, law schools in the Asia-Pacific region, including the Law Faculty at NUS, offered a course in environmental law, not even as a component in any of the subjects that called for a consideration of environmental sustainability, such as trade law or the law of the sea.

In the years that followed its establishment, APCEL achieved many milestones together with its partners, namely, IUCN-CEL (now IUCN-WCEL) and the United Nations Environment Programme (UNEP), and also with many other organisations. It has also jointly organised conferences, workshops with numerous other organisations, and its members have served as resource persons in activities organised by them. Some of its milestones include: training some 65 professors from 15 law schools in the Asia-Pacific region, with a multiplier effect where training was given by the alumni in "training the trainers" on their return to their respective countries; conducting for the Singapore Ministry of Foreign Affairs some 16 workshops on urban and industrial environmental management, and on marine protected areas. Altogether over 390 government officials from developing countries

---

4 Pavez Hassan, personal conversation with Koh Kheng-Lian, March 10, 2017, Bonn, Germany. The authors would like to thank Dr Pavez for permitting the use of this quote.

from the region and other parts of the world participated in these workshops, organising numerous workshops on a wide range of topics including biodiversity and climate change. Its members have left footprints in over 50 cities and locations all over the world, participating in conferences, seminars and workshops and conducting lectures. They have also contributed to environmental jurisprudence in wide-ranging topics covering biodiversity, marine environment, climate change, zoonotic diseases, trade and environment, to name a few. All this has been made possible with APCEL's vast network of environmental experts, which Tommy and other friends have helped APCEL to connect and nurture. While APCEL has reached part of the vision of what was contemplated that October afternoon of 1992 when Tommy and Parvez met, more can be expected of the future regarding challenges of the environment posed by the 2015 Sustainable Development Goals and the 2030 Agenda.

Tommy was one of the awardees for tokens of appreciation at the APCEL 20th anniversary celebrations for his role in its establishment. In her citation of Tommy for the award, Koh Kheng-Lian, Honorary Director of APCEL, paid tribute to him as one of the "twin fathers of APCEL" (the other is Dr Parvez Hassan).

Tommy continues to inspire APCEL and we can count on him to give advice, write a foreword for our publications, be a keynote speaker at our conferences, recommend speakers for conferences and workshops — anything, and he will always lend a willing ear and assist. We in APCEL, Singapore and the world continue to look up to him not only as the great negotiator of UNCED but the progenitor of capacity building for the environment in the modern era.

The NUS Master of Science (Environmental Management) [MEM] Programme

In 2001, five years after the establishment of APCEL, NUS launched a unique multi-disciplinary and inter-disciplinary graduate programme, the M.Sc. (Environmental Management), or MEM programme. It involves the collaboration of nine faculties and schools at NUS — the

Faculties of Arts & Social Sciences, Engineering, Law, and Science; and the NUS Business School, the Lee Kuan Yew School of Public Policy, the Saw Swee Hock School of Public Health, the Yong Loo Lin School of Medicine, and the School of Design & Environment (SDE) which hosts the programme.

Prior to its launch, the programme's Steering Committee sought the help of Tommy Koh. Tommy endorsed the programme and agreed to chair and appoint members of the Advisory Committee. The programme's Advisory Committee comprises eminent persons from Singapore and abroad, in academia, government and industry. The programme is administered by a director, appointed by the SDE from among its staff. Policies and implementation are managed by a programme management committee comprising a representative from each faculty and school.

The programme plays an important role in helping to build capacity in environmental education for developing countries. It has been extremely fortunate to have Prof. Tommy Koh as Chair. He has been extremely supportive and has helped it in numerous ways. Of particular importance is Tommy's help in securing sponsors for scholarships, bursaries and prizes. This is particularly important as university fees and the cost of living in Singapore continue to rise.

Tommy also takes a keen personal interest in the programme, attending the welcome ceremony for new students at the start of each academic year. Indeed, in the 15 years since the programme began, Tommy missed only one such event, as he was called away by affairs of state. Tommy would also help us with guest speakers for our events.

The MEM programme now has some 250 graduates from over 30 countries, including China, the Czech Republic, France, Greece, India, Iran, New Zealand, Sweden, the US and of course, the countries of Southeast Asia. They work with government ministries and institutions in a multitude of countries, as well as in international, regional and national organisations, NGOs and multinational and national corporations. The programme recently celebrated its 15th anniversary in

November 2016, together with APCEL's 20th anniversary, and the Bachelor in Environmental Studies (BES) programme's fifth anniversary.

The Asia Environment Lecture

Following the MEM's 10th anniversary celebrations, Tommy suggested an annual Asia Environment Lecture (AEL) for NUS. This was again, an excellent initiative, bringing global leaders on the environment to NUS to share their expertise, with a special focus on the challenges that confront Asia. The lecture is co-hosted by the MEM programme, APCEL and the Bachelor in Environmental Studies (BES) programme, with generous sponsors, particularly Heinrich Jessen, CEO of Jebsen & Jessen and City Developments Ltd.

The speaker for the inaugural lecture was Dr Bindu Lohani, Vice President for Knowledge Management and Sustainable Development, Asian Development Bank. Since then, speakers have included Dr Marco Lambertini, Director-General, World Wide Fund for Nature (WWF) International (2nd AEL); Christine Ervin, First President and CEO, US Green Building Council (3rd AEL); and Dr Andrew Steer, President & CEO, World Resources institute (4th AEL).

In 2014, in the MEM's 13th year, Tommy said:

> For Singapore and other countries, the tension between development and conservation will become more acute and it will have to be handled with greater knowledge, balance and sensitivity.... At the tertiary level, much can be done to enhance this awareness and develop the solutions and skills to successfully manage the environment while pursuing our many activities. The MEM programme has attempted to do this: to produce the next generation of leaders for Asia and the world, who will do their part in helping to steer the course of development towards sustainability, imbued with a core of knowledge gleaned from many disciplines.[5]

---

5 Tommy Koh, Foreword in *Sustainability Matters — Asia's Green Challenges* (Singapore: World Scientific, 2014), x–xiii.

In his message at APCEL's 20th anniversary and MEM's 15th anniversary celebrations, Tommy, as Co-Chair of the APCEL Advisory Committee and Chair of the MEM Advisory Committee, said:

> I wish that we will adopt a new ambition for Singapore, and not just for NUS. The ambition is to make Singapore the regional hub for teaching and research on the environment. This will be a very important contribution to ASEAN and to nature and sustainable development.[6]

We hope that future generations will work towards making Tommy's dream a reality.

APCEL and the MEM programme wish to thank Prof. Tommy Koh for his sterling leadership in leading not just Singapore, but the world community, in environmental stewardship. We are much privileged to have worked closely with him and to have learned much from him. We celebrate his life and we wish for many more happy years with him to mentor and guide us with his wealth of knowledge and infinite wisdom.

---

6 Cited in *Celebrating Environmental Education and Capacity Building* [commemorative magazine], (National University of Education, 2016), 3.

CHAPTER 36

Tommy Koh and the NUS Centre for International Law

~~~

ROBERT BECKMAN

I first met Tommy in 1976, when I came down from Harvard Law School to New York to be interviewed by the then Dean of the Faculty of Law of the University of Singapore, Professor S Jayakumar, for a teaching position in the Faculty. Tommy was Singapore's Permanent Representative to the United Nations, and I met him after my lunch and interview with Professor Jayakumar. I remember Tommy as very friendly and unassuming, but I also remember being very surprised that that he looked so young. I later learned that the reason he looked so young was because he became Singapore's Permanent Representative at the age of 30. After meeting Tommy and Jaya, I decided to accept a position with the Faculty of Law.

I had very little contact with Tommy until the late 1980s, when he was the Singapore Ambassador to the United States. I accompanied the National University of Singapore (NUS) Jessup Moot Team to the international rounds of the Jessup Moot Competition in Washington. Because Tommy was a former Dean of the NUS Faculty of Law, he offered to meet the NUS team and treat them to lunch. I will never forget the time when one of our team members came down with a bad case of the flu, and Tommy personally delivered to the hotel a bowl of soup that his wife had specially prepared. I was simply astounded that the Singapore Ambassador would personally drive to the hotel in the evening to deliver soup to a visiting student.

The first experience I had of working with Tommy was in two conferences organised by the Institute for Policy Studies in the 1990s on the Straits of Malacca and Singapore. At these conferences I saw Tommy in action for the first time. I was most impressed with his skill in chairing the sessions, as he used just the right mix of leadership, humility and humour. I immediately understood why he had been so successful as a diplomat and negotiator.

The same two persons who I met in 1976 were instrumental in establishing the NUS Centre for International Law (CIL) in 2009. The main reason I agreed to serve as CIL's founding Director was that I was advised that Tommy Koh had agreed to serve as chairman of CIL's Board of Governors. This would finally give me the opportunity to work closely with Tommy Koh and ensure that CIL would be a success.

To mark its official launch on October 30, 2009, CIL organised a "Colloquium on Singapore and International Law: The Early Years". Tommy was one of the speakers at the Colloquium, and the title of his paper was "My Adventure with International Law". The closing line in his paper aptly summarises in one sentence why CIL was established and why Tommy was willing to serve as the chairman of its Governing Board:

> ... we, the teachers and practitioners of international law, have a lot to do in convincing a sceptical world that, however imperfect, international law exists and that it impacts many aspects of our lives. We must continue to believe in a world ruled by power and law, and not by power alone.

Tommy was very supportive of CIL from the outset, and was a pleasure to work with. We learned early on that we should never be late for meetings. If we scheduled a meeting for 9.00 a.m., we knew that we could expect Tommy to arrive no later than 8.40. We also learned that he had more confidence in our little "start-up" than we did. He was willing to make commitments to others that CIL was ready, willing and able to take on new tasks and responsibilities, even when the staff at CIL were not sure we were either ready or able to do so. Following his lead, we soon adopted his "can do" attitude as our own, and this is one of the main reasons for our success.

The CIL secretarial, administrative and research staff came to learn of and appreciate the many charms of Tommy Koh. He was always polite, always friendly and always unassuming, no matter who he was dealing with. For official lunches or dinners, we could be assured that he would want to select the meal in advance (always healthy options, on his wife's orders) and that he would arrive early to rearrange the seating assignments. We also knew that we could count on him to charm the guests with interesting stories and anecdotes of his vast experience in the international arena.

Tommy has continued to write on the rule of international law. In an opinion piece in *The Straits Times* on May 26, 2010 entitled "Role for Law in a World Ruled by Power" he made the following comment:

> *The inescapable conclusion is that international law permeates many aspects of our lives. It provides the framework for international coopera-tion. It helps to make this a rules-based world.*
>
> *It is, of course, true that, unlike in a domestic legal system, there is no officer empowered to enforce the judgments of the International Court of Justice, the International Tribunal for the Law of the Sea, WTO's dispute settlement body, and so on. But does this mean the judg-ments have no force? The truth is that most states choose to comply most of the time.*
>
> *Why? Because they consider it to be in their own self-interest to do so.*

Tommy returned to the rule of international law theme again in the 2015 Biennial Lecture of the Law Society of Singapore. In this closing paragraph, he not only followed his long-established practice of making "three points", but he also made a direct link between Singapore's inter-est in promoting the rule of international law and the establishment of CIL:

> *I have three key messages. First, Singapore must be strong economically and militarily in order to be able to defend its independence and ter-ritorial integrity. Second, we should work assiduously to strengthen the International Rule of Law because we want to live in a world which is ruled by law rather than by force. Third, where appropriate, we will*

use international law as our shield to defend our interests and as our sword to advance our interests. In order to do this successfully, we need good international lawyers, in the government, private sector and academia. This is why we have established the Centre for International Law at NUS.

One of Tommy Koh's major contributions to CIL was to launch the "Fireside Chat" series on International Law and Diplomacy in 2012, together with Professor S Jayakumar. The CIL Fireside Chat Series explores the interplay between diplomacy and international law by inviting leading international lawyers and diplomats to share their insights on the legal and political considerations that shape a state's conduct in international relations. The sessions are chaired by Tommy Koh and Professor S Jayakumar, two of Singapore's eminent diplomats.

Another major contribution Tommy has made to CIL was to serve as chair of its major conferences on international law. As chair he provides leadership in planning the conferences and in persuading prominent persons to agree to participate. The conferences have also led to a CIL International Law Series of highly regarded books by publisher Edward Elgar.

Last but not least, Tommy's contributions to CIL has been to serve as a role model for the young members of CIL's research staff. His impact can be seen in the following comments from current or former researchers at CIL:

Working with Professor Tommy Koh is every young Law of the Sea scholar's dream. As the President of UNCLOS III, his work throughout the Conference and his declaration of the Convention as the "Constitution of the Ocean" is legendary. But the best part about working with Professor Koh is getting to know him on a personal level. For someone of his stature and with his deep knowledge on almost any issue, what I learned and appreciate most from him is his ethics and his positive outlook on life. Stay humble; always show respect for others; accept that others may have different opinions; appreciate the simple things in life like art, music, food and the people around you; and that living a healthy and happy life is not difficult. When I was leaving CIL to pursue my doctorate degree, he took me out for lunch to show his appreciation for my work at CIL. No lunch I could offer him could ever show my appreciation for all the things he had taught me and how he had inspired me to live my life better.

Leonardo Bernard, CIL Research Fellow (2010–2015)

I have been a long-time admirer of Professor Tommy Koh's work and his contributions to the development of international law and the promotion of international diplomacy. My admiration has only grown after I started working at the Centre for International Law in 2012 — this time it's not just for his work but for him personally as a great professor, mentor and leader. The breadth of his knowledge, the depth of his expertise, and the optimism in his positive outlook and approach to work and life are truly a source of inspiration for me. Part of what makes Professor Tommy Koh an amazing mentor and leader is the way he cares about his staff and makes people feel valued, included and motivated. He always greets people around him with friendliness, treats them with warmth, and delights them with his charm and a great sense of humour. He constantly encourages his young staff and values the contributions and opinions of junior researchers. He generously gives them credit even when they are simply doing their work to assist him. He sends his staff books that he thinks they would be interested in. If he attends an event and notices his staff have not had the time to eat, he would get them food. His numerous gestures, big and small, invariably show his genuine care and kindness. It has been an incredible honour and an amazing opportunity to work with and for him and learn from him.

Hao Duy Phan, CIL Senior Research Fellow (2012–2017)

I first met Prof. Koh in 2009 at the official launch for CIL. Awestruck and nervous at meeting such a luminary, he immediately put me at ease with his down-to-earth charm and humour. Over the years, I have had several occasions to work with him in his tireless efforts to put CIL on the map. Watching his effortless delivery of speeches or his skilful chairing of conference sessions has made me swell with pride to be a Singaporean. Moreover, such opportunities have served as unparalleled learning experiences for a junior researcher and aspiring academic such as myself. I, following Prof. Koh's excellent example, will try and capture the lessons imparted by Prof Koh in four (not three) key points.

First, be concise (a skill I am still working on!). In his speeches and writing, Prof. Koh has an uncanny ability to express complex ideas simply and succinctly. To break down complicated issues while still conveying the depth and importance of such issues is no easy feat, and a skill that Prof. Koh has perfected to a tee. Second, be firm but courteous. In both diplomacy and academia, such a skill cannot be underestimated. I have seen Prof. Koh deliver "hard truths" or express firm opinions on Singapore's position on contentious issues in a way which never comes across as aggressive or antagonistic, but measured and reasonable. Third, be mindful of the fact that there are always multiple perspectives of an issue. Prof. Koh is adept at understanding these different perspectives and trying to find common ground between competing interests, a talent that has served him well in a range of different settings from the negotiations of international instruments to academic conferences. The fourth lesson I have learned from Prof. Koh, and if I may borrow a phrase from Rudyard Kipling, is to be able to "walk with Kings — nor lose the common touch." As my fellow researchers have attested, perhaps Prof. Koh's most wonderful quality is his kindness and graciousness to people from all walks of life, be it a dignitary or a student. He is always warm and inclusive and has a kind, warm word for everyone. In a nutshell, it has been a privilege and a pleasure to work with Prof. Tommy Koh and I hope to continue to do so in the years to come.

Tara Davenport, CIL Senior Research Fellow (2009–2013)

Chapter 37

Peacekeeper and Peace-Builder

—⚔—

Nassrine Azimi and Chang Li Lin

When the United Nations Institute for Training and Research (UNITAR) approached the Singapore government in 1994 to co-organise a peacekeeping seminar for the debriefing of the United Nations Transitional Authority in Cambodia (UNTAC) operation that had just ended, it had Professor Tommy Koh in mind. Prof. Koh was asked if he could convene such a seminar in partnership with Japan and with UNITAR. As the then Director of the Institute of Policy Studies (IPS), he saw an opportunity, indeed a necessity, for Singapore to offer itself as a neutral platform to conduct an exercise that everyone in the peacekeeping community agreed was essential, but one which no one had been able to undertake as yet.

It was a leap of faith. Singapore was neither a Troop Contributing Country nor directly vested in the UN operation in Cambodia then. Prof. Koh was undaunted. He had the goodwill and ear of every major actor, at the UN and in various capitals. It also helped that the Japanese partner he sought was Ambassador Hisashi Owada, a long-time colleague from the UN days and at the time president of the Japan Institute of International Affairs (JIIA). Together, alongside the Executive Director of UNITAR, the Swiss Marcel Boisard, the three leaders joined forces to form a wonderfully effective troika.

One of the significant outcomes of the first meeting on UNTAC, held in Singapore in August 1994, was the eventual establishment of a Lessons Learned Unit at the Department of Peacekeeping Operations (DPKO). A common refrain repeatedly heard at the seminar had been that when the UN ended its operation in Cambodia, there was no systematic, official debriefing conducted to allow various stakeholders to share what they had learned or observed. Neither was there any platform, to allow the individuals directly involved in the operation to reflect on how their particular mandates could be improved in future undertakings. Therefore, for many of the participants, the Singapore seminar was to be, astonishingly, the first time they had come together again with their fellow administrators since leaving Cambodia.

With the support of the then UN Secretary-General, Boutros Boutros-Ghali and thanks to the co-chairs' commitment and efforts to raise its profile, the Singapore seminar could be developed into a longer-term series, with the specific objective of contributing to lessons-learnt efforts of UN Peacekeeping Operations (UNPKO). Alongside our three co-chairs we saw this as a closed-door debriefing type of exercise, which would allow for honest and frank discussions. Thus, over the next 10 years the series addressed a number of topics related to UN peacekeeping. These included Civilian Police; Humanitarian Action; Peacekeeping and Peace-Building; Reform of the UN Peace Operations; the UN Transitional Administration in East Timor, and concluding in 2005 with an over-arching reflection on the role of the UN as Peacekeeper and Nation-Builder.

From the late 1990s to mid-2000s, the size and nature of UN peacekeeping operations were changing dramatically, shifting from peacekeeping proper to nation-building. Over the decade of their involvement, Professor Koh and the co-chairs too sought to engage on these broader themes and issues directly relevant to UNPKOs, ensuring that the series mirrored developments on how UN peacekeeping was conceived, supported, implemented and assessed around the world.

Hisashi Owada, now a judge on the International Court of Justice describes succinctly the originality of the enterprise.

In the highly analytical as well as pragmatic study of these novel peacekeeping experiments, the combined contributions of UNITAR on the comparative analysis of past peacekeeping efforts of the United Nations, of IPS on the theoretical analysis of dichotomies inherent in them, and of JIIA on the practical lessons learnt by the Japanese participation in these hybrid activities made these seminars uniquely effective.[1]

Of his friendship with Professor Koh, Judge Owada says:

Our friendship dates back to 40 years ago, when Ambassador Koh visited Tokyo on his way to the United Nations to assume his new assignment as Singapore's Permanent Representative. At the time I was working as a diplomatic aide to Prime Minister Fukuda. Since that time, we have cooperated closely on many memorable occasions, in addition to our joint commitment to the UNITAR-IPS-JIIA Seminar. In all these efforts, Tommy's power of intellect, his intuitive insight and his warm-hearted openness, combined with a sense of commitment to worthy causes, have always been my source of encouragement. To this day he remains my best intellectual and personal "comrade-in-arms".[2]

The good offices of the co-chairs also meant that the Peacekeeping series was attended by the most senior and appropriate officials directly involved in the operations, even ongoing ones. As members of the secretariat we, alongside other participants, became privy to many moving first-hand accounts of what went well in the field, what could have been done better and what went horribly wrong. To hear about the inability to protect the vulnerable in the face of genocide, to hear from experienced leaders, some of whom ultimately perished in the line of duty, was sobering. Each seminar had it its own challenges but also immensely useful lessons. The co-chairs brought to the series not just their impressive intellectual and professional abilities but also their personal qualities. Dr Boisard recalls vividly, the impressions Professor Koh made on him:

Behind the peacekeeping seminars, I also came to admire Tommy Koh's unique personality. His career had been so brilliant and versatile — diplomat, high-level negotiator, intellectual — yet he retained a deep simplicity, respect

---

1 Hisashi Owada, e-mail message to authors, January 11, 2017.
2 Ibid.

for his colleagues and tolerance vis-à-vis different opinions that were impressive. Maybe this capacity for consensus is due to his being a citizen of a small multicultural country without much natural resources (as I am myself). His personal intelligence and inimitable smile just made him admired across borders. He is truly a great figure in the field of international relations, his success due, beyond all else, to a certain desire and dedication to serve, an ability to be always well prepared, and to his agility of mind, able to make a perfect synthesis of very complex issues. And I must add, like his writing, Tommy's verbal interventions during our conferences were masterpieces of brevity and clarity![3]

While Professor Koh may not have donned a blue helmet, he and his fellow co-chairs and colleagues did their best to ensure that the UN peacekeepers could discharge their duties well, and if not, then to learn from the mistakes and improve. That vision has proved truly essential.

---

3 Marcel A. Boisard, e-mail message to authors, January 3, 2017

CHAPTER 38

WTO Dispute Settlement System: Singapore's Involvement

⟋⟍

MARGARET LIANG

Introduction

The World Trade Organization (WTO) Dispute Settlement Understanding (DSU) that emerged from the Uruguay Round was described by the former WTO Director-General Mike Moore as the crown jewel of the WTO. This mechanism provides security and predictability to the multilateral trading system. It lays down clear rules and procedures to help WTO members settle trade disputes. Hence, any WTO member, big or small, has the right to seek recourse under the WTO dispute settlement mechanism if another member imposes trade measures that affect their trade interests and that are deemed to be a violation of any of the WTO Agreements.

This mechanism has been very effectively used by WTO members since it came into force in January 1995. It has helped settle trade disputes between developed countries, between developed and developing and between developing countries. What is significant is that many small developing countries have complained against larger developed countries and have had rulings in their favour. Examples of such trade disputes could be seen in the EU-Peru case on "Sardines" where Peru complained against the EU; and the US/Vietnam case on "Shrimps" where Vietnam complained against the US. It is an effective tool to help WTO members, irrespective of size or clout, solve their trade disputes under multilaterally agreed rules. Singapore was in fact the first WTO member to seek recourse under the WTO Dispute Settlement Mechanism when we complained against Malaysia shortly after the WTO came into force on January 1, 1995. The trade dispute was over import restrictions imposed by Malaysia on Singapore's exports of petrochemicals, namely, Poly-Ethylene (PE) and Poly-Propylene (PP).

How Does the WTO Dispute Settlement Mechanism Work?

The process consists of four broad stages: (1) consultations; (2) panel process and, if requested, (3) appellate body review; and (4) surveillance of implementation. There are clear prescribed time frames for each stage of the process. This is to ensure that parties do not block or delay the completion of the dispute settlement process. The mechanism has thus been effectively strengthened and given more "teeth" during the Uruguay Round negotiations.

Singapore's Involvement in WTO Dispute Cases[1]

Why is the WTO Dispute Settlement Mechanism important to Singapore?

Singapore was among those countries that strongly supported the negotiations to reform the GATT procedures and to strengthen the dispute settlement mechanism during the Uruguay Round. As a small country whose economy is heavily dependent on access to the global markets, it is important to have trade rules that provide for an open and predictable multilateral trading system, where the rights and interests of small countries could be protected, in particular, by an efficient dispute settlement mechanism. It was thus in Singapore's interest to strengthen the rules on dispute settlement, which would discourage countries from taking unilateral actions outside the GATT and WTO. In particular, as

---

1 Margaret Liang, "Singapore's Contribution to the WTO Dispute Settlement Mechanism: Reflections of a Singapore Negotiator," in eds. Tommy Koh, Li Lin Chang, Joanna Koh, *50 Years of Singapore and the United Nations* (Singapore: World Scientific, 2015).

a small trading nation with little economic clout, we needed to have strengthened dispute settlement rules that could protect Singapore against restrictive measures taken by our trading partners.

An example could be illustrated by the first trade dispute case that Singapore brought against Malaysia under the WTO Dispute Settlement Mechanism. After having failed to settle the trade dispute through bilateral/diplomatic means, Singapore initiated a complaint against Malaysia on January 10, 1995 under the WTO Dispute Settlement Mechanism. The Malaysian measure prohibited all imports of Poly-Ethylene (PE) and Poly-Propylene (PP) unless an import licence known as an Approved Permit was granted by the Malaysian Director-General of Customs, acting on behalf of the Ministry of International Trade and Industry. This was known as the "AP Scheme". Malaysia was a major market for Singapore's producers of PE and PP and Singapore's manufacturers and exporters were adversely affected by the Malaysian measure. Pursuant to the WTO rules and procedures laid down, Singapore held consultations with Malaysia under the first phase, which were compulsory. Although the DSU provides for two consultations within the 60-day time frame, Singapore had an additional third round at the request of Malaysia. Singapore's dispute with Malaysia was resolved after the third round of consultations when Malaysia decided to withdraw its AP Scheme and eventually replaced it with an automatic licensing scheme consistent with the GATT/WTO. Singapore did not need to proceed to the next phase, which was to request for a panel. The WTO Dispute Settlement Mechanism has thus worked well for Singapore.

Singapore's involvement in WTO dispute cases: Singapore panellists

Singapore has been a reliable and useful source of supply for the selection of panellists for the early GATT dispute cases and now for WTO dispute cases. Singapore is generally considered as neutral and non-partisan in many WTO disputes and is well respected by the WTO members at large. Hence, Singapore officials have been asked by the WTO Director-General to serve on WTO dispute cases, either as chairman or panellists.

Since the GATT days, several Ministry of Foreign Affairs, Ministry of Trade and Industry and Attorney-General's Chambers officials have served as chairmen or panellists of various dispute cases initiated under the GATT and WTO. These included Ambassadors Tommy Koh, See Chak Mun and Chew Tai Soo; S Tiwari, Elizabeth Chelliah, Minn Naing Oo and myself. We served as panellists in our personal capacity and were appointed because of our experience and expertise in the various WTO issues.

Workings of a panel

How are panels composed and what are the procedures for panel hearings? Under the DSU rules, the disputing parties are given a specific period of time to mutually agree to names that they propose to serve as panellists. If the parties fail to agree, the complainant can request the WTO Director-General to compose the panel, based on certain criteria set by the parties. The panel has, as a general rule, six months to complete its work according to the procedures laid down in the DSU. A first organisational meeting with the parties is held to work out the timetable for the work of the panel. During the six month time frame, there will be two substantive meetings with the parties, with each meeting lasting about one to two days. The panellists will meet among themselves for the next five days or so after each of the substantive meetings to deliberate on the case. In between these sessions, the panellists will be in constant communication via emails and tele-conference.

Panel procedures are confidential and the panel meets in closed sessions. Deliberations and documents submitted to the panel are kept confidential. The panel has to make an objective assessment, based on the facts of the case and the applicability of the various WTO Agreements, and determine whether the measure at issue conforms to these WTO Agreements and provisions. It is a long-drawn process of presenting one's legal arguments and interpretations, in order to persuade or convince one another. The final objective is to reach a consensus among the panellists on their findings. The Chair and the two panellists would need to work as a team. The Chair cannot and will not impose his views on the other two panellists. Should there be a strong dissent from any one of the panellists, the dissenting view would be elaborated in the panel report, but without naming the dissenting panellist. However this should be avoided as far as possible as a dissenting voice would weaken the panel findings.

Ambassador Koh's contributions

Ambassador Tommy Koh has served on three dispute panels, twice as chairman. These were as follows:

a) US: The Cuban Liberty and Democratic Act or Helms-Burton Act: Complaint brought by the EC (European Commission) against the US.[2] (Ambassador Koh served as panellist)
b) Canada: Measures Affecting the Importation and the Exportation of Dairy Products. Complaint brought by the US and New Zealand against Canada.[3] (Ambassador Koh served as chairman)
c) US: Safeguard Measure on Imports of Fresh, Chilled or Frozen Lamb Meat from New Zealand and Australia. Complaint brought by New Zealand and Australia against the US.[4] (Ambassador Koh served as chairman)

The deliberations of the panel are highly confidential given the sensitive nature of the issues and there are no public documents available as yet on the deliberations of the respective panellists. However, Ambassador Tommy Koh did share his own insights of the three panels he was part of in *Economic Diplomacy: Essays and Reflections by Singapore Negotiators.*[5] He found the WTO dispute settlement system "an admirable one. It is mandatory and not voluntary. No member of the WTO, no matter how powerful, can block the establishment of a panel or the adoption of a panel's report."

---

2 For more about the case, see https://www.wto.org/english/tratop_e/dispu_e/cases_e/ds38_e.htm
3 For more about the case, see https://www.wto.org/english/tratop_e/dispu_e/cases_e/ds113_e.htm
4 For more about the case, see https://www.wto.org/english/tratop_e/dispu_e/cases_e/ds177_e.htm
5 Tommy Koh, "My Experiences with the WTO Dispute Settlement System," in *Economic Diploma-cy: Essays and Reflections by Singapore Negotiators*, eds. C. L. Lim and Margaret Liang (Singapore: Institute of Policy Studies and World Scientific, 2010), 141–155.

Having been invited by the parties involved to be a panellist and chairman, it is an affirmation of Ambassador Koh as a trusted and skilled negotiator that the parties felt that the process and outcomes would be given due consideration and be fair. Ambassador Koh was invited to three subsequent panels but had to turn them down due to time constraints.

To that end, even though the Singapore panellists are acting in their personal capacity, they are helping Singapore to raise its profile in the WTO and to contribute to the WTO International Trading System through facilitating the resolution of trade disputes.

Conclusion

The WTO Dispute Settlement System will continue to be central to Singapore's trade policy approaches. Singapore has had only one experience as a complainant in a WTO trade dispute. Nevertheless, should Singapore face trade problems with our major trading partners in future, which cannot be resolved through diplomatic means, we will always have the WTO Dispute Settlement Mechanism to fall back on, to be used wisely, either as a complainant or respondent. The WTO Dispute Settlement Mechanism has worked well for Singapore.

CHAPTER 39

Malaysia and Singapore: The Reclamation Case — From Dispute to Settlement

CHEONG KOON HEAN

The Reclamation Areas in Dispute

For more than 100 years, Singapore had carried out reclamation within its waters, creating land to meet its development needs. Extensive studies were always done before reclamation took place and careful measures were put in place during reclamation to ensure that the construction works would not adversely impact the environment.

The reclamation works at Tuas View extension and Pulau Tekong commenced in 2000. However, in January 2002, the Malaysian government protested that the reclamation activities at Tuas View extension were encroaching into Malaysian territorial waters at a position marked "Point 20", based on a map issued by Malaysia in December 1979. This 1979 Malaysian map had all along been rejected by many of Malaysia's neighbours, including Singapore. The Malaysian protest was even more surprising given that by January 2002, Singapore had already reclaimed land well beyond "Point 20".

After several written exchanges over one and a half years, the dispute widened when Malaysia, in April 2002, went on to protest against Singapore's reclamation around Pulau Tekong and Pulau Ubin as well, claiming that these works had caused transboundary environmental

289

damage to Malaysia's waters and had affected its navigation channels. The Singapore technical agencies carrying out the reclamation works were puzzled by the allegations as their technical studies and their close monitoring of the works did not show any harmful effects in Singapore waters and the adjacent areas. Singapore therefore asked Malaysia for more information and the basis for these allegations. However, the information was not forthcoming.

As the diplomatic exchanges continued, Malaysia became more explicit in relying on its international law rights under the 1982 United Nations Convention on the Law of the Sea (UNCLOS). As both Malaysia and Singapore were party to this Convention, both were bound to observe its provisions.

In July 2003, Malaysia suddenly informed Singapore that it was formally referring the dispute to arbitration under UNCLOS and requesting for provisional measures, one of which was to require Singapore to suspend all land reclamation activities. If Singapore did not agree to these measures within 14 days, Malaysia would seek the International Tribunal for Law of the Sea's (ITLOS) decision to prescribe these measures. In response, Singapore expressed that it was unreasonable for Malaysia to deliver the technical reports and at the same time start arbitration proceedings. Singapore therefore invited Malaysia to meet so as to resolve the issues amicably. Malaysia subsequently agreed to meet Singapore in August 2003. In this meeting, Malaysia set out its concerns. Singapore presented its land use planning process, explained how reclamation was carried out and also addressed Malaysia's queries. It appeared that an amicable way forward might be found.

However, things did not turn out that way. Malaysia proceeded to insist on the immediate stoppage of reclamation works as a precondition for further talks. Singapore responded that Malaysia's demand was not justifiable as the studies had demonstrated that the reclamation works had not caused and would not cause any significant impact on Malaysia. Three days later on September 5, 2003, Malaysia abruptly informed Singapore that it had brought the dispute to ITLOS.

With this move, Singapore would face its first international court case before ITLOS, having to defend its legal rights to carry out reclamation.

The Singapore Team

The dispute had political, legal and technical ramifications. Multiple agencies were involved in preparing Singapore's defence. The efforts were spearheaded by a Reclamation Executive Committee (EXCO) consisting then of Minister of Foreign Affairs Professor S Jayakumar, Minister for National Development Mah Bow Tan and Attorney-General Chan Sek Keong. The EXCO was supported by a multi-agency committee comprising officers from the Ministry of Foreign Affairs, the Attorney-General's Chambers, the Ministry of National Development, the Housing and Development Board, the Maritime Port Authority, the Jurong Town Corporation and the Urban Redevelopment Authority. This committee was led by Ambassador-at-Large Professor Tommy Koh, myself as Deputy Secretary of Ministry of National Development and the Principal Senior State Council S Tiwari of the Attorney-General's Chambers.

As Ambassador Koh was the President of the United National Conference which adopted the 1982 UNCLOS, he was naturally appointed the Agent or lead representative of Singapore in the legal proceedings.

The multi-agency group was supported by external legal experts (Professors Michael Reisman and Vaughan Lowe) and technical experts (Professors Kees d'Angremond and William Kamphuis).

Once the dispute was brought before ITLOS, the Singapore team faced extreme time pressure to prepare its written response within 15 days. Preparations also commenced in earnest to prepare for adjudication.

Proceedings at ITLOS in Hamburg

The ITLOS proceedings were to take place on September 25, 2003 in Hamburg. The Singapore team arrived in Hamburg and had only three days to make their preparations.

On September 25, Malaysia presented its arguments and evidence before the 25 judges of ITLOS. The Malaysian side painted Singapore's reclamation activities as having caused serious impacts, and argued for provisional measures to be imposed, chiefly to stop the reclamation activities.

On the second day, Singapore presented its oral response to Malaysia's application for provisional measures. I was part of the team who spoke, which included Ambassador Tommy Koh, Attorney-General Chan Sek Keong, and Professors Michael Reisman and Vaughan Lowe. I explained how Singapore's reclamation was planned and carefully executed with great care taken to protect the environment. The lawyers argued that Malaysia's application was (a) neither admissible nor within the jurisdiction of the Tribunal; (b) that Malaysia failed to produce sufficient evidence of a real risk of harm to Malaysia or the marine environment if the reclamation works were not stopped immediately and (c) that Malaysia cannot demonstrate the urgency for provisional measures. Ambassador Koh also put forth why there was no basis to Malaysia's claim to "Point 20".

On the third and final day of oral proceedings, Malaysia surprisingly made no mention of "Point 20" or the Tuas reclamation. Instead, it sought Singapore's undertaking not to infill part of the Tekong reclamation works at an area called "Area D" pending decision of the Arbitral Tribunal. Malaysia's Agent, Tan Sri Ahmad Fuzi, also repeated an earlier offer to jointly sponsor a study to assess the impact of the reclamation projects.

At Singapore's closing submission, Ambassador Koh reiterated that the Singapore government was willing to, among other things, jointly sponsor and fund a scientific study by independent experts. In fact, Singapore had informed the Tribunal that Singapore had accepted such a joint study at a meeting in Singapore in August 2003. Regarding "Area D", Singapore was prepared to give an assurance that no irreversible action would be taken to construct the stone revetment around Area D, pending the completion of the joint study.

ITLOS delivered its judgement on October 8, 2003. ITLOS did not order Singapore to stop its land reclamation works either at Pulau Tekong or Tuas. Instead, the Tribunal prescribed that Malaysia and Singapore cooperate and promptly establish a group of independent experts to conduct a joint study on the effects of Singapore's land reclamation works, and to propose measures to deal with any adverse effects of such reclamation works. The study was to be completed within a year.

Joint Study Proceedings

To follow up on the Tribunal's decision, Malaysia and Singapore established a Joint Working Group (JWG) to oversee the joint study. Two officers were appointed as liaison officers. I was appointed as Singapore's representative, and Malaysia appointed Madam Rosnani Ibrahim, Director-General of the Department of Environment. In view of the complexity of the study, the JWG comprised some 50 experts who were engineers, marine scientists, port officials, legal counsels and Foreign Service officers.

Malaysia also appointed Professors Roger Falconer and Christopher Fleming from the United Kingdom as its two technical experts, whilst Singapore appointed Professor Kees d'Angremond from the Netherlands and Professor William Kamphuis from Canada. They jointly formed the independent group of experts (GOE), and were assisted by DHI Water and Environment from Denmark to carry out the detail technical studies.

The JWG and the GOE met multiple times over the course of the year. Intensive, and inevitably difficult and contentious discussions took place, sometimes late into the night. Finally, after a year, the GOE completed the joint study and concluded that there were no major impacts arising from Singapore's land reclamation. To reduce hydrodynamic changes, current velocities and any impact to the navigation of ships/boats, the GOE proposed some changes to the final reclamation profile of Pulau Tekong as well as the streamlining of "Changi Finger" as part of the future Changi Reclamation.

Settlement Agreement

Both governments accepted the experts' findings and recommendations, paving the way for negotiations to agree on a final Settlement Agreement. A signing ceremony was then held in Singapore on April 29, 2005 at the Ministry of Foreign Affairs. The two agents, Tan Sri Ahmad Fuzi and Ambassador Tommy Koh signed the Settlement Agreement, witnessed by Dato' Seri Syed Hamid and George Yeo, the two foreign ministers.

To bring closure to the case, the Arbitral Tribunal agreed to adopt the text of the Settlement Agreement as the award of the Tribunal. The Settlement Agreement was also registered with the United Nations Secretariat through the Permanent Missions of Malaysia and Singapore to the United Nations.

Reflections on Working with Ambassador Tommy Koh

Ambassador Tommy Koh played a very key role in the resolution of the reclamation dispute.

First, Ambassador Koh's background as an international lawyer and a seasoned diplomat made him an excellent choice to lead the working team towards a good outcome for Singapore. He provided wise counsel during many hours of deliberation on the strategies we should adopt to make Singapore's case.

Ambassador Koh's view was that international law is important to all states, especially small states, as it levels the playing field on which big and small states interact with one another. If negotiations proved to be ineffective, referring such a dispute to third party could enable a peaceful settlement of disputes.

His familiarity with the intent and proceedings of ITLOS guided us on many aspects of the case. In Hamburg, it was evident that many of the judges at ITLOS and even Malaysia's foreign legal counsels held Ambassador Koh in high regard.

Second, as a seasoned diplomat, Ambassador Koh's belief in the importance of good inter-personal relations set the tone for the process of negotiations. He had said, "Negotiators interact with one another not only intellectually, but also emotionally." Ambassador Koh's soft spoken and polite manner was balanced with firm, well-argued comments. This earned him the trust and respect of colleagues and even those who sparred with him and helped to achieve "win-win" outcomes.

Ambassador Koh also took the time to cultivate warmer relationships. After the Settlement Agreement was signed in Singapore, Ambassador Koh arranged for the Malaysian delegation to be hosted to lunch at one of their favourite restaurants in Singapore, Samy's Curry. On the same evening, the Malaysians were invited to the opening of a beautiful exhibition at the Asian Civilisations Museum entitled "Nonya Kebaya: A Living Art," on loan from the collection of the Malaysian prime minister's wife, Datin Paduka Seri Endon Mahmood. The opening was co-officiated by the wives of the two prime ministers. These little touches were the hallmark of Ambassador Koh, and helped to conclude the contentious dispute on a much warmer note.

A third trait of Ambassador Koh was that, beyond focusing on tasks at hand, he took care to feed the "needs of the soul". For example, during intense preparations for the ITLOS hearings at Hamburg, the Singapore team subsisted largely on cold sandwiches and salads for much of the time. To re-energise the team, Ambassador Koh arranged for hot Chinese food to be brought in, which instantly lifted morale. At the end of the Hamburg hearings, Ambassador Koh took the opportunity to attend a classical concert, which was unsurprising, given his love for the arts as a chairman of Singapore's National Arts Council. Though not everyone in the team shared in his enthusiasm, I was happy to join him and we both thoroughly enjoyed the beautiful concert, ending our time in Hamburg on a happy note.

CHAPTER 40

Tommy Koh and Pedra Branca

CHAN SEK KEONG

On May 23, 2008, the International Court of Justice (ICJ) rendered its decision on the dispute between Malaysia and Singapore over the sovereignty of Pedra Branca Middle Rocks and South Ledge, a group of three maritime features at the eastern end of the Straits of Singapore. The dispute arose when Malaysia published a map in 1979 that showed Pedra Branca as being located within Malaysia's territorial waters.

After an eight-day hearing, the ICJ held (by a majority vote of 12 : 4) that Pedra Branca belonged to Singapore, but not Middle Rocks and South Ledge. As Pedra Branca was the main island in the group, it was still a notable victory for Singapore. Prime Minister Lee Hsien Loong said: "The litigation over Pedra Branca was unprecedented in its scale and complexity. The disputed facts spanned 300 years."[1]

Tommy Koh and Professor Jayakumar have written, from the Singapore's perspective, a very readable account of the case. The book, *Pedra Branca — The Road to the World Court*, was published in 2008.

The book gives an accurate and objective account of Singapore's lengthy and intensive preparations over many years for the case, without seeking to embellish their efforts. The Singapore team's professionalism was highly praised by our external counsel who had never before seen such excellent research and other preparatory work from any national team they had worked with. The book also gives a very fair account of

---

1 Speech given at the 150th Anniversary Dinner of the Attorney-General's Chambers on March 31, 2017.

Malaysia's preparations and arguments in their attempt to convince the ICJ of the merits of its case.[2]

Tommy is known for moderation, empathy and, most of all, absolute fairness to his opponents in his diplomatic, litigation and academic encounters. Tommy's objectivity, verging on neutrality, can be seen in his account of a distorted photograph, which Malaysia suddenly produced in the course of the hearing. Tommy merely described the photograph, which inaccurately showed the small island against a nearby dominating Bukit Berbukit on Johor mainland, as "mysterious", and commented sympathetically that it was "a public relations disaster for Malaysia."

The Pedra Branca case is an affirmation of Tommy's lifelong belief that next to mutual agreement through diplomacy, acceptance of the rule of law in settling disputes between states is the best way to advance peaceful international relations. Hence, for Tommy, the reference to the world court was a happy occasion for him.

Tommy's achievements as a diplomat are legendary. He is a diplomat *par excellence,* by nature, temperament and practice. If war is an uncivilised and cruel form of diplomacy by force, arbitration before an international neutral tribunal is, as Lee Kuan Yew has said in his foreword to the book, the best way not to allow state disputes "to fester and sour bilateral relations." That Malaysia and Singapore agreed to refer the dispute to the ICJ is testimony of the two countries' desire to maintain good and enduring relations.

Once Malaysia and Singapore signed a special agreement to refer the Pedra Branca dispute to the ICJ in February 2003, Tommy was in the enviable position of being qualified to represent Singapore in one of four ways: (i) as scholar, (ii) as counsel, (iii) as agent, or (iv) as ad hoc judge. Under the ICJ statutes, a state party has the right to nominate an ad hoc judge if she does not have a national as a member of the court. Tommy was therefore qualified to be appointed an ad hoc judge for Singapore. He was initially considered for nomination, but the idea was dropped for prudential reasons. First, he would have to vote, and if he voted in favour of Singapore, it would have diminished his personal

---

2 The Agent for Malaysia, Kadir Mohamd, has also written, from Malaysia's perspective, an account of the case. See *Malaysia Singapore: Fifty Years of Contentions 1965–2015* (The Other Press, 2015), 89–133.

stature as an international lawyer, and also Singapore's reputation for avoiding conflicts of interest. Second, his nomination might also be perceived as a sign of Singapore's lack of confidence in the merits of its legal case. Third, if Malaysia were to object, it could irk some members of the court to be called upon to decide the issue.

That decision left Tommy with three remaining roles.[3] By that time, we had already appointed international counsel and had assigned them the legal issues to address at the hearing. Tommy's expertise was then deployed to critiquing the legal research done by the AGC's in-house team. However, in so far as Singapore needed Tommy to have a speaking role at the hearing, it would have to be that of Agent. And so Tommy was appointed Agent for Singapore.

As expected, the role of Agent suited Tommy's experience and talents. Also Tommy was already well known and respected in international law and relations through his work in the adoption of the United Nations Convention on the Law of the Sea, and also the Rio Summit on climate change. The Agent represents the state party and is the head of the delegation that includes counsel and advocates. His statements to the ICJ bind the state. He makes the first speech for the state, in which he introduces the members of his delegation and summarises the case for the state. He also makes the closing submission for Singapore, which is a highly important role.

In his opening speech, Tommy introduced Singapore's team, and gave a clear and succinct summary of Singapore's claim to sovereignty over Pedra Branca and its satellite features. Equally important, he re-affirmed Singapore's strong support for international law in the peaceful settlement of international disputes. He said:

> *Singapore attaches great importance to international law and we have always sought to conduct ourselves in conformity with it. We have worked with other like-minded States to strengthen the rule of law in the*

---

3 Eventually, Tommy took upon himself two additional roles: (v) as a publicist, by requesting *The Straits Times* to send Lydia Lim and Channel NewsAsia (CNA) to send May Wong to report the proceedings for the Singapore public, and (vi) as our in-house epicurean who took our team on a two-hour drive to eat at a (very disappointing) one Michelin starred Dutch restaurant, in the belief that if we were to fight well, we should eat well! The CNA recordings are available on YouTube, and are worth listening to for their day-to-day dramatic accounts of the Parties' arguments.

world. We believe in the peaceful settlement of disputes. We believe that States should seek to resolve their differences by consultations, negotiations and mediation. When a dispute cannot be resolved by those means, we believe that, instead of allowing the dispute to adversely affect the overall bilateral relationship of the two countries concerned, it is preferable to refer a dispute to a binding third party procedure, namely, to arbitration or adjudication. It is for this reason that Singapore and Malaysia have agreed to submit our dispute to this honourable Court.[4]

In his closing speech, Tommy showed his mastery of his brief. He delivered a clear and concise summation of Singapore's case in his customary pointed style to make 10 points as set out below:

(1) In 1847, Pedra Branca was terra nullius when Singapore took possession of it. Malaysia failed to show: (a) that Pedra Branca was part of the Sultanate of Johor; or (b) that an original title had been transmitted to the State of Johor.

(2) Between 1847 and 1851, Britain was in possession of Pedra Branca without the consent of any native ruler.

(3) Between 1847 and 1851, the British acquired sovereignty over Pedra Branca by satisfying the two requisite criteria: animus or intention, and corpus or activities undertaken *à titre de souverain*.

(4) From 1847 to 1979, Singapore's sovereignty over Pedra Branca was open, continuous and notorious. It was acknowledged by all concerned and challenged by none. Malaysia only claimed Pedra Branca in 1979 by publishing a map showing the island within its territorial boundary.

(5) In 1953, the State Secretary of Johor (which was a sovereign state under international law) wrote in his official capacity to the Singapore Government "the Johore Government does not claim ownership of Pedra Branca." This disclaimer was binding on Malaysia under international law.

(6) In 1968, the Malaysian Government demanded that Singapore

---

4 Oral argument by Tommy Koh on November 6, 2007, retrieved from: https://www.mfa.gov.sg/content/mfa/media_centre/special_events/pedrabranca/press_room/sp_tr/2007/200711/press_200711_26.html

lower its marine ensign from its lighthouse on Pulau Pisang, but not from Horsburgh Lighthouse on Pedra Branca.

(7) Between 1962 and 1975, Malaysia published six maps which attributed sovereignty of Pedra Branca to Singapore. Singapore did not publish any map acknowledging Pedra Branca as belonging to Malaysia.

(8) Pedra Branca, Middle Rocks and South Ledge were inseparable maritime features on the basis of geographical proximity, geology, history and law. They should be treated as a group, and whoever owned Pedra Branca should also have title over the other two features.

(9) Even if Malaysia had a historic title to Pedra Branca, its title was extinguished by Singapore's effectivités and assertion of sovereignty over the island from 1847 onwards. Malaysia had zero effectivités since 1847.

(10) Malaysia's magnanimous concession that Singapore would be allowed to continue to operate Horsburgh Lighthouse, in the event she was awarded title to Pedra Branca, was in reality an attempt to change a legal order which had existed for 160 years.

The Court held that Malaysia had original title over Pedra Branca[5] but by a majority accepted Tommy's main point that Singapore's effectivités, which Malaysia had acknowledged by her own conduct, were sufficient to extinguish Malaysia's original title might have over Pedra Branca. That was what really counted for Singapore.

The ICJ hearing also brought out the best in Tommy's character — his deeply charitable and forgiving nature. In his second speech, Sir Elihu Lauterpacht, one of Malaysia's counsel, commented on the missing letter

---

5 Based primarily on two letters written by John Crawfurd on January 10, 1824 and October 1, 1824, and accounts of the *orang laut* (the subjects of the Sultanate) having sailed around Pedra Branca from time to time. Cf The case of "Sovereignty over Pulau Ligitan and Pulau Sipadan (Indon./Malay.)" 2002 ICJ REP. 625 (Dec. 17) at para. 110 where the ICJ pronounced:

Malaysia relies on the ties of allegiance which allegedly existed between the Sultan of Sulu and the Bajau Laut who inhabited the islands off the coast of North Borneo and who from time to time may have made use of the two uninhabited islands. The Court is of the opinion that such ties may well have existed but that they are in themselves not sufficient to provide evidence that the Sultan of Sulu claimed territorial title to these two small islands or considered them part of his possessions. Nor is there any evidence that the Sultan actually exercised authority over Ligitan and Sipadan.

from Governor Butterworth to Sultan Ali and the Temenggong seeking their permission for the East India Company to build a lighthouse "near" Point Romania. The Temenggong had replied in his letter dated November 25, 1844 that "the company are at full liberty to put up a Light House there, or any spot deemed eligible."[6] Malaysia's case was that Butterworth could have referred to Pedra Branca in his letter. Sir Elihu contended:

> In the circumstances we are obliged to consider two possible inferences that may be drawn from the available correspondence read as a whole.

And concluded his statement with this sting in the tail:

> And I leave entirely aside any suggestion of a third inference, namely that Singapore has deliberately concealed these letters.

Those members of the Singapore team who heard this statement were shocked that a Queen's Counsel of such high standing could resort to such forensic subterfuge to suggest the contrary.

How did Tommy react? In his concluding speech, Tommy expressed his "great pleasure in seeing my friend of 30 years... back with us in the Court today" and "wish[ed] him continued good health."[7]

---

6 After years of research in all the archives and libraries all over the world, Singapore was unable to find a copy of the letter.

This was not the first time that Sir Elihu had demonstrated his style of advocacy in this way. A few months before, in the Reclamation Case between Malaysia and Singapore before the International Tribunal of the Sea, Sir Elihu had made the following remarks in his submission:

> ... with all respect to my learned friend Professor Koh, though he played a critically important role in the achievement of the final text of UNCLOS, that does not carry with it any implication that his interpretation of the Convention should be given any special weight. The interpretation of the Convention is a matter for this high Tribunal and for no-one else.

It was, of course, not Singapore's case that Tommy's interpretation of the Convention carried any weight, much less special weight. Hence, the submission was completely gratuitous. Unknown to Sir Elihu, Tommy had in his possession a copy of a speech made by Sir Elihu, where he had argued that the Tribunal was a wholly unnecessary institution and that it was a waste of money to establish and maintain it. Tommy could have quoted Sir Elihu's views on the Tribunal, but he decided not to do so as he thought it was not cricket, even though Sir Elihu had already bowled a googly.

7 Sir Elihu fainted in the courtroom during Malaysia's first round of oral pleadings. He was rushed to hospital. One week later, Sir Elihu requested the Court to expunge from its records any reference to his fainting in court. The Ag President was of the view that it could not be done, and sought Tommy's view. Tommy agreed with the Ag President. They then went to the room where the Malaysian delegation's room and explained the decision to them.

Malaysia has recently made an application to the ICJ to review its previous judgment on the ground that that she had discovered "new facts" (which were not known to her before judgment was delivered) and which, if known to the Court, would have been decisive against Singapore's claim. Tommy is now part of the Singapore team to put Malaysia's claim to Pedra Branca to rest, once and for all.

Section V

Tributes

CHAPTER 41

Tommy Koh: Colleague and Friend

—— ❧ ——

GEORGE YEO

When I was an undergraduate in Cambridge in the 1970s, a Singaporean postgraduate student intimated to me that Tommy Koh was a potential prime minister and a rival to Lee Kuan Yew. Tommy Koh had become well known as Singapore's first Permanent Representative to the UN and especially for his remarkable leadership in drafting and securing global support for the UN Convention on the Law of the Sea.

I first met Tommy at an official function in Singapore in the late 1970s. His reputation preceded him. When he walked into the room, he looked the caricature of himself with a head shock full of hair, kind but intelligent eyes behind thick black-rimmed glasses and the softest of handshakes. I was surprised that he took the trouble to greet and shake hands with everyone in the room, including young me in Captain's uniform. From an admirer, I became a fan.

When I entered politics in 1988, Prime Minister Lee Kuan Yew appointed me as Minister of State for Finance and for Foreign Affairs. Tommy was then our Ambassador to the United States. As a junior minister, I learnt much from him about foreign affairs and diplomacy. I was struck most by his good heart and his willingness to see the good in others. Diplomats are expected to be cynical. Tommy was not, without being naive or idealistic. This made him an excellent negotiator. He is always in search of win-win solutions, which is only possible when one does not only see the worst in the other party.

I cannot remember who observed that diplomats are paid to lie for their country. I completely reject this view and, I am sure, Tommy too.

Diplomats have to assess and manage risks all the time. When there is greater trust, the circles of feasible negotiation widen, increasing the area of overlap. There is then more space for creative exploration and agreement. If one betrays a trust, the circles shrink and future negotiations become more difficult. Even those who disagree with Tommy acknowledge his fair dealing and trustworthiness. He is a valuable diplomatic asset for Singapore.

After Indonesia established diplomatic relations with China in 1990, Lee Kuan Yew decided that it was opportune for Singapore to follow suit. He appointed Tommy as our Chief Negotiator. The Singapore Armed Forces' training in Taiwan was an issue that had to be explicitly but delicately handled. Some of the details remain classified till today but it is an open secret that our soldiers continue to train in Taiwan and our unofficial relations with Taiwan remain excellent, even as we enjoy very good relations with the Mainland. Tommy's deft handling of negotiations made possible the historic Wang-Koo and Xi-Ma Talks[1] in Singapore.

After the Soviet Union collapsed, he was asked by UN Secretary-General Boutros Boutros-Ghali to lead a friendship mission to Russia and the Baltic Republics in 1993, principally to ease the withdrawal of Russian troops. By being hard and soft at the right moments, a potentially dangerous situation was averted.

Among senior diplomats around the world, Tommy is fondly remembered till today. I have been asked countless times, in and out of office, to convey good wishes from many of them to Tommy, which I happily do.

When Goh Chok Tong became Prime Minister in 1990, I was privileged to head a new Ministry for Information and the Arts. I knew Tommy had a passionate interest in the arts. When he returned to Singapore from Washington D.C. that year, I asked him to chair our newly established National Arts Council. He was the perfect man for the role. It was not an easy job because we had limited means to satisfy

---

1 In April 1993, Singapore hosted a high-level meeting between Taiwan and China, where Taiwan's Straits Exchange Foundation (SEF) Chief, Koo Chen-fu, met Wang Daohan, Chairman for China's Association for Relations Across the Taiwan Straits (Arats). In November 2015, Singapore hosted another high-level meeting between Mainland China and Taiwan, this time between Taiwanese president Ma Ying-jeou and Xi Jinping, General-Secretary of the Communist Party of China.

unlimited wants. He helped artists, encouraged them, cheered them on. But he could be firm. He left the management of the Substation in no doubt that the vulgarity of a particular exhibition was unacceptable. When a director of one of our arts schools took a racist line, Tommy advocated his removal at my ministerial staff meeting which he was member of. On another occasion, a young performer had performed a crude act on stage which horrified Singaporeans. It was during a performance supported by the National Arts Council. Tommy took action promptly, which made it unnecessary for me as Minister to become directly involved. I also appointed him to chair a politically-sensitive committee to review Singapore's censorship rules around the same time.

In November 2000, after a golf game in Brunei between Goh Chok Tong and US President Bill Clinton on a dark, thundery night, negotiations between Singapore and the United States for a free trade agreement were launched. It was a narrow window of opportunity made possible by uncertainty over who won the US Presidential Election, which then hung on floating chads in Florida. Because of this, Clinton was not yet a "lame duck". Trade Representative Charlene Barshefsky had asked me in Brunei before Clinton arrived whether Singapore was interested in a bilateral free trade agreement using the US-Jordan Free Trade Agreement as a template. As Minister for Trade and Industry, I was Barshefsky's counterpart. We quickly worked on the wording of an agreement to launch negotiations, which Goh Chok Tong then proposed to Clinton after the famous golf game. Once Clinton agreed, I called Tommy who was at a meeting in China and requested him to be our Chief Negotiator. He was the obvious choice. Knowing the importance of the free trade agreement to Singapore, he agreed immediately.

After over two years of intense negotiations, we reached agreement with the Bush Administration in early 2003. Tommy's role was indispensable. We negotiated the final round with US Trade Representative Robert Zoellick in Singapore. Zoellick could have insisted that it be held in Washington D.C. Instead, he gave us the home ground advantage partly because there was a meeting which both of us had to attend in Manila shortly thereafter. Negotiations, which went on all night, were tougher than I had anticipated. At one point, Zoellick complained that the air-conditioning where the American team had their internal meetings was too cold. He and his officials must have also suffered jet lag. Far from taking advantage of our American friends, Tommy got the temperature raised to a comfortable level and arranged for the supply of McDonald's hamburgers so that they were fortified with their own comfort food. The US-Singapore Free Trade Agreement has created many good jobs in Singapore and given many Singapore companies a leg up in the US market.

When Lee Hsien Loong became Prime Minister in 2004, he appointed me Foreign Minister, one of which pleasures was the opportunity to work closely with Tommy again. He attended all my staff meetings and was always the voice of conscience, appealing to our better side. When I became too negative about a particular country or issue, he would furnish an opposite argument to restore balance. He would not hesitate to disagree but was never disagreeable. I found his optimism a refreshing antidote to the pessimism of my other colleagues. But even as they opposed some of Tommy's suggestions, they thought the world of him. For a long time, Singapore's diplomats had to justify the death penalty at the UN and other international forums. When required, Tommy would explain Singapore's position but he never hid his personal opposition to it. He was utterly professional but he had his principles.

In 2007, Tommy represented Singapore on the High Level Task Force that drafted the ASEAN Charter. The Charter was intended to be the Constitution of ASEAN. It was an ambitious exercise that could have foundered over a number of sensitive issues like human rights and dispute resolution. Tommy played a key role. He has this remarkable, almost effortless ability to broker differences and forge consensus.

Tommy's amiability belies a core within which enables him to stand up for what is right. He is never intimidated except, in charming self-admission, by his wife. I observed with some fascination the interaction between Tommy Koh and Lee Kuan Yew over dinner on a couple of occasions. With the greatest politeness, he would disagree with Lee Kuan Yew to his face, like the latter's views on the performance of Hispanics in the United States. Lee Kuan Yew appreciated Tommy's honesty but I also thought that Lee Kuan Yew knew he could not browbeat Tommy to agreement on any subject he did not believe in.

Tommy's willingness to speak truth to power, gently and politely, plus his negotiating skills, would have made him an excellent UN Secretary-General. When the turn came to Asia to throw up candidates for the post in 2005, he was a potential serious contender. Thailand was fielding Surakiart Sathirathai and asked for Singapore's support but we were for a few months unsure whether we ourselves were putting up a candidate. Tommy would have been our best candidate and would have won had he ran. This was the view of many pundits. But his doting wife, Siew Aing, advised against his running for good reasons. Siew Aing, while a medical student, fell in love with a young Tommy in shining armour. In order to marry and accompany him to New York following a fairytale courtship, she gave up her housemanship after graduating with an MBBS, and therefore her chance ever to practise as a doctor. As a faithful husband, Tommy abided Siew Aing's wish and disqualified himself. Their faithfulness to each other has always been an inspiration to me and my wife.

After I lost the elections in 2001 and retired from politics, Tommy wrote a tribute which touched me deeply. I am grateful to him for speaking at my book launch in 2013. I have often said that God put Tommy among us to make us better. He has been a mentor to me, a wonderful colleague and a dear friend. On his 80th birthday, I add my congratulations to the many he must be receiving and wish him many, many more happy, healthy years.

CHAPTER 42

Working with Ambassador Tommy Koh

JENNY HO-TAN

I had the privilege of working with Ambassador Tommy Koh when I was posted to our Embassy in Washington D.C. in 1984 to be his personal assistant.

My first encounter with him was the day I reported for work at the Embassy. After being introduced to him and after a short chat, he gave me a list containing names of international schools in Washington D.C. to choose a school for my then six-year-old son. When I told him that Ministry of Foreign Affairs (MFA) had told me that my son could only go to a public school and only children of Heads of Missions were entitled to attend international schools, he was taken aback. He added that all Singaporeans should be treated equally under the Constitution. He told me not to worry but to go ahead and pick a school for my son, as he would write to MFA to seek approval for my son to go to an international school. He explained to MFA that the standard of public schools in Washington D.C. was not consistent and may not be suitable for Singaporean kids. I was very touched by his concern for my son's welfare. He also made sure that my family and I were properly settled in.

I had heard wonderful things about Ambassador Koh before I met him in person in Washington D.C. What he did for my son's schooling fully convinced me that Ambassador Koh is a man who really cares for those around him, and it is no wonder that he commanded great respect from people who came into contact with him. He fought hard for the rights of his staff and was ever ready to help anyone who needed his assistance. When my family and I arrived in Washington D.C. that wintry day, I learned from Ambassador Koh's chauffeur — who had come to the airport with the other office chauffeur to pick up my family and me, that Ambassador Koh had anticipated that one vehicle would not be enough for a family of four and a domestic helper as well as several luggage bags. I marvelled at his foresight and thoughtfulness, which I had not seen in many senior office holders with whom I had worked or met. His thoughtfulness and kindness are so admirable and up to now, I feel honoured to have had the opportunity to know him and work with him. My husband and I are grateful for all the care and concern he showered on us. Needless to say, my family and I had an enjoyable and most unforgettable four-year stay in Washington D.C.

My second opportunity in working with Ambassador Koh came in 1991. I had resigned from MFA as I didn't want my husband to take no-pay leave again just to accompany me on another overseas posting. Spouses of Mission staff then were not allowed to work in the country where their husbands or wives were posted. At the time, Ambassador Koh was holding two portfolios as Ambassador-at-Large at MFA and Director of the Institute of Policy Studies (IPS). When his personal assistant at IPS left, he asked if I would work for him at the Institute.

After I submitted my resignation at MFA, I went to see the then Director of Administration to inform her that I was going to be the Personal Assistant to Ambassador Tommy Koh at IPS. The Director was upset because there had been a number of resignations from personal assistants and stenographers, and I was one of the most senior to resign. Learning this, Ambassador Koh very generously offered to help uncover the cause for the high turnover and find a solution. It was a gracious gesture, reflecting his character and professionalism.

In 1997, Ambassador Koh was asked to help set up the Asia-Europe Foundation (ASEF) in Singapore and was appointed as the first Executive Director of the Foundation. He had to relinquish his post as Director of IPS, and he approached me to help him set up ASEF together with another staff member Leigh Pascual, who was seconded from MFA. When the Deputy Executive Director (from France) and other foreign departmental heads (from Germany, Britain and China) were appointed and came to Singapore, he made sure that they were all made to feel welcome. Ambassador Koh, Leigh and I did our best to help these officers find accommodation and also gave them whatever assistance they needed. It was important to Ambassador Koh to make sure that these newcomers felt comfortable and were able to travel about in Singapore with ease. He would go to their offices to see if they were getting on all right and he asked them to approach him should they need any help. I have not found another person who can match Ambassador Koh's gentlemanly, patient, caring and understanding nature.

Ambassador Koh's appointment as Executive Director of ASEF was only for a period of three and a half years, as there was a three-year rotational system for all the senior positions in ASEF. He returned to MFA while I stayed on at the Foundation. Life was not the same in ASEF after he left. I missed his friendly and approachable presence. At the same time I feel privileged to have worked with him for over a decade, from Washington to IPS and ASEF.

CHAPTER 43

Tommy Koh: Young Boss and Man Sans Pareil

GEOFFREY YU

Balmy Evening in Manhattan

On my way to meet Tommy Koh for the first time in June 1974, I was buoyed up by elation and excitement.

It was a balmy evening in Manhattan, a place I had dreamt of visiting since my mid-teens. There I was finally, the dream come true, walking in the shadow of skyscrapers up mid-town East Side, hardly believing that I was en route to spending 10 weeks in exotic Caracas. Dinner had been arranged at the home of the man who was to lead Singapore's delegation to the epochal United Nations Conference on the Law of the Sea (UNCLOS). The man was none other than Ambassador Tommy Koh, Singapore's Permanent Representative to the United Nations. At 36 years of age, a mere 10 years older than me, he was already ensconced in his second tour as Singapore's Ambassador and Permanent Representative to the United Nations.

Forty-three years later, I can still recall the details of meeting over dinner in his home: outside an aubergine sky, inside a loving young couple — Tommy and his beautiful wife Siew Aing, offering the ravenous, jet-lagged delegates from Singapore the comfort food of chicken rice, wanton noodles and laksa. Close by us, their young sons played. The atmosphere was relaxed, convivial and warm. No one stood on ceremony nor was there any barrier of hierarchy and seniority. The host and hostess put everyone at ease and it felt like a wonderful evening among new friends, who included, among others, Chao Hick Tin, then a young legal officer prone to infectious laughter.

What a wonderful start to my adventure in distant lands, I told myself on walking back to the hotel after dinner. Little did I know then that the happy evening was the overture to more than 40 years of work and friendship with Tommy as well as to my friendship with Siew Aing, his wife and life companion. I mention Siew Aing because anyone knowing them knows how inseparable they are.

Let me briefly highlight here the early years, when Tommy was my young boss, from 1974 to 1981. He was between 36 and 43 years old.

Inspiring Mentor

Over a period of seven years, I worked for Tommy in Caracas, Geneva and New York.

Less than two days after the introduction to Tommy, the delegation flew to Caracas, capital of a then resurgent Venezuela. How often does a young man have an opportunity, within two days of a first meeting, to interact and learn from a new boss at close proximity over 10 intense weeks? And it was not any boss, but a young man already known for his brilliant mind, oratorical skill and disarming charm. Over those packed weeks, Tommy and his delegation spent hours together daily, in huddles and over meals. The work was varied and the hours were often long. As much as I possibly could, I observed our leader, opening mental files on Tommy's panoply of skills and tools as a top negotiator. I saw how, as the head, Tommy set out the delegation's goals, devised a strategic game plan, and put the delegation members to best use, network, seize opportunities, and win over friends and opponents alike. Everything he did appeared effortless. He was never hurried, and spoke in a calm voice and soft tone. It was a voice that was never raised. His demeanour was relaxed, a smile invariably present. Whenever someone spoke to him, he listened intently. Whenever the debate among negotiators became tense, he could be counted on to thaw the ice by drawing on an inexhaustible trove of jokes. Of themselves, these qualities would not suffice in bridging opposing national interests. That Tommy often succeeded in moving opponents closer to each other was equally due to his capacity to project fairness, objectivity and integrity at all times. These are not skills that can be easily learned, if at all. It calls for someone who is self-confident, poised, patient, tolerant, and open-minded, with a genuine curiosity about people and the world. Without exaggeration, I can say that Tommy possessed all those qualities. He transformed them into accomplishments, an inimitable art form. I was privileged to see them deployed to great effect — not merely in Caracas, but throughout the protracted negotiation period that culminated in a binding treaty in 1982.

As a member of the UNCLOS negotiating team, I spent three years in four extended negotiating sessions, observing and learning from Tommy, not just in Caracas, but also in Geneva in 1975 and New York in 1976. Within his team, Tommy never asserted authority or seniority. He did not need recourse to such means. His method was to lead from the rear. Each of us was left to find our own way to reach the delegation's desired outcome. As leader and boss, he merely made sure that we knew he was available and supporting us, shepherding with a light hand, ready to back us when this was needed. In many ways, he was the ideal mentor for bright, enterprising, eager youngsters, for his guidance was deft, handling everyone almost as if each was his equal, just less experienced and nimble. In brief, he led by example, and in conference settings, his example was inspiring. This set him apart from many other bosses, for he empowered his juniors by example and by delegation of responsibility.

In Caracas, Tommy assigned me to cover alone Committee Three, which dealt with scientific research and pollution. Despite being an utter novice in international negotiations, not once did I feel him looking over my shoulders as I manoeuvred my course in that Committee. Every initiative I took was approved by him. It was immensely empowering to a young diplomat. Occasionally, he would pop into my committee room to see what was going on. Those visits were a source of comfort for me. Not once did I see him, whether in Caracas or elsewhere, generating tension or intimidation.

The gratification of working with Tommy was again renewed in 1978, when I took a break from work in our Tokyo Embassy to integrate into Tommy's team for that year's UN General Assembly. Although there would be no outcomes binding our country, Tommy, nevertheless, conducted daily morning meetings in which the events of the previous day and the day ahead were reviewed. In these gatherings, Tommy demonstrated the benefits of transparency and information sharing. They were occasions for tactical planning. In this way, he promoted cooperation, coordination and solidarity; all members were treated as equals.

It seemed a matter of time before my working for Tommy would become more formalised. In the autumn of 1980, I was appointed Tommy's number two. During the year that I was there, I worked alongside Tommy on three notable projects: UN involvement in the upheavals in Indochina arising from the Vietnam-Kampuchea (as Cambodia was then called) conflict and the China-Vietnam conflict; the lead-up to and the conduct of the UN International Conference on Kampuchea; and Singapore's campaign for the Presidency of the UN General Assembly. These projects entailed working to narrow mandates from home, tight deadlines and delicate dealings with diplomats from the direct protagonists in the two conflicts on the one hand, and our ASEAN friends on the other. Tommy was at the top of his game — cool, calm and collected, inspiring confidence in his younger colleagues who were proud to work for him. His skills in the conference room were masterly. When he spoke, the room would fall into a hush. His summing-up of issues was legendary. All in the room listened for they knew he would speak with the impartiality, fairness and sagacity of a Solomon. Such moments, and there were many, never failed to fill me with pride to be part of his team.

Administration work would be a wasteful drain on Tommy's gifts. So I was glad to relieve him of the mundane tasks of running an office, knowing that his delegation of responsibility was a demonstration of trust and dependence. However, one administrative project which he took personal charge of was the purchase of a residential property for the Ambassador. We spent many interesting hours visiting brownstone houses and apartments, and found the property which 35 years later, continues to house his successors.

No one who worked for him wanted to fail him. His team members always worked in a horizontal setting; it was a management approach that led everyone to greater productivity, professional empowerment at its most potent. It was a signal indication of his effective management style that I was often told by people who worked for him in his New York years, that they accomplished this or that. With profound generosity, he let them take the credit for successful outcomes.

Long Hair, Slim Suits and Ladies

Yet, working for him extended beyond seeking to emulate and acquiring some of his unique diplomatic arsenal. He became a friend and companion outside of work, given to laughter and jokes, sharing good meals, exercising together and exchanging books, among other common pursuits. The mid-1970s was the era of bell bottoms, long hair and slim suits, when youths sought to distance themselves from their baby-boomer parents. I was part of the rising generation, while Tommy, my near contemporary, straddled both generations comfortably. His hair then, as now, was much closer to the Beatles cut than his peers among the Ambassadors. I harboured the feeling that if he had not been a young father and husband occupying such a responsible position, he might well have sported considerably longer hair and worn brighter clothes! As it were, he showed an interest in my sartorial preferences and was happy to accompany me occasionally on my shopping expeditions in New York, offering comments on the clothes that I contemplated buying. A little incident comes to mind. During the spring break in 1975, I was on graduate study leave at Oxford when I was summoned to join the UNCLOS delegation in Geneva. I arrived sporting longish hair, then quite in keeping with my contemporaries on campus. Only on the third day in Geneva did Tommy casually mentioned, as we walked up a flight of stairs, that my hair seemed long. I gave him a smile and the matter did not come up again.

The camaraderie that came from working together over 10 weeks in Caracas was renewed in spring 1975, in Geneva, when the delegation was strengthened by the addition of S Jayakumar. The experience was repeated in New York in 1976, over two periods totalling eight weeks. As Ambassador based in the Big Apple, Tommy no longer had breakfast with us, but the delegation met daily in the morning before negotiations resumed during the working week. By then, the bonds had been firmly soldered. Chao Hick Tin was the undisputed chef of the delegation, cheerfully preparing breakfast each morning. In New York, dinner choices were abundant, so he was less busy as chef. However, in Caracas and Geneva, because the local cuisine was unappealing, he happily cooked dinner as well as shopped for the food. Everyone else played dishwasher, a far easier task. By way of compensation, Siew Aing and Tommy regularly invited us to their home for a Singaporean repast, in the company of their two lively boys. On weekends, as a relief from the intense meetings and caucuses, we made group visits to museums and eating excursions to Chinatown.

Of Tommy's legendary approachability and inimitable charm, there are stories galore. Among the secrets to them are his astounding capacity to remember names, faces and places. In conference rooms, receptions, corridors and the street, he greeted warmly statesmen and janitors alike by name. And he never failed to introduce strangers to one another in a group. His manners were impeccable. Over and above all else, ladies held a special place for him. Old or young, ravishing or otherwise, simple or sophisticated, he had a compliment for each of them, well-placed, sincerely meant. Without exception, they adored him. Secure in her position in his heart, Siew Aing was most generous with her ladies' man.

The Hand of Friendship

Let me end my account by describing the hand of friendship, which Tommy and Siew Aing extended to me. In October 1980, he welcomed me as his number two in New York although he knew that I was unlikely to complete the full term of my posting. Beyond the professional confidence that he extended to me, Siew Aing and he made me feel that I was not merely a staff member, but also a good family friend. Often, I was included in family weekend outings they organised for their two sons, including to Central Park and watching a performance of the New York Christmas favourite, *The Nutcracker*, by the New York City Ballet. Knowing that I was a rookie cook, Siew Aing took me grocery shopping with her in Chinatown on Saturday mornings.

This single man shared many meals with the family. In July 1981, I had the privilege and pleasure of accompanying them both to Mexico City for his presentation of credentials as Singapore's first Ambassador to Mexico. Once, Tommy returned from a trip to South America with the gift of an alpaca pullover. When he handed it to me, he said simply, "Thank you for looking after Siew Aing in my absence."

Wishes

Tommy Koh is a true patriot. He loves his country, devoting half a century so far to championing its interests and winning for it as many foreign friends as possible. It is an honour for me to join many in saluting him. I send him my warmest affectionate wishes for many more years of good health, joy, laughter, and, not least, continuing challenges to his razor-sharp intellect.

CHAPTER 44

Tommy Koh: Reflections of a Friend

— ·ᴗ· —

Gopinath Pillai

In the late 1950s if you had seen an article on the Preservation of Public Security Ordinance (PPSO) in any publication of the University of Malaya, it was very likely that Tommy Koh was the writer. No one was so appalled by this piece of legislation as Tommy was. The cause of his unhappiness was that the law allowed for the arrest and detention of persons the government considered a threat to national security, without trial. This law was passed during David Marshall's tenure in office as the first Chief Minister of Singapore. What prompted him to enact this law was the Hock Lee riots, one of the few violent events in Singapore's history that shocked the nation. Tommy's objection to the law was that it deprived a person the opportunity to defend himself in a court of law, which was the constitutional right of every citizen. This reflected probably the most important trait in Tommy's character.

Tommy and I joined the University of Malaya, then located in Singapore, in the same year, 1957. Although I did one week of orientation in Singapore before going to Kuala Lumpur to do my first year of the Arts course, we did not have an opportunity to meet. On my return to Singapore in the second year I met Tommy at the University Socialist Club, a leftist political club that was anti-colonial and pro-independence. He was the Secretary General and I was elected into the Central Working Committee as the Publication Secretary overseeing the Club's well known monthly, the *Fajar*.

What was obvious to me about Tommy from our early interaction was his strong sense of justice and fairplay. Another example of this trait was his stand on the Club's membership. Our membership was rather small for two reasons. First, many of the undergraduates, while participating in our activities, were unwilling to become members of the Club for fear of offending the colonial government. The second reason was that the Club on its part was also highly selective in allowing new members to enrol. Tommy was against the committee vetting application for membership. He maintained that any student of the University has the right to be a member of any club in the University. After long discussion Tommy was able to persuade the committee to allow any matriculated student to be a member of the Club.

Apart from the Socialist Club, Tommy was also active in the University Law Society — the first student organisation to invite S. Rajaratnam as guest speaker when he became Minister of Culture after the 1959 election. An event that the University Law Society organised annually was the inter-hall debates. In one of these debates the Raffles Hall team, in which I was a member, proposed the motion: "That the University of Malaya was established to train lower level civil servants to provide bureaucratic support for their colonial masters." I am not sure that this is the exact wording but it conveys the thrust of the motion. Tommy chaired the debate and the chairman of the panel of judges was Professor Wang Gungwu. The highlight of the debate was the walkout by one of the opposition speakers because there was a fair amount of heckling by the Raffles supporters. I am narrating these stories of events that happened more than 50 years ago, to give the reader an idea how campus life was in Singapore in the late 1950s and early 1960s — and how fully immersed Tommy was in that life. I do not have much information about his earlier school life. In this connection I must say I was disappointed that he did not agree to be featured in a book written by his classmate, Tan Guan Heng, on prominent Rafflesians, although he did agree to launch the book.

After graduation Tommy and I went our separate ways. Tommy's chosen path was academia and later diplomacy. I went off to work for a bank in Thailand and after that in a development finance institution in Malaysia. While in Malaysia, I read in the papers that Tommy had been appointed Singapore's Permanent Representative to the United Nations. I was thrilled because I felt the government was recognising his talent and also that they did not hold his leftist leanings against him. The credit for this, I feel, goes to S. Rajaratnam who by then had become Foreign Minister. He also set politics aside and appointed David Marshall as Singapore's Ambassador to France.

Tommy and I reconnected after I returned to Singapore in 1970. When I became the Research Secretary of the University of Singapore Society, I went to pick Tommy's brains. He suggested that I ask the deans of the various faculties to submit their five-year plans to the graduate body in closed-door meetings where the Chatham House Rule would apply. I soon learnt a new lesson. You can have good rules but they mean little unless people respect them or you have strong ways of enforcing them. In the first session the dean was quite frank and made some provocative statements. A member present who was a newspaper reporter felt that it was too good an opportunity to miss and reported the entire proceedings in a tabloid with a sensational headline. The dean was understandably furious and in spite of my apologies, the damage was done. I decided to abandon the programme, which was a pity as Tommy's idea was to get the graduates more closely involved in the workings of the university. It reflected his inclusive approach to nurture a sense of belonging.

Tommy was a staunch supporter of having an ombudsman in Singapore. Considering Singapore's ethnic diversity as well as the fact that multiple players with varying interests are engaged in its economy, the idea of an ombudsman makes a great deal of sense. Many of us felt Tommy himself would have made an excellent ombudsman. However, the idea did not gain traction with the government and it is unlikely to materialise.

Another cause that Tommy espoused was the concept of the minimum wage. He felt that the income disparity was widening and the minimum wage will help to narrow the gap. Personally I am not sure whether the minimum wage will actually narrow the gap. Unless labour organisations are vigilant, the concept of the minimum wage can be abused.

At the risk of repeating myself I would say that both ideas of having an ombudsman and a minimum wage emanate from Tommy's deep-rooted desire for justice and fairplay.

Tommy told me when he returned to Singapore after his first assignment at the UN that he was going to devote all his time from then on building the Law Faculty at the National University of Singapore, to be one of the top law schools in the world. Unfortunately, he did not have much time to embark on this as his services were needed elsewhere. The Singapore Ministry of Foreign Affairs was not about to lose this talented diplomat to academia even though I am sure he would have also been a very successful academic. He was to be sent back to the United States for another stint as Singapore's Permanent Representative to the UN.

Tommy has two qualities that make him a consummate diplomat. First is his ability to present his famous "three points" in as gentle a manner as possible irrespective of how charged the atmosphere was, or how heated the arguments were. To borrow from Shakespeare I would say his words "fall like the gentle rain", which causes no offence to anyone but at the same time it does not dilute the strength of his argument.

The second quality is his ability to downplay his own knowledge of any subject or his own vast experience of a situation so that he never appears intimidating. I have never known anybody being uneasy in his presence. The best testimony to his diplomatic skills is the fact that he heads the Singapore delegations for dialogues with three important countries, namely, China, India and Japan. I have been on the delegation for the Singapore-India strategic dialogue from the time it started, and in 2015 Tommy nominated me as a member of the other two delegations. He chooses members of the delegation carefully and he is meticulous in his choice of topics. I have seen in the case of the dialogue with India, for example, that he keeps himself abreast of political events there and makes substantive contributions in the discussions. The country he knows best is perhaps the United States, but for India he built fairly quickly a network of key players and through them was able to acquire an in-depth understanding of the issues facing the country. Because of this understanding, he also developed an empathy for India. I would say that today he is one of the most respected Singaporeans in India.

One other diplomatic achievement of Tommy that Singapore can be proud of is his chairmanship of two important UN conferences, one of which pertained to the agreement on the Law of the Sea. As Chairman of the UN Conference on the Law of the Sea, he painstakingly worked on the parties with conflicting interests and got them to agree to a set of rules that was acceptable to the majority of the members of UN. This Agreement has tremendous impact on all maritime activity, particularly on international trade. Someone who worked closely with Tommy at the Conference told me that a lesser man would not have been able to achieve what Tommy had achieved.

One of our leaders once referred to Tommy as Singapore's national treasure. Many of us who were his contemporaries in the university and those of us who have worked with him would fully recognise his contributions to our nation. He always worked on the principle that a good deal must be a fair deal and an endurable deal. On a personal note I would say that it has been my privilege to be his friend. This friendship is almost 60 years now, and I take this occasion to wish him a very happy 80th birthday.

CHAPTER 45

My Friend of 65 Years, Professor Tommy Koh

WAN HUSSIN ZOOHRI

I am delighted and honoured indeed to contribute this essay in celebration of my dear friend Professor Tommy Koh's 80th birthday.

My friendship with Tommy began in 1952 when we were both young students at Raffles Institution (RI). We had been posted to RI after passing the Secondary Schools' Entrance Examination in 1951. Tommy was in Standard 6A, and I in Standard 6B, which is today's equivalent of Secondary 1. Our classes were adjacent to each other and the design of the classrooms was such that every time Tommy entered or left his classroom, he had to pass through mine.

As busy schoolboys, we did not have much interaction then. But he made a first big impression on me during an inter-class debate; needless to say, he was a top debater. At that early age, Tommy was already showing signs of an outstanding talent with fast thinking and communicating skills.

For the next three years, in what was then known as Standard 7, 8 and 9, we were in the same class. As part of our extra-curricular activities, he was in the Scout movement while I was in the Army Cadet Corps. He became a First Class Scout. Up until then we were, what I would call, "ordinary friends" — just as we were with the rest of our classmates. The turning point came during one Hari Raya celebration. I invited him to my kampung house at Jalan Eunos and we bonded over beef rendang and ketupat. I would like to think that this acknowledged Singapore foodie today remembers my mother's cooking!

An activity I particularly enjoyed at RI was playing soccer for the school team. I was in the Colts, a junior team known for playing barefoot. As a kampung boy, I relished it. From Second Team, I made it to First Team, eventually becoming soccer captain in 1955.

The interschool soccer matches were played at our soccer pitch, an open field located at Bras Basah Road. What a thrill it was for the RI team when our fellow Rafflesians came out in full force to support us. I am happy to report that Tommy was one of our regular supporters. He even described me as "… one of the heroes of my class, the school soccer star… Wan Hussin Zoohri." Tommy, I take that as an ultimate compliment, thank you!

After we completed our Cambridge School Certificate Examination in 1955, we unavoidably went our separate ways. Tommy went on to read law at the then University of Malaya, now known as the National University of Singapore, where he secured a First Class Honours degree. Space does not allow me to list all his academic accomplishments here, but I will mention just two: an LLM from Harvard University and a post-graduate diploma in Criminology from Cambridge University.

As for me, I joined the Ministry of Education as a trainee teacher in 1957 and stayed in the teaching service for 23 years, later becoming Senior Inspector of Schools. I joined politics in 1980 as a member of the ruling People's Action Party.

In the years after RI, as both Tommy and I pursued our careers separately, set up home, started families and raised our children, we all but lost touch with each other. But I continued to admire his achievements from afar, especially his roles and contributions as a diplomat, reports of which I would read in the newspapers. When he returned to Singapore in 1990 after serving as Singapore's Permanent Representative to the United Nations and Ambassador to the United States for almost 20 years, he became chairman of various government entities such as the National Arts Council and later, the National Heritage Board.

Serendipity connected us again in 1991. On June 28 of that year, Parliament was in session and one of the topics discussed was the National Arts Council Bill — there had been plans to set up the first-ever arts council. As Member of Parliament, I spoke in favour of the Bill, mentioning three main points: I requested the NAC to state clearly its policy towards the evolution of Singapore arts in particular, and Singapore's culture in general; I appealed to NAC to take cognizance of the different ethnic cultures in its journey towards a unique Singaporean culture; and I reminded the NAC to establish a functional link with the schools and junior colleges, as the youths would be both the beneficiaries and the talents for Singapore's future cultural renaissance.

The next day, I was pleasantly surprised to receive a letter from Tommy, thanking me for my speech in Parliament. His letter, a keepsake I still treasure, reflects his meticulous approach and firm direction in steering the NAC towards achieving its cultural mission. NAC was officially formed in September 1991, with Tommy as its founding chairman.

With Tommy based in Singapore, we did meet up occasionally. On November 4, 2013, he gave me a copy of *The Tommy Koh Reader: Favourite Essays and Lectures*. In his note, he very kindly described me as a "distinguished Rafflesian". This was an epithet of which I was undeserving, but I appreciated it nonetheless. Just as I did his glowing account of me in his foreword in my autobiography, *Memories and Musings*, published in 2015.

It is a joy reading Tommy's book. Although it is not an autobiography, it mirrors his many qualities as an intellectual, a diplomat, a cultural activist, a concerned and engaged citizen, and most of all a man with integrity, honesty and selflessness and, in his own words, a "happy warrior for peace." His collection of essays and lectures covers diverse topics from family and friends to nature and the environment. From the eight broad subjects explored in his book, one not only gains an insight into Tommy's values and the beliefs he holds dear, but also gleans gems of advice and wisdom.

My essay cannot do justice to this man of exceptional calibre. So I will conclude by selecting and reiterating just five of his many outstanding qualities.

First: his intellectual prowess. This is clearly evident from the speeches he has made in both the national and international arenas. I would say he is equal to, if not better than, many world-class diplomats. The many successful negotiations he has conducted at international levels are testimony to his cogent, logical and persuasive arguments.

Second: his intellectual dissent. He is unafraid to express his disagreement with Singapore's current policies. A case in point is his argument for a minimum wage scheme for the lowest-earning 20 per cent of our workers. He rebutted the official view that this scheme would increase unemployment, reduce foreign investment and affect economic competitiveness. He substantiated his arguments by saying he found no evidence of this happening in Japan, South Korea and Taiwan, countries that had adopted the minimum wage scheme much earlier. He has also written to disagree with some of the "hard truths" mentioned in Lee Kuan Yew's book, *Hard Truths to Keep Singapore Going*.

Third: his unparalleled diplomatic acumen. Tommy stands out as a distinguished diplomat, as evidenced by his representation at international forums. He has successfully steered through difficult situations between opposing parties. One example was when he took on a "mission impossible" to negotiate between Russia and the Baltics in 1993 as the United Nation's Special Envoy. On the strength of his credentials, I am of the opinion that he is an eminent candidate for the post of Secretary-General for the United Nations.

Fourth: his role as a Renaissance man. His diverse interests in cultural matters and concern for inclusiveness among the many strata of society ingrained in his psyche. No group in our society escapes his attention. He respects the elites, appreciates the contributions of the middle class, and feels deeply the plight of the less privileged. This makes him a wholesome man. Much credit must surely go to him for his contributions in setting Singapore's cultural roadmap during his chairmanships in the National Arts Council from 1991 to 1996, and the National Heritage Board from 2002 to 2011.

Fifth: his modesty. Having known Tommy for the past 65 years, his natural modesty stands out every time we meet; it is not only seen but also felt. I feel extremely at ease with him and enjoy his company immensely. He is still the same Tommy I knew when we were at RI. His high position in society does not in any way affect his true modesty.

Truly, he is the Immaculate Asian Gentleman. This is the man I salute till today.

CHAPTER 46

A Tribute to Tommy

S JAYAKUMAR

Introduction

Some individuals are so outstanding that they are icons of Singapore. In the field of diplomacy, law and scholarship, Professor Tommy Koh has become so renowned both in Singapore and internationally that he can be truly described as an iconic Singapore personality.

My relationship with Tommy goes a long way back, to 1957. In our lifetime, our paths have intersected in many places. There is no other individual with whom I have worked so closely over such a long period. It is therefore an honour and privilege for me to contribute to this book tribute to Tommy for his 80th birthday.

Raffles Institution

Tommy and I first met at Raffles Institution (RI). We were very much involved in the Literary and Debating Society and used to arrange debates within the school as well as debates with other schools. Even in those early days in RI, I could witness his exceptional oratorical skills and intellectual prowess. Our days in RI marked the beginning of a unique close collaboration and friendship that has lasted a lifetime.

Student Days in the University of Singapore Law Faculty

We were both involved in student activities in the University of Singapore. He was active in the Socialist Club while I was in the Student Union and Law Club. Tommy was in the first batch of law students. He was head and shoulders above others in his class and graduated with a First Class Honours.

I recall two particularly memorable incidents that took place during our student days.

First, Tommy was accused of being involved in the 1961 protests involving 10 Chinese secondary schools; the protests were against the reforms to the examination system. The students considered the proposals to be unreasonable. Tommy was mistakenly identified to have visited Whampoa Chinese Secondary School in support of these protests. David Marshall (whose firm Tommy was attached) stated in the Legislative Assembly that Tommy was not even in Singapore at the relevant time. Then Minister of Education Yong Nyuk Lin later apologised in Parliament:

> *I tender full and ample apology for having misinformed this House because of the mistaken identity. I also tender full and ample apology to Tommy Koh Thong Bee for any pain and suffering the wrong identification caused him.*[1]

Second, in the context of the Professor DJ Enright issue in the 1960s (who had been castigated by the government for a lecture he had given), Tommy, the President of the Student Union Ernest Devadason and I were taken on a boat ride by Political Secretary Sidney Woodhull. The purpose was to give us a gentle warning that we students should not step into the realm of politics. I found that Tommy, as a student activist and leader, was very principled and prepared to stand up for his views. He did so in the persuasive and dignified manner that has become his trademark.

---

1 "Tommy Koh: A Govt Apology, Second Day Exam Goes On Despite Barricades," *The Straits Times*, November 29, 1961, 11. Retrieved from: http://eresources.nlb.gov.sg/newspapers/Digitised/Article/straitstimes19611129.2.82

Teaching Staff in the NUS Law Faculty

We were colleagues on the teaching staff in NUS. He became a staff in 1962 while I became a staff in 1964. He was elected as Dean of the Faculty in 1971 after returning from his stint as Singapore's Permanent Representative to the United Nations.

As Dean, as he himself stated in his oral history, he wanted to be a good leader and to be a leader by example. He taught as many courses as he assigned to his colleagues. He published as much as any other colleague.

I followed in Tommy's footsteps by first succeeding him as UN Permanent Representative (1971–1974) and then, on my return, succeeding him as Dean of the Law Faculty. I was fortunate because he had led improvements to the Law School in terms of both teaching and research. He brought about very close rapport between teachers and students. The overseas reputation of NUS Law grew under his care and leadership.

Ambassadors to the United Nations

Elsewhere, I have recounted how in 1968 Tommy consulted me about then Foreign Minister S. Rajaratnam's offer to him to be Singapore's next Permanent Representative to the United Nations in New York.[2] Tommy's immediate response was to demur as he felt he was not qualified for the post. I told Tommy that he was being overly modest and that he should not decline the offer as I felt he could have a real impact in New York. Tommy eventually accepted the appointment after discussing it, as he always has at every important juncture, with his wife Siew Aing.

As I knew he would, Tommy went on to do an outstanding job as our Permanent Representative in New York. At 31, he was our youngest-ever Head of Mission. He set the high standards, which every other Permanent Representative, including myself, aspired to meet.

---

2 S Jayakumar, *Diplomacy* (Straits Times Press, 2011).

Delegation to the UN Conference on the Law of the Sea (UNCLOS)

For many years, Tommy, myself, Chao Hick Tin, Geoffrey Yu, Michael Cheok and the late Sivakant Tiwari were core members of the Singapore delegation to the UN Seabed Committee, which later morphed into the Preparatory Commission for the International Seabed Authority and for the International Tribunal for the Law of the Sea. This Preparatory Commission was established, prior to the entry into force of the UNCLOS, to prepare for the setting up of both institutions and to implement an interim regime adopted by the Third United Nations Conference on the Law of the Sea.

Tommy established himself not only as an advocate of Singapore's interests but also for his wider negotiating and mediating skills. Most importantly, he emerged as one of the leading lights at UNCLOS. He was viewed not only as a highly competent lawyer and negotiator, but also as an honest broker who could be counted on to resolve issues whenever there was an impasse or bottleneck. Not surprisingly this led him to become President of UNCLOS.

Working Together on International Cases

We worked closely on the Land Reclamation and Pedra Branca cases involving Singapore that appeared before international tribunals. Tommy handled these two cases as Singapore's representative and agent.

I witnessed how effectively he could galvanise and enthuse a team from many different government ministries and agencies to work as a cohesive unit. He had almost natural skills as well as ability to establish the all-important comfort level with his opposing Malaysian counterparts in these cases. On the Land Reclamation case for instance, the personal relationship between him, our agent, and the Malaysian agent Tan Sri Ahmad Fuzi was an important factor in reaching the Settlement Agreement.

ASEAN Charter

Tommy and I were both involved in various stages of drafting the ASEAN Charter. I was Singapore's representative to the Eminent Persons Group — formed to make key recommendations on the Charter to the ASEAN leaders. Later, in 2007, Tommy took up the task of drafting and fleshing out the details of the ASEAN Charter when he was Singapore's Representative to the High Level Task Force. Together with Solicitor-General Walter Woon, Tommy worked assiduously with the representatives from the other ASEAN countries to reach the ASEAN Charter. It helped that Tommy has always been a strong believer in the ASEAN cause.

Co-Authorship of Books and Articles

Together, we co-authored at least four books — a leading commentary on UNCLOS for the Virginia University Centre for Oceans Law and Policy; a book on transboundary pollution; a book calling for joint development in the South China Sea; and a book on Singapore's experience in the Pedra Branca case. We have also co-authored several op-eds in *The Straits Times*. Of course, Tommy, on his own, is a prolific op-ed contributor to *The Straits Times*.

Working with Tommy as a co-author is a gratifying experience. More often than not, we start on the same page. Where, on occasions, we have differences of view, we discuss the issues at length and in depth. In this process of intellectual give-and-take, one of us would always be able to persuade the other.

Co-Chairing of Conferences

In recent years, both of us returned to academia in the NUS Faculty of Law. We were responsible for setting up the NUS Centre for International Law (CIL). Tommy serves as Chairman of the Board of Governors of the

Centre for International Law while I am Chairman of the International Advisory Panel.

We have co-chaired many CIL conferences. In 2012, we started the CIL Fireside Chat series, where we invite experts to explore pressing issues of international law and international affairs. We have hosted almost 20 Fireside Chats to date.

Closing Words

I am only one of the many people on whom Tommy has left a lasting impact, in many fields. He has worn many other hats and has championed many other causes ranging from the arts to environmental matters. No doubt, others will attest to his contributions in those areas. Having worked with him over 50 years in various capacities, these are the qualities that most strike me — his intellectual prowess, oratorical skills, charming disposition, diplomatic skills and integrity.

I join others in sending Tommy greetings on his 80th birthday and thanking him for his outstanding contributions to the nation building of Singapore. I especially thank him for showing us how Singapore can punch above its weight in this wide and complex world.

List of Contributors

⸺

Nassrine Azimi

Nassrine Azimi is currently a visiting scholar at the Terasaki Center for Japanese Studies, University of California in Los Angeles (UCLA). She co-founded and coordinates the Green Legacy Hiroshima Initiative (http:www.unitar.org/greenlegacyhiroshima), a global campaign to disseminate and plant worldwide seeds and saplings of trees that survived the 1945 atomic bombing of Hiroshima. At the United Nations Institute for Training and Research (UNITAR). Nassrine established the Hiroshima Office for Asia and the Pacific in 2003, and was its first director until 2009. Prior to her work in Hiroshima she had been UNITAR's coordinator of environmental training programmes and deputy to the executive director in Geneva, and chief of the Institute's New York Office, which she reopened in 1996 and directed for five years. She remains a senior advisor at the Institute. Nassrine has published extensively on UN peacekeeping and peace-building, post-conflict reconstruction, environmental and cultural governance, and Asia. Her latest book, *Last Boat to Yokohama*, is about Beate Sirota Gordon and her father Leo, both prominent artistic and cultural figures in Japan and the United States. She is now working on a book about the American experts who helped protect Japan's cultural property under Occupation, in the aftermath of WWII.

Robert Beckman

Robert Beckman is founding Director of the Centre for International Law (CIL), a university-level centre at the National University of Singapore. He served as the director of CIL from September 2009 to June 2016, and he continues to head its programme in Ocean Law and Policy. Prof. Beckman is an associate professor in the NUS Faculty of Law, and has been with the Faculty since 1977. He is a director of the Rhodes Academy of Oceans Law and Policy, a summer diploma programme held in Rhodes, Greece. He is also an adjunct senior fellow in the Maritime Security Programme at the Institute for Defence and Strategic Studies of the S. Rajaratnam School of International Studies (RSIS) at Nanyang Technological University (NTU).

Manu Bhaskaran

Manu Bhaskaran is Director of Centennial Group International and founding Director and Chief Executive Officer of Centennial Asia Advisors. Mr Bhaskaran has more than 30 years of expertise in economic and political risk assessment and forecasting in Asia. Before joining the Centennial Group, he was Chief Economist for Asia of a leading international investment bank and managed its Singapore-based economic advisory group. Mr Bhaskaran has regular columns in business weeklies such as *The Edge* in Singapore/Malaysia. He serves as Member of the Regional Advisory Board for Asia of the International Monetary Fund; Senior Adjunct Fellow, Institute of Policy Studies, Singapore; Council Member of the Singapore Institute of International Affairs; and Vice-President of the Economics Society of Singapore. Mr Bhaskaran has a Master's degree in Public Administration from the John F. Kennedy School of Government at Harvard University and a Bachelor's degree in Economics from Cambridge University. He has also qualified as a Chartered Financial Analyst. He is based in Singapore.

Chan Heng Chee

Ambassador Chan Heng Chee is currently Ambassador-at-Large with the Singapore Foreign Ministry and Chairman of the Lee Kuan Yew

Centre for Innovative Cities in the Singapore University of Technology and Design (SUTD). She is Chairman of the National Arts Council, a Member of the Presidential Council for Minority Rights, a Member of the Constitutional Commission 2016, and Deputy Chairman of the Social Science Research Council.

Ambassador Chan served as Singapore's Ambassador to the United States from 1996 to 2012 and Singapore's Permanent Representative to the United Nations from 1989 to 1991. She was concurrently High Commissioner to Canada and Ambassador to Mexico. Previously, she was Executive Director of the Singapore International Foundation (which created a Singapore version of the Peace Corps) and Director of the Institute of Southeast Asian Studies. She was founding Director of the Institute of Policy Studies and Head of the Department of Political Science, National University of Singapore.

Ambassador Chan was named Singapore's first "Woman of the Year" in 1991, and was twice awarded the National Book Awards in 1986 for *A Sensation of Independence: A Political Biography of David Marshall* and in 1978 for *The Dynamics of One Party Dominance: The PAP at the Grassroots*.

When Ambassador Chan left Washington at the end of her appointment, she received the Inaugural Asia Society Outstanding Diplomatic Achievement Award, the Inaugural Foreign Policy Outstanding Diplomatic Achievement Award 2012 and the United States Navy Distinguished Public Service Award.

Chan Sek Keong

Chan Sek Keong was born in 1937. He received his LL.M (Honours) from the University of Malaya in Singapore in 1961. He was admitted a year later as an advocate and solicitor in Malaya and in Singapore where he practised until 1986. He was Member of the Military Court of Appeal from 1971–1986. He was offered appointment as a judge, but chose appointment as a judicial commissioner in 1986. In 1988, he was appointed a judge of the Supreme Court. He was appointed as Attorney General of Singapore in 1992, and returned to the Bench in 2006 as Chief Justice and retired in 2012. He was reappointed Senior Judge in 2015 for a term of three years.

Chang Li Lin

Chang Li Lin is a civil servant. Prior to her current appointment in the public service, she was Deputy Director for Public Affairs at the Institute of Policy Studies (IPS) at the Lee Kuan Yew School of Public Policy, National University of Singapore. She first worked with Prof. Tommy Koh as an intern at IPS. At the Institute, she covered policy research in the areas of international relations. Thereafter, she took over the public affairs portfolio started by Peggy Kek, which included managing donor and media relations, and special projects. A graduate of University of Reading and University of Kent at Canterbury, in the United Kingdom, Ms Chang has a Masters in International Relations (IR) and a B.A. in Sociology and IR. She has written articles and edited a number of publications with Prof. Tommy Koh on Singapore's foreign policy, including *The Little Red Dot* series featuring essays by Singapore and foreign diplomats; on the USSFTA; Singapore and the United Nations; and Singapore and ASEAN.

Chao Hick Tin

Chao Hick Tin served for 28 years on the Singapore Supreme Court Bench when he retired from the Court of Appeal as its Vice-President. He was elevated to the High Court in 1987 and was promoted to Judge of Appeal in 1999. From 2006 to 2008, he served as Attorney-General for two years and thereafter returned to the Bench. Before his elevation to the Bench in 1987, he served as Head of the Civil Division at the Attorney-General's Chambers. He was a Singapore delegate to the UN Seabed Committee (1971–1973) and the UN Law of the Sea Conference (1974–1981). In 2007, he was a member of the Singapore team who appeared before the International Court of Justice at The Hague in relation to the Pedra Branca case.

Cheong Koon Hean

Dr Cheong Koon Hean has been CEO of the Housing and Development Board (HDB) since 2010 and was the CEO of the Urban Redevelopment

Authority (URA) from 2004 to 2010. She was also the Deputy Secretary in the Ministry of National Development from 2001 to 2016. Dr Cheong is currently on the boards of HDB, National University of Singapore and the Civil Service College. She is a member of the World Economic Forum's Real Estate and Urbanisation Global Agenda Council; Deputy President of the International Federation for Housing and Planning; nominating committee member of the Lee Kuan Yew World City Prize; and an endowed professor in Nanyang Technological University. Dr Cheong has been conferred several awards, including the Meritorious Service Medal for outstanding public service; Doctor of Architecture honoris causa, and the Convocation Medal for Professional Excellence. In 2016, she was conferred the Urban Land Institute's JC Nichols Prize for Urban Visionaries, and the Council for Tall Buildings and Urban Habitat's Lynn S Beedle Lifetime Achievement Award.

Simon Chesterman

Professor Simon Chesterman is Dean of the National University of Singapore Faculty of Law. He is also Editor of the *Asian Journal of International Law* and Secretary-General of the Asian Society of International Law. Educated in Melbourne, Beijing, Amsterdam and Oxford, Professor Chesterman's teaching experience includes periods at the universities of Melbourne, Oxford, Southampton, Columbia and Sciences Po. From 2006 to 2011, he was Global Professor and Director of the New York University (NYU) School of Law Singapore Programme.

Prior to joining NYU, he was a senior associate at the International Peace Academy and Director of UN Relations at the International Crisis Group in New York. He has previously worked for the UN Office for the Coordination of Humanitarian Affairs in Yugoslavia and interned at the International Criminal Tribunal for Rwanda.

Professor Chesterman is the author or editor of 17 books, including *Law and Practice of the United Nations* (with Ian Johnstone and David M. Malone, Oxford University Press, 2016); *One Nation Under Surveillance* (Oxford University Press, 2011); *You, the People* (Oxford University Press, 2004); and *Just War or Just Peace?* (Oxford University Press, 2001). He is a recognised authority on international law, whose work has opened up new areas of research on conceptions of public authority — including the rules and institutions of global governance, state-building and post-conflict reconstruction, and the changing role of intelligence agencies.

Chua Mui Hoong

Chua Mui Hoong is a journalist with *The Straits Times*, where she is now Opinion Editor. She has been with the newspaper since 1991, writing and editing articles on political and social issues. She is the author of several books, including *A Defining Moment: How Singapore Beat SARS*; and *Pioneers Once More: The Singapore Public Service 1959–2009*. She was also part of a team from *The Straits Times* that interviewed Mr Lee Kuan Yew for the book *Hard Truths*. She is a graduate of Cambridge and Harvard universities.

Gregory Clancey

Dr Gregory Clancey is Associate Professor in the Department of History, the Leader of the STS (Science, Technology, and Society) Cluster at the Asia Research Institute (ARI), and the founding Master of Tembusu College, all at the National University of Singapore (NUS).

Dr Clancey received his Ph.D. in the Historical and Social Study of Science and Technology from the Massachusetts Institute of Technology. He has been a Fulbright Graduate Scholar at the University of Tokyo, and a Lars Hierta Scholar at the Royal Institute of Technology (KtH) in Stockholm.

Dr Clancey's research centres on the cultural history of science and technology particularly in modern Japan and East Asia. His book *Earthquake Nation: The Cultural Politics of Japanese Seismicity* (University of California Press, 2006) won the Sidney Edelstein Prize from the Society for the History of Technology in 2007, and was selected as one of the "11 Best Books about Science" in the UC Berkeley Summer Reading List in 2009. Clancey is the 2012 recipient of the Morison Prize from MIT for "combining humanistic values with effectiveness in the world of practical affairs, and in particular, in science and technology."

Geh Min

Dr Geh Min (MBBS, FRCS, FAMS) is a staunch supporter and spokes-person for the environment. She was President of the Nature Society (Singapore) from 2000 to August 2008 and was sworn in as a Nominated Member of Parliament on 29 November 2004 with serving term from 1 January 2005 to 19 April 2006. She received the 2006 President's Award for the Environment and is currently a board member of BirdLife International (Asia) and a member of The Nature Conservancy's Asia Pacific Council.

Jenny Ho-Tan

Jenny Ho-Tan joined the Ministry of Foreign Affairs (MFA) in January 1969 and worked with Ambassador Tommy Koh as his personal assis-tant in the Singapore Embassy in Washington DC (1984–1988). She left MFA and joined the Institute of Policy Studies (IPS) in 1991 serving as Office Administrator and Personal Assistant to Ambassador Tommy Koh, who was Director of IPS.

When Ambassador Tommy Koh became the founding Director of the Asia-Europe Foundation (ASEF) in 1997, she left IPS so that she could continue to serve as Personal Assistant to Tommy until 2000.

She had an enjoyable, happy and memorable working relationship with Ambassador Tommy Koh for almost 14 years, four years with him in Washington D.C., six years at the Institute of Policy Studies and three and a half years at the Asia-Europe Foundation.

After leaving ASEF, she rejoined MFA and continued to work there until her retirement in 2014.

S Jayakumar

Professor S Jayakumar was Singapore's Deputy Prime Minister and Senior Minister. He also served as Minister for Home Affairs, Minister for Foreign Affairs, Minister for Labour, and was also Minister for Law. He was Singapore's Permanent Representative to the United Nations, and High Commissioner to Canada (1971–1974) and a member of Singapore's delegation to UNCLOS. He has written several books, the most recent being *Be at the Table or Be on the Menu — A Singapore Memoir, Pedra Branca — The Road to the World Court* (together with Prof. Tommy Koh) and *Diplomacy — A Singapore Experience.*

Before his political career, he was Dean of the National University of Singapore's Faculty of Law. He is now Chairman of the Law Faculty's Advisory Council and Chairman of the International Advisory Panel of the Centre for International Law (CIL).

Peggy Kek

Peggy Kek is Director of Development and Partnerships at the Singapore Symphony Orchestra. She first met Tommy Koh in 1997 when he hired her as the head of Public Affairs at the Asia-Europe Foundation and subsequently the Institute of Policy Studies. In 2004, she left Singapore to work at the World Bank in Washington D.C. Upon her return, she held positions at the Singapore International Foundation and the Lee Kuan Yew School of Public Policy at the National University of Singapore. Peggy also worked with the United Nations Children's Fund (UNICEF) in the 1990s and early 2000s. She is a graduate of NUS and holds a Masters in International Studies from SOAS. She is the co-author of *Singapore and UNICEF: Working for Children* (2016) and editor of *20 Years of Asia-Europe Relations* (2016).

Khor Kok Wah

Khor Kok Wah is Vice-President (Industry and Projects) and Dean, Centre for Lifelong Education at the Nanyang Academy of Fine Arts. He was previously Deputy CEO at the National Arts Council, having served as Senior Director for Literary Arts and Director for Arts Facilities. He was also Director for Arts and Heritage at the Ministry of Information, Communications and the Arts.

Koh Buck Song

Koh Buck Song works as a writer, editor and consultant in brand-building, leadership and corporate social responsibility. He has authored and edited more than 25 books, including three poetry collections, several literary anthologies and publications including *Brand Singapore* on its country brand-building. He has served as a member of three Censorship Review Committees — in 1991–1992 chaired by Tommy Koh, in 2002–2003 and in 2009–2010 as Deputy Chairman. He was a board member of the National Arts Council and the Media Development Authority, and has chaired and served on many citizens' panels on the regulation of films, theatre, publications and online media. He read English at Cambridge, and was literary editor, regular columnist and political commentator with *The Straits Times*. He has worked at the Economic Development Board on global media relations and strategic planning, and as a public affairs consultant in Southeast Asia. A master's graduate in public administration from Harvard, he taught leadership as Adjunct Associate Professor at the Lee Kuan Yew School of Public Policy and in the Social Leadership Singapore executive education programme for the social sector. He has also lectured on media policy as Adjunct Faculty at the Singapore Management University. He represented Singapore as poet-in-residence at the Scottish Poetry Library in Edinburgh and in Japan on a Japan Foundation cultural leaders programme. An artist who practises the art form *haiga* (poetry and painting), he has exhibited at Esplanade's Super Japan Festival, the National Poetry Festival and the Singapore Writers Festival.

Gillian Koh

Dr Gillian Koh is Deputy Director (Research) at the Institute of Policy Studies, whose research interests lie in the discipline of political sociology and in the specific areas of electoral politics, the development of civil society, state-society relations, and Singapore's national identity.

She has published articles on civil society and political development in Singapore, co-edited *Civil Society and the State in Singapore* (World Scientific Publishing Europe Ltd, 2017); *Migration and Integration in Singapore: Policies and Practice* (Routledge, 2015); *State-Society Relations in Singapore* (IPS & Oxford University Press, 2000); and co-authored *Civil Society*, which is part of the IPS Singapore

Chronicles Series (Straits Times Press, 2016). Gillian gained her Ph.D. in Sociological Studies from the University of Sheffield (UK) in 1995 and has been at IPS since.

Koh Kheng-Lian

Koh Kheng-Lian is Emeritus Professor of the Law Faculty, National University of Singapore. She was formerly Director of the Asia-Pacific Centre for Environmental Law (APCEL) (1996–2013). She was also IUCN-CEL Regional Vice-Chair for South and East Asia, and a member of its Steering Committee (1996–2004). She is the Singapore representative of IUCN Asia Regional Committee, and national correspondent for Singapore for the Centre International de droit Compare de l'environment. She is the 2012 Laureate of the Elizabeth Haub Prize in Environmental Law conferred jointly by the University of Stockholm, Université Libre de Bruxelles and the International Council of Environmental Law (http://www.juridicum.su.se/ehp/news.html). She is an inductee to the Singapore Women's Hall of Fame 2014 for her pioneering work in the development of environmental law in the region (http://www.swhf.sg/the-inductees/17-environment conservation/138-koh-kheng-lian)

Michael Koh

Michael Koh is currently a Fellow with the Centre For Liveable Cities. He was previously Head of Projects and Design at SC Global overseeing Singapore and overseas development projects. Prior to that, he had 25 years of experience in the public service. He served six-and-a-half years as CEO of the National Heritage Board (NHB) where he is credited and publicly recognised for rebranding and repositioning the museums to new highs, and making heritage accessible to the people. He increased museum visitorship from 1 million to 4 million through many new initiatives and outreach events. He also served three-and-a-half years as concurrent CEO of the National Art Gallery and was responsible for the planning and design of the project. Prior to NHB, Mr Koh held appointments at the Urban Redevelopment Authority where he spearheaded the city planning and urban design of Singapore's Central Area, which included the new Downtown at Marina Bay, Orchard Road, Bras Basah and Bugis. He led the planning team for key development projects such as the Business and Financial Centre and the Integrated Resort, now Marina Bay Sands. Michael has also held appointments at Mapletree Holdings and Singbridge. He currently serves as a board member of the National Library Board and has served on the boards of NHB, Land Transport Authority, Singapore Tourism Board, Civil Service College and the National Art Gallery, and a member of the Hotel Licensing Board and the Street and Building Naming Committee. He is an alumnus of the National University of Singapore and Harvard University.

Melissa Kwee

Melissa Kwee is Chief Executive Officer of the National Volunteer and Philanthropy Centre (NVPC). She has assumed roles including Chairman of Halogen Foundation and President of UN Women Singapore (formerly known as Unifem Singapore), where she tackled human trafficking issues and initiated community campaigns to engage and empower youth as civic advocates.

She received the Singapore Youth Award in 2007 and Asean Youth Award 2009 for her leadership and service. To help teenage girls at risk, she co-founded Beautiful People, a programme of Beyond Social Services, which pairs teenage girls with mentors to offer guidance, life skills and friendship. Prior to that, she started Project Access, a values-based leadership education initiative to inspire and equip girls and young women to be role models of positive change.

Ms Kwee has served on many public service and community boards to advance causes she believes in, including the National Arts Council, the Singapore Repertory Theatre, the ITE Board of Governors and Prison Fellowship International. She is currently on the boards of Crest Secondary, a specialised school for technical education in Singapore; 70x7, an initiative by the Prison Fellowship Singapore; Pontiac Land Group; and Honestbee.

She holds a degree in anthropology from Harvard University and received a Fulbright Scholarship to study ethnic-based community leadership in Nepal.

Kenson Kwok

Kenson Kwok trained as an architect and earned a Ph.D. in environmental psychology.

During an 18-year career with the museums in Singapore he established three new institutions — the first phase of the Asian Civilisations Museum (ACM) at Armenian Street (1997), the flagship ACM at Empress Place (2003), and the Peranakan Museum (2008). He oversaw the conversion of two historic buildings in the Civic District into museums, helped build the museums' collections and sponsorship base, secured high-profile long-term loans, and set new standards for museum curating, display and design. During his time at ACM, over 60 special exhibitions were mounted, some attracting record-breaking attendance.

He was the co-curator of the exhibition "A Passage to Asia", staged at Bozar in Brussels to mark the 8th Asia-Europe Summit in 2010, and commissioner for "Baba Bling: Signes Intérieurs de Richesse" at the Musée du Quai Branly, Paris in the same year.

In retirement, he remains active in the museum sector as a member of committees at the National Gallery Singapore, the National Museum of Singapore, the NUS Museums, and ICOM (International Council of Museums).

His awards include the Public Administration Medal, and the Chevalier de la Légion d'Honneur.

Kwok Kian Chow

Kwok Kian Chow was Director of Singapore Art Museum (1994–2009), and Director (2009–2011) and Senior Advisor of National Gallery Singapore (2011–2015). He is currently Programme Leader for Arts and Culture Management at the Singapore Management University.

Kwok Kian-Woon

Kwok Kian-Woon is Professor of Sociology at Nanyang Technological University, where he has served as a founding member of the School of Humanities and Social Sciences, the first Senate Chair, and the Associate Provost of Student Life. His research areas include the following: social memory, war and violence, the Chinese overseas, and mental health. He has chaired the National Archives of Singapore board and serves as a board member of the National Arts Council (and the Singapore Art Museum) and the National Heritage Board (and the Asian Civilisations Museum), as well as on their many committees. Professor Kwok was the co-chair of the steering committee for the first Singapore Biennale and a member of the first steering committee for the establishment of the National Gallery, including as chair of its museological committee. He was a member on the academic panel of the Institute of Policy Studies and an external advisor to the Nanyang Academy of Fine Arts. He is the current chair of the steering committee for the Singapore Writers Festival. Professor Kwok is actively involved in civil society, participating in public discussion and serving on the boards of independent groups such as the Intercultural Theatre Institute and Temenggong Artists-in-Residence Ltd. He is a former president of the Singapore Heritage Society, a non-governmental organisation, which has over decades shaped the national agenda on heritage conservation.

Margaret Liang

Margaret Liang is Adjunct Senior Fellow of the S. Rajaratnam School of International Studies (RSIS), Nanyang Technological University Singapore; Associate Trainer for Singapore Ministry of Foreign Affairs (MFA); and Senior Fellow of the MFA Diplomatic Academy. She was Consultant to MFA for WTO/Trade Issues (2004–2014); Adjunct Professor of the National University of Singapore Law Faculty (2008–2013); and Senior Fellow of the Ministry of Trade and Industry's Trade Academy (2013–2014). She has served in Singapore

Missions in Bonn and in Geneva. She was actively involved in GATT/WTO negotiations during the Uruguay Round. From 1985 to 1992, she was Singapore's negotiator in the Uruguay Round, *inter-alia*, in the areas of Anti-Dumping, Subsidies and Countervailing Duty Measures, Safeguards, Dispute Settlement, GATT Articles and Government Procurement. Ms Liang was a member of the Singapore team in the WTO dispute settlement case on Singapore/Malaysia-Import measures on certain petrochemical products and has served in several dispute panels. She has conducted WTO Trade Policy courses for RSIS in Cambodia, Laos, Vietnam, Indonesia, Malaysia, the Philippines, Thailand, Sri Lanka, Bhutan, Mongolia, Abu Dhabi and Timor-Leste; and under Singapore's technical assistance programmes for Cambodia, Laos, Myanmar and Vietnam. She was Academic Coordinator for the WTO Regional Trade Policy Course, for Asia-Pacific, a joint cooperation between the WTO and the National University of Singapore from 2008–2010.

Donald Low

Donald Low is Associate Dean (Executive Education) at the Lee Kuan Yew School of Public Policy, National University of Singapore. His research interests at the School include economics in public policy, inequality and social spending, behavioural economics, public finance, organisational change, and governance and politics in Singapore.

Prior to his current appointment, Mr Low spent 15 years in the Singapore Public Service. Mr Low is the editor of *Behavioural Economics and Policy Design: Examples from Singapore* (2011), a pioneering book that details how the Singapore government has applied ideas from behavioural economics in the design of public policies. His 2014 book, *Hard Choices: Challenging the Singapore Consensus* raises searching questions about the long-term viability of many aspects of governance in Singapore, and argues that a far-reaching rethinking of the country's policies and institutions is necessary, even if it weakens the very consensus that enabled Singapore to succeed in its first 50 years.

Lye Liang Fook

Lye Liang Fook is Research Fellow and Assistant Director at the East Asian Institute, National University of Singapore. His research interests cover China's foreign policy, China's One Road, One Belt initiative, China-ASEAN relations and China-Singapore relations. He was part of a team that completed a review of the Suzhou Industrial Park, the first flagship project between China and Singapore, to distil lessons from this collaboration. His research interests extend into other government-to-government projects between the two countries such as the Sino-Singapore Tianjin Eco-city project and the China-Singapore (Chongqing) Demonstration Initiative on Strategic Connectivity. His publications have appeared in Routledge, *International Relations of the Asia Pacific, Journal of Chinese Political Science, Copenhagen Journal of Asian Studies*, Eastern Universities Press, Institute of Southeast Asian Studies (ISEAS) Publishing, Konrad Adenauer Stiftung Publishing, World Scientific Publishing, and *China: An International Journal*. Besides the academia, he manages the Singapore Secretariat of the Network of East Asian Think Tanks (NEAT) and the Network of ASEAN-China Think Tanks (NACT), two Track II bodies that aim to promote regional cooperation.

Irene Lye Lin-Heng

Lye Lin-Heng is Director of the NUS Law Faculty's Asia-Pacific Centre of Environmental Law (APCEL) and Chair of the Management Committee for the multi-disciplinary NUS M.Sc. (Environmental Management), or MEM programme. She is a member of the Board of Governors of WWF (Singapore) and Visiting Associate Professor at Yale University's School of Forestry & Environmental Studies. She is a member of the Governing Board, IUCN Academy of Environmental Law and former co-chair of its Research and Committees. She was Honorary Legal Advisor to the Nature Society (Singapore) for many years. She is a member of the National Committee on Drinking Water Quality Standards, a member of the Strata Titles Board, and a former board member of the Housing and Development Board (HDB). She was awarded the PBM in 2016 for her work with the Ministry of National Development.

Kishore Mahbubani

Kishore Mahbubani was with the Singapore Foreign Service for 33 years (1971–2004), serving, among other senior positions, as the Permanent Secretary of the Ministry of Foreign Affairs (1993–1998) and Singapore's Ambassador to the UN (twice from 1984–1989 and 1998–2004). He has been Dean of the Lee Kuan Yew School of Public Policy, NUS from August 2004.

He has published six books: *Can Asians Think?* (1998), *Beyond the Age of Innocence* (2005), *The New Asian Hemisphere* (2008), *The Great Convergence* (2013), *Can Singapore Survive?* (2015) and *The ASEAN Miracle: A Catalyst for Peace* (2017). His articles have appeared in leading journals and newspapers.

Prof. Mahbubani was awarded the President's Scholarship in 1967. He graduated with a First Class Honours degree in Philosophy from the University of Singapore in 1971. From Dalhousie University, Canada, he received a Master's degree in Philosophy in 1976 and an honorary doctorate in 1995. He spent a year as a Fellow at the Center for International Affairs at Harvard University from 1991 to 1992. He was conferred the Public Administration Medal (Gold) by the Singapore Government in 1998. He was listed as one of the top 100 public intellectuals in the world by *Foreign Policy* and *Prospect* magazines in 2005, and among *Foreign Policy*'s Top Global Thinkers in 2010 and 2011. Most recently, he was selected by *Prospect* magazine as one of the top 50 world thinkers for 2014.

Arun Mahizhnan

Arun Mahizhnan is Special Research Adviser at the Institute of Policy Studies (IPS). Prior to that, he served as Deputy Director and Acting Director at the Institute. He is concurrently an Adjunct Professor at the Wee Kim Wee School of Communication and Information at the Nanyang Technological University. Before joining IPS, he held senior positions in the public communications field in both the public and private sectors.

Jeremy Monteiro

Jeremy Monteiro (pianist, vocalist, composer, jazz educator) has won critical acclaim in many parts of the world. He has performed all over the globe in addition to numerous occasions at home in Singapore, where he has been dubbed "Singapore's King of Swing" by the local press. He currently acts as an International Arts Ambassador for EFG Bank, headquartered in Zurich, Switzerland, in addition to running his production company Showtime Productions Pte. Ltd.

Mr Monteiro has performed at some of the most prestigious international jazz festivals and stages. In November 2014, he performed on one of the main stages of the EFG London Jazz Festival at the Queen Elizabeth Hall. In June 2015, he performed at the City of London Festival at the top of the Walkie Talkie Tower and in November that same year, he returned to the EFG London Jazz Festival to play at the Royal Albert Hall's Elgar Room with his group "Jeremy Monteiro & Alberto Marsico with the Jazz-Blues Brothers".

Mr Monteiro commemorated his 40th anniversary as a professional musician, and staged a celebration concert on 30 September 2016 at the Esplanade with many of his past and current collaborators from Singapore and overseas. In August 2016, he was made a Visiting Professor of the University of West London to assist in research and teaching projects at the London College of Music. He is a co-founder and director at the Composers & Authors of Singapore Limited and a co-founder and executive director of the Singapore Jazz Foundation Limited.

Elaine Ng

Elaine Ng is Chief Executive Officer of the National Library Board (NLB) of Singapore. As CEO of NLB, Elaine oversees the strategic development of the National Library, the network of 26 public libraries, and the National Archives of Singapore. Prior to joining the NLB in April 2011, Elaine was Deputy Chief Executive Officer of the National Heritage Board (NHB) where she was responsible for heritage development.

Mrs Ng sees Prof. Tommy Koh as the rock star of the cultural scene in Singapore, playing the role of advocate, mentor and "loving critic".

Ong Keng Yong

Ambassador Ong Keng Yong is Executive Deputy Chairman of the S. Rajaratnam School of International Studies at the Nanyang Technological University in Singapore. Concurrently, he is Ambassador-at-Large at the Singapore Ministry of Foreign Affairs, non-resident High Commissioner to Pakistan and non-resident Ambassador to Iran. Mr Ong also serves as Chairman of the Singapore International Foundation (SIF).

Mr Ong was High Commissioner of Singapore to Malaysia from 2011 to 2014. He served as Secretary-General of ASEAN (Association of Southeast Asian Nations), based in Jakarta, Indonesia from January 2003 to January 2008.

Mr Ong started his diplomatic career in 1979 and was posted to Singapore embassies in Saudi Arabia, Malaysia and the United States of America. He was Singapore's High Commissioner to India and concurrently Ambassador to Nepal from 1996 to 1998. From September 1998 to December 2002, he was Press Secretary to the then Prime Minister of Singapore, Mr Goh Chok Tong. At the same time, Mr Ong held senior appointments in the Ministry of Information, Communications and the Arts, and the People's Association in Singapore. From 2008 to 2011, he served as Director of the Institute of Policy Studies (IPS) in the Lee Kuan Yew School of Public Policy at the National University of Singapore.

Mr Ong graduated from the then University of Singapore with a LL.B (Hons) and the Georgetown University (Washington D.C.) with an M.A. in Arab Studies.

Pang Khang Chau

Pang Khang Chau is currently a Judicial Commissioner of the Supreme Court. He practised public international law from 2003 to 2016 as a member of the International Affairs Division (IAD) of the Attorney-General's Chambers (AGC), and headed the IAD from 2012 to 2016 as its Director-General. Officers of the IAD advise government depart-ments on international law matters and represent the government in international negotiations and international disputes. During his time in IAD, Mr Pang was involved in the Land Reclamation dispute before the International Tribunal on the Law of the Sea, the Pedra Branca dispute before the International Court of Justice and the Railway Land arbitration before the Permanent Court of Arbitration at The Hague. He also led the Singapore delegation in negotiating the maritime boundary with Indonesia in the eastern part of the Singapore Strait. Before joining IAD, he served as State Counsel in the Civil Division of AGC from 1995 to 1998 and as Deputy Director, Legal Policy Division of the Ministry of Law from 1998 to 2002. He is also President of the Singapore Branch of the International Law Association.

Gopinath Pillai

Gopinath Pillai has had a varied career as a journalist, teacher, entre-preneur and diplomat. He is founding Chairman of the Management Board of the Institute of South Asian Studies, Ambassador-at-Large in the Ministry of Foreign Affairs since August 2008, and Singapore's Special Envoy to Andhra Pradesh. He was Singapore's longest-serv-ing non-resident Ambassador to Iran between 1989 and 2008, and also served as Singapore's High Commissioner to Pakistan. He was recently appointed as Chairman of the Indian Heritage Centre Advi-sory Board.

His business interests include education, logistics and information technology. He is Chairman of Malvern International Plc, listed on AIM in London, UK, and Chairman of Playware Studios Pte Ltd, an EdTech company focused on game-based learning and education.

Mr Pillai has been involved in organisations connected to social development. He was the founding Chairman of the NTUC FairPrice Co-operative Limited, Chairman of the Hindu Advisory Board, and President of the National University of Singapore Society.

For his contributions to public service, Mr Pillai has received several awards. The Singapore government has awarded him the Public Service Star Award (BBM) in 1999, BBM (BAR) in 2009 and the Meritorious Service Medal in 2015. For his efforts in bridging and advancing Singapore-India relations, the Indian government conferred on him the Padma Shri Award at the 2012 Republic Day. In 2015, the National University of Singapore bestowed on him the Outstanding Service Award.

Francis Seow-Choen

Dr Francis Seow-Choen is a colorectal surgeon in private practice in Singapore. He was variously Head of the Department of Colorectal Surgery, Singapore General Hospital; Head of Surgical Oncology, National Cancer Centre; and Adjunct Associate Professor at both the National University of Singapore and the Nanyang Technological University. He is Visiting Professor to several universities and hospitals overseas and is well-known internationally as a teacher and trainer in colorectal surgery. He received the Excellence for Singapore Award in 2000 for his contributions to international colorectal surgery.

Dr Seow-Choen is also a well-known in the study of stick insects, with four books on them to his name and two more to be published in 2017. He is an Honorary Research Associate with the Lee Kong Chian Natural History Museum, the National Biodiversity Centre of the National Parks Board, Singapore, as well as the Sabah Forestry Department.

Dr Seow-Choen is also active in social work. He was a member of the first international team to reach and assist Aceh during the Aceh Tsunami in December 2004. He was the founding Chairman of Guide Dogs Association of the Blind in Singapore until 2015, before passing the reins to the next generation of leaders.

Paul Tan

Paul has previously worked in broadcast and print media as well as at the Singapore Tourism Board, where he held various appointments including Regional Director, North Asia.

He joined the National Arts Council in February 2011 as the Festival Director of the Singapore Writers Festival (SWF) and Director, Literary Arts. He helmed four successful editions of the SWF while championing the development of Singapore creative writing. After a two-year stint as Deputy Chief Executive, in November 2016, he was appointed Covering Chief Executive of the National Arts Council.

Paul has published four collections of poetry. The first two, *Curious Roads* (1994) and *Driving into Rain* (1998), won the Commendation and the Merit Prizes at the Singapore Literature Prize competition respectively. His most recent volume, *Seasonal Disorders/Impractical Lessons* was published in 2014.

Tan Tai Yong

Tan Tai Yong is Professor of Humanities (History) and President of Yale-NUS College. Prior to this, he served as Executive Vice-President (Academic Affairs) at Yale-NUS; Vice Provost (Student Life); and Dean of the Faculty of Arts and Social Sciences at the National University of Singapore. He helmed the Institute of South Asian Studies as Director from 2004 to 2015.

Professor Tan is Honorary Chairman of the National Museum of Singapore and chairs the National Collection Advisory Panel at the National Heritage Board. He is a member of the ISEAS-Yusof Ishak Institute Board of Trustees. He is a member of the Singapore Social Sciences Research Council, and serves on the editorial boards of *Modern Asian Studies, India Review* and the *Journal of Southeast Asian Studies*. Professor Tan has published extensively on South Asian, Southeast Asian and Singapore history.

Daren Tang

Daren Tang has been the Chief Executive of the Intellectual Property Office of Singapore (IPOS) since November 2015. He leads IPOS in its new vision of being an innovation agency that uses its networks and expertise to help drive Singapore's future growth.

In recent years, Mr Tang led the IP negotiations for Singapore in three major free trade agreements: the Trans-Pacific Partnership (TPP) agreement, the Regional Comprehensive Economic Partnership (RCEP) agreement, and the European Union-Singapore Free Trade Agreement. In the

TPP and RCEP agreements, Mr Tang was tasked with the Chairmanship of the overall IP negotiations. In May 2017, he was elected as Chairman of the WIPO (World Intellectual Property Organization) Standing Committee on Copyright and Related Rights for a two-year term.

Formerly, Mr Tang was a Senior State Counsel with the International Affairs Division of the Attorney-General's Chambers. He was the lead services negotiator in the US-Singapore FTA, and a member of the team that argued the Pedra Branca case before the International Court of Justice, where he worked closely with Tommy Koh in both instances.

Mr Tang holds a LL.B from the National University of Singapore, and an LL.M from Georgetown University, where he was also a Fellow of the Institute of International Economic Law. He attended the Advanced Management Program at the Harvard Business School in 2013.

Simon SC Tay

Simon SC Tay is a public intellectual as well as an advisor to major corporations and policymakers.

He is Chairman of the Singapore Institute of International Affairs, and concurrently a tenured Associate Professor, teaching international law at the National University of Singapore. He was Visiting Professor at Harvard Law School, the Fletcher School and Yale University.

Prof. Tay is also Senior Consultant at WongPartnership, a leading Asian law firm of some 300 lawyers and with offices in Singapore, China and the Middle East. He serves as independent director or advisor on boards for global companies such as Mitsubishi UFJ Financial Group of Japan, the LGT Private Bank, and Eurex Clearing Asia, and leading regional companies — Far East Organization and Hyflux Ltd of Singapore, and Top Glove Corporation of Malaysia.

His previous corporate advisory appointments include the Toyota Motor Corporation Global Advisory Board (2010–2015) and Temasek Holdings (2006–2009). From 1992 to 2008, he served in a number of public appointments, as Chairman of the National Environment Agency (2002–2008); and as a Nominated Member of Parliament (1997–2001).

He is a prize-winning author of fiction and poetry. In 2010, his novel *City of Small Blessings* was awarded the Singapore Literature Prize, and his most recent collection of stories, *Middle & First*, was published in 2016. He holds a Masters in Law from Harvard Law School (1993–1994), which he attended on a Fulbright Scholarship and where he won the Laylin Prize for the best thesis in international law.

Wee Yeow Chin

Dr Wee Yeow Chin is a botanist by training. He obtained his B.Sc. (Hons.) in 1961 and M.Sc. in 1964 from the University of Malaya in Singapore and University of Singapore, respectively. He then joined the Malayan Pineapple Industry Board as an agronomist, spending the next 12 years in Pekan Nenas, Johor, Malaysia. His work on pineapple flowering earned him his Ph.D. in 1976. A few years later, he returned to Singapore to teach botany in the then Department of Botany, National University of Singapore, retiring in 1997 as Associate Professor.

Dr Wee's involvement in nature education and conservation began when, as a newly recruited lecturer, he was "volunteered" to the post of Honorary Secretary of the then Malayan Nature Society (Singapore Branch). From 1978–1990, he spent his time in the society popularising local nature through conducted walks and writing nature-related articles and books. This was at a time when people were more familiar with temperate plants than the local species.

In 1990, he was thrust into the post of Honorary Chairman when the incumbent went on sabbatical. At Patron Tommy Koh's prompting, he took the society out of the Malayan Nature Society to form the Nature Society (Singapore). He remained as the founding President for the next five years.

Dr Wee was also involved in various nature-related committees: Nature Reserves Board (1987–1989), Nature Reserves Committee (1989), National Council on the Environment (1992–1996) and Singapore Green Plan's Work-Group on Nature Conservation (1992).

Danny Yeo

Prior to retiring in February 2015, Danny Yeo was Assistant Vice President of Branding and Promotions at Singapore Press Holdings. He joined the company in 1972, when it was still known as The Straits Times (Malaya) Berhad.

During his 43 years with SPH, he held positions in various areas including operations, advertising, customer service, and branding and promotions. Together with his colleagues, he pioneered major events like The New Paper Big Walk, The New Paper SUVival Challenge, The Business Times Leadership Conference, The Business Times Wine Challenge, CATS CARnival, The Straits Times Global Outlook Forum and of course, Singapore Hawker Masters. At 67 years old, the sprightly retiree is busier than ever, acting in films and commercials, growing his own vegetables and fruits, jamming with a band, and cycling around the country. The father of three has a name card, which aptly reads: "REtireless — If it's legal, I'll do it!"

When it comes to food, Danny is a slave to char kway teow — but not just any char kway teow. He eats from only what he thinks are three of the best char kway teow stalls in Singapore — Outram Park Fried Kway Teow Mee, Guan Kee Fried Kway Teow and Hill Street Char Kway Teow. He would have the dish once a week if not for the watchful eyes of his loving wife. He now settles for twice a month — once without his wife's knowledge.

George Yeo

George Yeo is Chairman of Kerry Logistics Network and a director of Kerry Holdings.

From 1988 to 2011, he served 23 years in government, as Minister for Information and the Arts, Health, Trade & Industry, and Foreign Affairs.

Mr Yeo has a B.A. in Engineering (Double First) from Cambridge University and an MBA (Baker Scholar) from Harvard University.

He started as a Signals Officer in the Singapore Army, crossed over to the Air Force, became Chief-of-Staff of the Air Staff, and attained the rank of Brigadier-General as Director of Joint Operations and Planning in the Defence Ministry before resigning to enter politics in 1988.

Mr Yeo was a member of the Mentor Group and Governing Board of Nalanda University and its second Chancellor. He is a member of the Board of Trustees of World Economic Forum, Berggruen Institute on Governance, Harvard Business School Board of Dean's Advisors, International Advisory Panel of Peking University, International Advisory Board of IESE Business School, International Advisory Council of China's Eco Forum Global Guiyang, International Advisory Board of Japan's National Graduate School for International Policy Studies (GRIPS), International Advisory Committee of Mitsubishi Corporation and Hong Kong Economic Development Commission. He is an independent director of AIA Group and Wilmar International.

Mr Yeo served as a member of the Pontifical Commission for Reference on the Economic-Administrative Structure of the Holy See from 2013–2014. From February 2014, he became a member of the Vatican Council for the Economy.

Yeo Lay Hwee

Dr Yeo Lay Hwee has been Director of the European Union Centre in Singapore since 2009. She is also Council Secretary and Senior Research Fellow at the Singapore Institute of International Affairs (SIIA), and Adjunct Fellow at the S. Rajaratnam School of International Studies (RSIS). Since 2011, she has also taken on the role of Co-Editor in Chief for the *Asia Europe Journal.*

Dr Yeo sits on several academic advisory boards: the Centre for European Studies at the Australian National University (ANUCES), the KU Leuven's Master in European Studies (MAES) Programme; the Centre for Asia-Pacific Studies, Tallinn University of Technology, and Leiden Asia Centre, University of Leiden.

An international relations expert, her research interests revolve around comparative regionalism, principles of multilateralism and governance networks. She has written extensively on issues pertaining to Asia-Europe relations in general, and in particular, the ASEM process and relations between the European Union and ASEAN. She participates actively both in policy dialogues and academic workshops and conferences, and contributes regularly to commentaries and journals. She has also been involved in several EU-funded initiatives and actions such as the EU and Asia — Integration of Policy and Practice (EuropeAid/130829/C/ACT/ CAI), and also worked with other government agencies on training, public diplomacy and policy advocacy programmes related to governance, EU-ASEAN and ASEM. For her exemplary record in research and policy work on peace and developments in ASEAN and the EU, she was awarded the Nakasone Yasuhiro Award in June 2007.

Geoffrey Yu

Geoffrey Yu joined the Singapore Administrative Service in 1969 and was in the Singapore Foreign Service until 1981, when he resigned to join the World Intellectual Property Organization (WIPO), a United Nations Specialized Agency. He retired in 2006 as its Deputy Director General to return to Singapore.

From 2007 to 2010, he was concurrently Senior Specialist Advisor in the Ministry of Foreign Affairs and the Ministry of Law, as well as Deputy Chairman, Singapore Intellectual Property Academy, and Senior Fellow and Academic Panel Member, Ministry of Foreign Affairs' Diplomatic Academy.

Other positions he has held include Senior Advisor, Lee Kuan Yew School of Public Policy, National University of Singapore; Visiting Professor, Intellectual Property Research Centre, People's University (Renmin), Beijing; Chairman, Global Agenda Council on Intellectual Property of the World Economic Forum; and Chairman, Wild Rice Theatre Company.

He is currently Adjunct Professor, Lee Kuan Yew School of Public Policy; Adjunct Senior Fellow, S. Rajaratnam School of International Studies, Nanyang Technological University; and Chairman, Select Centre.

Wan Hussin Zoohri

Wan Hussin Zoohri is a retired Member of Parliament. He was in the education service for 23 years from 1957–1980. He was appointed Principal in 1973 and Senior Inspector of Schools in 1978. He entered politics in 1980 and was appointed Parliamentary Secretary from 1981–1985. After retiring from politics in 1991, he continued his involvement in NGOs. He was Secretary-General of Singapore Malay Teachers' Union from 1970–1978, Chairman of Prophet Muhammad's Birthday Memorial Scholarship Fund Board from 1995–2012, Chairman of Singapore Malay Badminton Association from 2000–2010, and Chairman of Aidilfitri Trust Fund from 2003–2008.

He is founding Chairman of Al-Zuhri Institute of Higher Learning in 2000 and is currently Chairman of its Board of Directors.

He was Tommy Koh's schoolmate from 1952 to 1955.